# GIANTS, CANNIBALS & MONSTERS

# GIANTS, CANNIBALS & MONSTERS

## BIGFOOT IN NATIVE CULTURE

Kathy Moskowitz Strain

hancock

house

ISBN-10: 0-88839-650-3
ISBN-13: 978-0-88839-650-1

**Cataloging in Publication Data**

Strain, Kathy Moskowitz, 1968–
    Giants, cannibals & monsters : Bigfoot in native culture / Kathy Moskowitz Strain.

Includes index.
ISBN 978-0-88839-650-1

    1. Indians of North America—Folklore.  2. Indian mythology—North America.
3. Sasquatch—Folklore.  4. Giants—Folklore.  5. Cannibalism—Folklore.
6. Monsters—Folklore.  I. Title.  II. Title: Giants, cannibals and monsters.

E98.F6S867 2008          398.2089'97          C2008-901593-2

Editor: Robert E. Strain
Production: Christopher L. Murphy, Ingrid Luters
Front cover: A depiction of Native American pictograph images showing a "hairy man, woman and child" — artwork by Brenden Bannon.

Published simultaneously in Canada and the United States by

**HANCOCK HOUSE PUBLISHERS LTD.**
19313 Zero Avenue, Surrey, B.C. Canada V3S 9R9

**HANCOCK HOUSE PUBLISHERS**
#104-4550 Birch Bay Lynden Rd, Blaine, WA U.S.A 98230

(800) 938-1114  Fax (800) 983-2262

**www.hancockhouse.com**
**sales@hancockhouse.com**

*This work is dedicated to the Native people of North America.*

*These are your stories.*
*Thank you for giving us a piece of your knowledge about a creature that you have always known.*

Look out.
Get ready.
Prepare yourself, for Yayali comes.

— TRADITIONAL ME-WUK STORY

# Contents

# Acknowledgements

There are many people I wish to thank for helping with this book.

Montra Freitas was my first field partner and was always there to hold my snacks when the going got tough. We have been though a lot together, and without you, I am sure I would not be the person I am today. Thank you for coming into my life when I needed a light. Her husband, John, was the first to experiment with call-blasting. He paved the way for many bigfooters to scream in the dark.

My friends in the Alliance of Independent Bigfoot Researchers (www.bigfootresearch.com) kept me laughing until my sides hurt. Teresa Hall, Kathy Harper, Rebecca Bridges, Paul Vella, Tim Cullen, Jerry Riedel, Tom Yamarone, and Scott Schubbe—thank you for your friendships over the years.

Thank you to Brain Brown for creating Bigfoot Forums as a place where I have met so many friends and shared so many ideas over the years.

Alton Higgins has been my greatest mentor—thank you for your patience.

Brenden Bannon and Tom Yamarone provided artwork and photos. Christopher Murphy worked very hard on the layout of the book. He kept me on track and provided vital advice, photos, and assistance. Words can't express enough how thankful I am for all of their help.

My wonderful family—mom, dad, Brenda, Jerry, Josh, Joe, Linda, Doug, Andrew, Samantha, Steven, Paula, Rachel, and Ethan—have stood by me all these years with encouragement and support. Thank you for your love and support.

My sons, Zackary and Jacob, never complained about the long hours in the field, the scary night sounds, or eating my campfire food. Though I know that sometimes you would have preferred to be somewhere else, thank you for being by my side.

Lastly, without my husband, Bob, none of this would have been possible. He encouraged me to gather these stories and read each one to help me decide which ones should be shared. Bobby—your wisdom has awed me; your humor uplifted me; and your love surrounded me. You are my soul. Thank you.

# North American Native Cultural Regions

# Introduction

As an anthropologist in California, I am very familiar with the traditional stories of our local tribes. I noted, as have others, a common motif of a child-stealing giant with a basket on his/her back. However, I was surprised to find a similar motif in tribes outside of California, such as in Idaho and the South. Intrigued, I began to find other similarities throughout the U.S.–cannibal giants, hairy monsters and human-like beings that lived in the woods. Could these characters be bigfoot? Of course, none of these stories directly used the term "bigfoot," but that would be expected since that term was only invented in the 1950s. But if these stories were about a bigfoot-like creature, what would it mean?

Native Americans and First Nation peoples have been in North America for thousands of years. Their interaction with the environment left them as experts of nature, including the soil, rocks, trees, plants, and animals. If bigfoot is real, native people would have had the earliest and longest contact with the species. Their experiences would be recorded in their stories and traditions. However, if bigfoot is not real, then these widespread stories would represent something else, perhaps the native version of a "boogyman," intended to keep children in at night and well-behaved.

The stories are presented as recorded and are categorized by the ten cultural areas of North America. The bigfoot-like characters are very obvious in some stories and less so in others. For example, the Cherokee story of "The Snake with the Big Feet," is about a snake with big feet that becomes human and marries the chief's daughter. Clearly, snakes do not have feet; nor do they turn human and marry human females. This story is included because after careful analysis of Cherokee stories, I believe the snake "represents" a bigfoot (as denoted by the big feet) and the story is designed to help the reader accept that a bigfoot "married" a human female.

It is very common in Native American traditions to "alter" or "hide" the true subject of the story in order to avoid taboos or taboo characters. In order to ease you into acceptance of the taboo creature, elements of a taboo character are often mixed with common animals or humans. You will see this often in this collection of stories where the bigfoot-like character can talk, has a home, and can do other human activities. While some will take these characteristics literally, one should be cautioned that the true intent of the storyteller may not be available for us to know.

These stories do not constitute proof that bigfoot exists. They simply represent a collection of stories told by Native people about a human-like giant, who at times is a man-eating cannibal, horrible monster, a thief, a trickster, a helper, and in a few stories, our creator.

Throughout this work I have provided images of the various native people discussed together with their artifacts and scenes from the regions in which they live. My purpose for this is to provide some insights into their culture and, thereby, bring about a better understanding of their stories and traditions.

# THE
# ARCTIC
# CULTURE

# Arctic Cultural Area

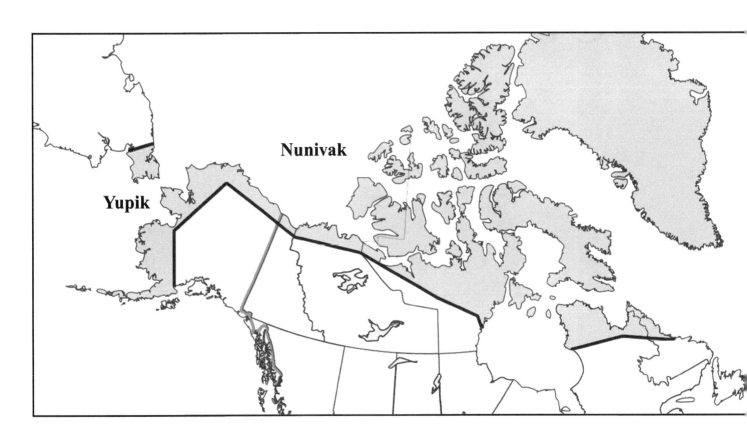

Yupik

Nunivak

# The Nunivak

The Nunivak are located in Alaska and along the coastline from the Aleutian Islands to eastern Greenland. Their traditional language is in the Eskimaun family. Please note that although the following story may not seem to be related to bigfoot, the story is included because of the cannibal aspect of the creature.

## The Cannibal Dwarfs

Source: *The North American Indian,* Vol. 20, by Edward S. Curtis, 1930. Massachusetts: The Plimpton Press, pp. 83–85.

A young woman and her brother lived so far inland that they had no knowledge of the ocean. While still young, the boy accompanied his sister, who provided for both by fishing, snaring mink, and netting squirrels; but, after attaining manhood, he hunted while she remained at home. The young man became a great hunter, and his caches were filled with squirrel and caribou-skins.

One day, late in the afternoon, when in need of meat, the young man set off for caribou, though his sister objected because of the lateness of the hour. Not far from home, he found a herd and shot one, which limped away wounded. He gave chase, but it was long after dark before he killed and skinned the animal. Unable to find the trail home, he wrapped himself in the fresh skin and slept. All winter he roved about the country, vainly endeavoring to reach home. Summer came, and by then he had reached the water, which was so vast in extent that he was unable to see the opposite shore. Now his boots were worn through, and his parka was tattered because he had cut strips from it to bind on his feet. One day, exhausted, he fell beside a stack of freshly piled driftwood. Not long afterward, he heard dogs howling, and soon two men, brothers, came by. Seeing him, they stopped, and noting his weak, emaciated condition, carried him to the men's house in their village. There, after being clothed and fed, he told the rescuers his story. He was sad because his sister was alone, except for a dog.

After the young man had recuperated, his rescuers told him: "You are just breathing [your life is in danger]. Some day some people here will cause you trouble."

Not long after, the men heard shouting outside and knew that a visitor was approaching the village. When near enough to be recognized, the young man saw that the stranger was his sister with her dog. She said to him, "The dog smelled your tracks and trailed you here."

Later, when sitting in the men's house, the young man was approached by a youth, a messenger, who said, "You, the stranger, must come with me."

The two brothers, the rescuers, asked the messenger, "Who wants him?"

"My sister wants him."

The two then informed the young man, "You may go with this messenger, but if you see his sister, you will never return alive."

He followed the messenger to the home of the sister, where he saw the girl crying. She sobbed, "When shall I see you again?"

The young man saw her parents in the room, two dwarfs [*jusfihhat*, little people], who said to him, "We pity you when you go out."

When they began to prepare food for him, their future son-in-law, the girl said to him: "Do not eat their food. Come and sit with me on this bench."

The dwarfs brought food to the young man, saying, "Our son-in-law, you must eat."

After giving him the dish, they returned to their side of the room. The girl said to her new husband: "Do not eat their food. Pour it out close to the wall."

On inspecting the food, he saw that it was composed of human fat. In place of it he ate caribou meat, which the girl handed him. After going to bed, his new wife said, "I wonder how long you and I shall be able to live together."

For a long while he was unable to sleep, but thought of what the dwarfs might do to him. Toward morning he was awakened by a crackling sound and the sting of smoke in his nostrils. Then he saw that the house was blazing furiously. He dashed through the entrance, his clothing and skin scorched. Outside, his wife was crying because she thought him burned to death, but the dwarfs were dancing and laughing: "Why are you crying so? Did you not give a thought to your parents and uncles who might need fresh meat?"

Upon hearing those words, the young man, enraged, threw the two dwarfs into the fire and turned to his wife, "Were you crying for them?"

"No. You can not kill them, no matter how hard you try. They will be back again soon."

He then went to the men's house, where his sister and his two rescuers were glad to see him alive and whole. The following day the messenger entered and again asked him to go to the girl. He went to his wife's home against the wishes of his sister and his rescuers. There he found his wife, eyes swollen with much crying, and the dwarfs, his parents-in-law. Again they prepared food and brought it to him, but he ate caribou meat instead, when he saw that the dish contained human hands.

At midnight he awoke just as the house, in flames, collapsed, and he was overcome. He came to consciousness in a strange men's house. All about him he saw dwarfs, uncles of his wife, sharpening flint knives and exclaiming gleefully to each other, "How glad we are that our niece has brought us meat!"

He noticed his own dog beside him. On discovering the dog, the dwarfs in glee shouted, "Our niece has brought us a relish to go with the man meat!"

The dog, very large and vicious, was an *ahlgalunuh* [polar bear] in a dog's form. The young man asked the dog: "What shall we do? What shall we do?"

After much thought of escape, he mounted the dog's back and the two floated up through the smoke-hole, escaping the clutching hands of the dwarfs. Outside he saw his two dwarf parents-in-law dancing, and singing: "Now our brothers are going to feast! Now our brothers are going to feast!"

The young man angrily exclaimed: "What mean little people! They are always playing tricks on me!" Snatching a club, he beat his parents-in-law, smashing their bodies and throwing the pieces in their men's house. They were never seen again in the village. He went to his own men's house, where he found his two rescuers, his sister, his wife, and his wife's brother, the messenger. With the last he often hunted, going out with him in a kaiak in the spring to catch seal. One time, when the two were hunting together, the young man killed a seal and stepped out of the kaiak onto an ice-floe to skin and cut up the carcass. Then the messenger paddled off. "Why are you paddling away in my kaiak?" he called.

"You killed my father and mother," was the answer, and the messenger started back for the village, leaving his companion on a drifting ice-floe. When he did not return, his sister and the dog traversed the shore, searching. At each village they inquired for the missing man. At one they told her, "We saw some one on the ice very far out, but it was impossible to go out in kaiaks to get him." At another village she was informed, "Yes, we saw a man on an ice floe during a heavy storm."

While traveling along shore, the dog suddenly stopped, sniffed the air, and plunged into the water, swimming until he disappeared from the sister's sight. After a long wait, she saw the dog again, carrying her brother on his back. They all then journeyed back to the village. Close to it they halted, and the young man instructed the dog: "The people here have played many tricks on us. Now we must do something to them, but my two rescuers and their wives are not to be harmed. You go to the village, select a man for a husband to my sister, and take a wife for yourself. Do as you please with the rest of the people."

When the dog returned, his jaws, flanks, and breast were flecked with blood. Entering the village, brother and sister found that all the people had been killed with the exception of those they had instructed the dog to let live. Their whole party then set out for the home of the young man and his sister.

# The Yupik

The Yupik are part of the larger Eskimo people. They still occupy their traditional homelands of western, southwestern, and southcentral Alaska and the Russian Far East. Their language is part of the Eskimaun family.

### The Strange Creature of the Mountains

Source: *Yupik Lore: Oral Tradition of an Eskimo People,* edited by Edward Tennant and Joseph Bitar, 1981. Albuquerque: Educational Research Associates, pp. 157–163.

Once upon a time there were some men herding reindeer up in the mountains along the Eek River. *Apatasok* was one of the herders at the time. The leader of the group was named Guy.

The men working with *Apatasok* said that they saw a man who made a loud hooting noise and who ran on his hands in the mountains and on the mountain tops. This was in the fall before the freeze. *Apatasok*, however, never saw this creature. He wished, even yearned, to see him.

Once as he was traveling downriver he heard a loud hoot coming from the mouth of the river. "I wonder what it will look like," he thought.

He kept going downriver at a slow pace, filled with curiosity. The hooting came from a distance towards where he was headed. Each sound was closer than the last. He was just coming around the bend when his backpack brushed against the limb of a tree. Because of this, he did not encounter anything after all. He was disappointed, because he wanted to see the creature.

Some time later, after herding reindeer, he was on his way home along the same river as before, when he heard a hoot ahead of him toward the mouth of the river.

"I suppose I won't see it this time either," *Apatasok* thought. In order to see it coming around a small point, he stopped above a bend and lay flat on his stomach in the grass. He loaded both of his twelve-gauge shot guns and cocked them.

He waited, very curious to see what it would look like. Then it came into view at the point. As the creature came into view, it hooted. Then it put its head down. When it put its head down, its eyes threw off fiery sparks. The creature stood about a foot off the ground. Its arms reached down below to its ankles.

It stopped and listened. Then it came toward *Apatasok*. It was not walking. Rather it was standing upright and propelling itself with its hands.

When it came to the bend, it stopped and hooted. As before, when it hooted its eyes threw off fiery sparks.

It was now about twelve feet from where *Apatasok* lay. *Apatasok* looked at the creature unafraid. As he watched, the creature stopped to listen.

After listening for a while, it slowly turned its head toward Apatasok and heard him breathing. When it caught sight of him it turned directly toward him and began to come closer.

As it came closer, *Apatasok* was suddenly filled with fear, because if the creature ever got him into its mouth, only his feet would show.

Full of fear, *Apatasok* stood up. He grabbed his guns, one on each side. He pulled both triggers at the same time, shooting the creature in the face. As the guns blasted, *Apatasok* passed out.

When he finally came to, he was in the middle of a field of short grass. The grass was flat and stretched as far as the eye could see. He looked around and saw some footprints going in one direction.

There would be one, two, three, and sometimes four footprints side by side, all going in the same direction. Apatasok followed them.

As he went along he thought, "The other workers may be worried about me. I should let them know first before I follow these footprints to see what is at the end of them."

He was thinking of going back to camp, but as he was about to turn back he passed out again. When he came to, he was in the middle of a small river. He could not move. He was paralyzed.

With much effort he moved his fingers until he could make a fist. He kept trying to move. When he could bend his arms, he took hold of one of his legs. He tried to limber his legs. He flexed it and stretched it. When the one leg improved, he did the same to the other.

As soon as he could, he stood up and began jumping up and down. The water in that small river was very shallow. Jumping up and down helped him warm himself, for he had been cold when he came to. He had forgotten about the creature he had shot.

Once he felt warm, he got thirsty. Looking around he saw a little stream. He went over to it and bent down to drink. As he bent down, he saw a hideous creature. It was his own reflection.

Filled with fear he stood up without drinking. He ran to his guns and fired all of his shells aiming in all directions.

When he was out of shells, he started for camp. He made a beeline to the workers' tents. They made tent camps in those days when herding reindeer.

Even if he came to any ponds, he headed straight for the middle and waded through them. He kept on a straight course.

Toward evening Guy began to worry about *Apatasok*. He went out looking for him from a vantage point. Presently, he saw him approaching. When Guy saw him, Apatasok was hidden in fog up to his waist.

As he came nearer the fog gradually went down. When he was only a short distance away, the fog totally disappeared. When he arrived, Guy asked him, "What happened to you?"

*Apatasok* said that nothing happened to him. Guy said, "Something had to happen to you. Anyone who is all right would not be coming in covered with fog."

*Apatasok* did not answer and they went down to the tent. When Apatasok entered, he drank water and ate. Only when he had finished eating did he speak about what he had seen.

# THE
# CALIFORNIA
# CULTURE

# California Cultural Area

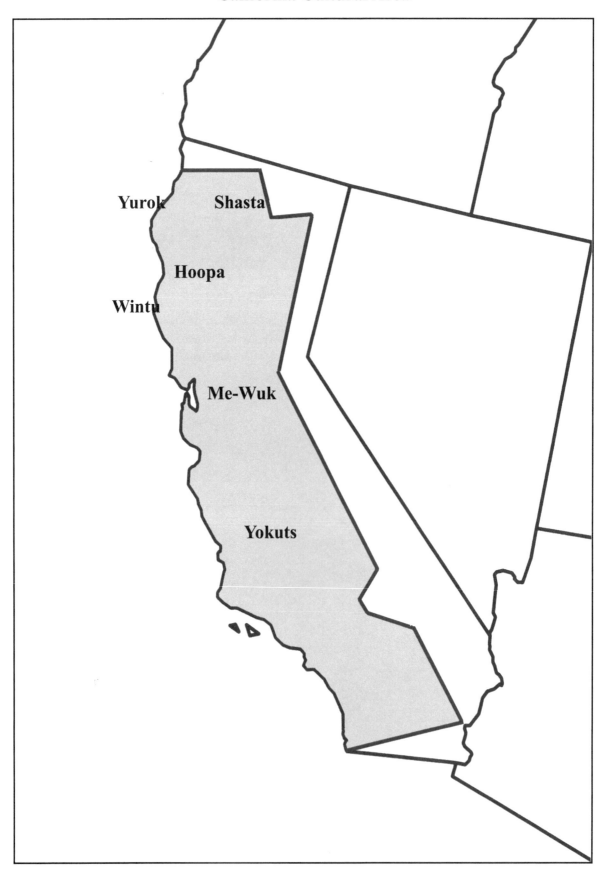

# The Hoopa

As in both prehistoric times and today, the Hoopa (also known as Hupa) inhabited the Trinity River area of northwestern California. They speak a language in the Athabaskan family. Their traditional words for bigfoot are *Oh Mah* ("boss of the woods") and *Wappeckquemow* (giant).

### *Wappeckquemow*

Source: *Legends Beyond Psychology,* by Henry James Franzoni III and Kyle Mizokami.

Among the tribes in the neighborhood of the Trinity River is found a legend relating to a certain *Wappeckquemow,* who was a giant, and apparently the father and leader of a pre-human race like himself. He was expelled from the country that he inhabited–near the mouth of the Klamath–for disobeying or offending the creator, and a curse was pronounced against him, so that not even his descendants should return to that land.

# The Me-Wuk

The Me-Wuk (also known as Miwok and Miwuk) occupied the foothills and valley plains of central California, as they still do today. Along with numerous tribes through the west, the Me-Wuk language is part of the Penutian stock.

The Me-Wuk are unique in that they have nine different names for bigfoot, depending on locations of the animal and behavioral characteristics. Names include *Ah-wah-Nee* (giant), *Che-ha-lum'che* ("Rock Giant of Calaveras County"), *Oo'-le* ("Rock Giant of the Chowchilla Foothills"), *Oo-wel'-lin* (rock giant), *Sachacha* (ogre), *Yalali* (hairy giant), *Yayali* (hairy giant), *La'-lum-me* ("Rock Giant of Wennok Valley"), and *Loo-poo-oi'yes* ("Rock Giant of Tamalpais").

### *Ke'-lok* and his Han-na-boo

Source: *The Dawn of the World–Myths and Tales of the Miwok Indians of California*, by C. Hart Merriam, 1910. Lincoln: University of Nebraska Press, pp. 75-82.

When *Wek'-wek* and *O-let'-te* were out hunting one day they went to *Tah-lah'wit* the North and came to a rocky hill where they saw a great and powerful giant named *Ke'-lok,* sitting by his *han-na-boo* or roundhouse. *Wek'-wek* flew close to him and saw him well.

That night, when they had gone home, *Wek'-wek* said to *O-let'-te,* "Grandfather, I want to play *al'-leh* [the hand-game] with *Ke'-lok.*"

When *O-let'-te* heard *Wek'-wek* say he wanted to play *al'-leh* with *Ke'-lok* he laughed and said, "You play hand-game with the Giant *Ke'-lok?*"

"Yes," answered *Wek'-wek,* "I want to play hand-game with *Ke'-lok.*"

Then his grandfather told him that *Ke'-lok* was his elder brother.

"All right," said *Wek'-wek,* "I'm going to play *al'-leh* with my brother."

After a while *Wek'-wek* arrived at *Ke'-lok's han-na-boo*, and when *Ke'-lok* came out, said to him, "Brother, I have come to play hand-game with you."

"All right," answered *Ke'-lok*, and he at once built a fire, and put eight round rocks in it and heated them until they were red hot. Then he said, "My young brother, you begin first."

"No," replied *Wek'-wek,* "I want to see you play first; you begin."

"All right," said *Ke'-lok,* and he immediately sprang up and darted up into the sky, for he was great and powerful and could do all things. As he went up he made a loud noise. Then he came down in a zigzag course, and as he came, sang a song.

Then *Wek'-wek* began to throw hot rocks at him but purposely missed him, for he did not want to kill his brother. His grandfather *O-let'-te* the Coy-

ote-man, called out to him from the south that if he hit *Ke'-lok* in his body it would not kill him, but that his heart [*wus'-ke*] was in his arm, under a white spot on the underside of the arm, and that if he hit that spot it would kill him; that was the only place on his body where a blow would kill him.

*Wek'-wek* answered, "I can easily hit that, but I don't want to kill him."

So he threw all the hot stones but took care not to hit the white spot under the arm. When he had fired all the rocks he picked them up and put them back in the fire to heat again.

Then it was *Ke'-lok's* turn.

When *Ke'-lok* was ready, *Wek'-wek* said, "All right, I will go now," and he shot up into the sky, making a great noise, just as *Ke'-lok* had done. Then he came down slowly, singing a song, and came toward *Ke'-lok's* roundhouse.

Then *Ke'-lok* began to throw the hot rocks at him and tried hard to hit him. But *Wek'-wek* dodged them easily and called out to *O-let'-te* his grandfather: "He can't hit me unless I let him, see me let him hit me"–for he thought he would not really be killed, believing that the magic of *O-let'-te* would keep him alive. So he let *Ke'-lok* hit him with the last rock.

*Ke'-lok* did hit him and he fell dead. Then *Ke'-lok* picked him up and hung him on his han-na-boo. *Ke'-lok's* place was at *Tah-lah'-wit,* the north.

When *Wek'-wek* set out to go there, his grandfather *O-let'-te* had told him to pluck out and take with him one of his father's long wing-feathers and stand it up on top of *Ke'-lok's han-na-boo* so it could be seen a long way off. *O-let'-te* said the feather would stand as long as *Wek'-wek* was alive, but if he were killed it would fall. While the hand-game was going on *O-let'-te* watched the feather, and when *Wek'-wek* was hit he saw it fall. Then he felt very sad and cried and told *Mol'-luk, Wek'-wek's* father, and they both mourned and cried.

Then *O-let'-te* said to *Mol'-luk,* "I'm going to play hand-game with *Ke'-*

*lok.*" So he took a long walking stick with a sharp point at one end and set out on the far journey to *Tah-lah'-wit*. When he arrived at *Ke'-lok's han-na-boo* he said, "Well, how are you getting along?"

*Ke'-lok* answered, "I'm getting along all right."

Then *O-let'-te* said, "I have come to play hand-game."

"All right," replied *Ke'-lok*; and he built a fire and heated the rocks red hot, just as he had done before. When the rocks were hot he asked, "Who will play first?"

*O-let'-te* answered, "I'm an old man, but I'll go first." So he shot up into the sky with a great noise, just as *Ke'-lok* and *Wek'-wek* had done before; and then circled around and came down slowly, singing a song of his own–different from the songs the others had sung.

Then *Ke'-lok* began picking up the hot rocks and throwing them at him. But *O-let'-te,* in spite of his age, was very agile and dodged all of the eight rocks so that not one hit him.

When *Ke'-lok* had fired all the rocks he said to himself, "Maybe my grandfather will beat me after all; I feel now that I am done for," and he was afraid.

*O-let'-te,* who was still in the air, then came down and said, "I'm old and tired of playing that way. Do you think old people can beat young people? I don't know, but I'll try anyhow."

It was now *Ke'-lok's* turn to go up and *O-let'-te's* turn to throw the hot rocks. *Ke'-lok* sprang up in the same way as before, and came down in the same way, singing his own song. *O-let'-te* picked up the hot stones and threw them at *Ke'-lok,* one after the other, until he had thrown four, but did not try to hit him. He then looked toward *Ke'-lok's han-na-boo* and saw *Wek'-wek* hanging there, and was very angry. When he picked up the fifth stone he said, "Now I am going to hit the white spot on his arm, over his heart," and he fired the rock straight and hit the white spot, and *Ke'-lok* fell dead.

As soon as *Ke'-lok* was dead his fire sprang up and began to burn and spread. Then *O-let'-te* went to *Wek'-wek* and took him in his hands. *Wek'-wek's* feathers moved a little; then his head drew in a little; then his eyes opened and he stood up and came to life and exclaimed, "The country is burning." And so it was, for the fire was now sweeping fiercely over the land, spreading swiftly to the east and west and south, roaring with a mighty roar, consuming everything in its way and filling the air with flame and smoke.

*O-let'-te* directed *Wek'-wek* to fly quickly to the ocean and dive under the water, where he had two sisters named *Hoo-soo'-pe* [the Mermaids], and stay with them while the world was burning. So *Wek'-wek* went into the ocean and found his sisters and remained with them until the fire had burnt over all the land and had burnt itself out. While with them he killed a great many ducks. His sisters did not like him to kill ducks, so after they had spoken to him he killed only what he needed to eat.

## *Oo-wel'-lin* the Rock Giant

Source: *The Dawn of the World–Myths and Tales of the Miwok Indians of California,* by C. Hart Merriam, 1910. Lincoln: University of Nebraska Press, pp. 169-172.

There was a great Giant who lived in the north. His name was *Oo-wel'-lin,* and he was as big as a pine tree. When he saw the country full of people he said they looked good to eat, and came and carried them off and ate them. He could catch ten men at a time and hold them between his fingers, and put more in a net on his back, and carry them off. He would visit a village and after eating all the people would move on to another, going southward from his home in the north. When he had gone to the south end of the world and had visited all the villages and eaten nearly all the people–not quite all, for a few had escaped–he turned back toward the north. He crossed the *Wah-kal'-mut-ta* [Merced River] at a narrow place in the canyon about six miles above *Op'-lah* [Merced Falls] where his huge footprints may still seen in the rocks, showing the exact place where he stepped from *Ang-e'-sa-wa-pah* on the south side to *Hik-ka-nah* on the north side. When night came he went into a cave in the side off a round-topped hill over the ridge from *Se-saw-che* [a little south of the present town of Coulterville].

The people who had escaped found his sleeping place in the cave and shot

their arrows at him but were not able to hurt him, for he was a rock giant.

When he awoke he was hungry and took the trail to go hunting. Then the people said to *Oo'-choom* the Fly: "Go follow *Oo-wel'-lin* and when he is hot bite him all over, on his head, on his eyes and ears, and all over his body, everywhere, all the way down to the bottoms of his feet, and find out where he can be hurt."

"All right," answered *Oo'-choom* the Fly, and he did as he was told. He followed *Oo-wel'-lin* and bit him everywhere from the top of his head all the way down to his feet without hurting him, till finally he bit him under the heel. This made *Oo'-wel-lin* kick. *Oo'-choom* waited, and when the giant had fallen asleep bit him under the heel of the other foot, and he kicked again. Then *Oo'-choom* told the people.

When the people heard this they took sharp sticks and long sharp splinters of stone and set them up firmly in the trail, and hid nearby and watched. After a while *Oo-wel'-lin* came back and stepped on the sharp points till the bottoms of his feet were stuck full of them. This hurt him dreadfully, and he fell down and died.

When he was dead the people asked, "Now he is dead, what are we to do with him?"

And they all answered that they did not know.

But a wise man said, "We will pack wood and make a big fire and burn him."

Then everyone said, "All right, let's burn him," and they brought a great quantity of dry wood and made a big fire and burned *Oo-wel'-lin* the Giant. When he began to burn, the wise man told everyone to watch closely all the time to see if any part should fly off to live again, and particularly to watch the whites of his eyes. So all the people watched closely all the time he was burning. His flesh did not fly off; his feet did not fly off; his hands did not fly off; but by and by the whites of his eye flew off quickly–so quickly indeed that no one but *Chik'-chik* saw them go. *Chik'-chik* was a small bird whose eyes looked sore, but his sight was keen and quick. He was watching from a branch about twenty feet above the Giant's head and saw the whites of the eyes fly out. He saw them fly out and saw where they went and quickly darted after them and brought them back and put them in the fire again, and put on more wood and burnt them until they were completely consumed.

The people now made a hole and put *Oo-wel'-lin's* ashes in it and piled rocks on the place and watched for two or three days. But *Oo-wel'-lin* was now dead and never came out.

Then the wise man asked each person what he would like to be, and called their names. Each answered what animal he would be, and forthwith turned into that animal and has remained the same to this day.

This was the beginning of the animals as they are now–the deer, the ground squirrel, the bear, and other furry animals; the blue jay, the quail, and other birds of all kinds, and snakes and frogs and the yellowjacket wasp and so on.

Before that they were *Hoi-ah-ko*, the First People.

## *Tim-me-la'-le* the Thunder

Source: *The Dawn of the World–Myths and Tales of the Miwok Indians of California,*
by C. Hart Merriam, 1910. Lincoln: University of Nebraska Press, pp. 173–178.

When *Oo-wel'-lin* the Giant was traveling south over the country eating people, there were two little boys, brothers, who were out hunting when he was at their village, and so escaped. When they came home they found that their father and mother and all the other people had been killed and eaten.

The younger one asked the other, "What shall we do? Shall we live here, only two of us? Maybe you are clever enough to turn into some other kind of thing and never die."

The elder brother did not know; he was stupid; the younger was the bright one.

For about a month they hunted birds and ate them; they had no acorn mush or other food, nothing but birds. One day they made a little hut of brush [called *o-hoo'-pe*] by a spring where the birds came to drink. Here they killed a great many birds of different kinds.

The younger brother said, "Let us save all the feathers of the birds we kill–wing feathers and tail feathers and all."

Soon they had enough for both, and the younger said, "We have enough. Let's be big birds and never die–never grow old."

"How are we to do it?" asked the elder brother.

The younger answered, "You know how the big birds spread their wings and go, without bothering to eat or drink."

In a few days they took the big wing-feathers they had saved and stuck them in a row along their arms, and soon had wings; and then they stuck other feathers all over their bodies and soon were covered with feathers, like big birds.

Then the younger brother said: "You fly; let me see you fly a little way." The elder brother tried but could not make his wings go.

"Try again and I'll help," said the younger, and he pushed his brother along; but though he tried again he could not fly, and dropped down.

Then they took more feathers and set them closer so they would not leak air. When they had done this the younger asked: "Do you think you can go this time?"

But the elder one replied, "Let's see you try."

"All right," the younger answered, and flew a little way.

"Now you try," he called, and lifted his brother up and pushed him to help him start, but when he had flown a little way he cried out that he could not go any farther.

"Go on, I'm coming," called the younger, and he soon caught up and came under his brother and sailed round and round and went up into the air and came down.

Then the younger said, "Now we can fly, what kind of animal shall we be?" The elder answered that he did not know. The younger said, "How about *We-ho'-whe-mah* [waterbird], who lives on the water in the back country?" "All right," replied the other. So they flew again, and the younger helped start the elder and flew under him so as to catch him if he fell, and they flew up and down and around.

The younger again asked his brother if he would like to be *We-ho'-whe-mah.* The brother replied, "No, I don't want to live on the water."

"Then how would you like to be *Tim-me-la-le* the Thunder," asked the younger. "We could come back sometimes and make a big noise and frighten the people. In summer we could go up through the north hole in the sky and stay up above the sky, and in winter come back here and make a big noise and rain to make the country green. Then maybe the people would come back and live again. We once had a father and mother and sister and uncle and grandfather and others. Maybe they would come back. We want to help them; we could make good rain to make things grow–acorns, pine nuts, grass, and all. Then maybe the people would come back and eat. We should never use food, never drink water, never grow old, and never be killed."

"All right," answered the elder, "We shall live always. But how are we going to make rain?"

"I'll show you," answered the younger. And they started again and went up very slowly, way up to the sky, and went north and found the north hole and went through it. When near the sky, but before they had gone through, the younger began to make a loud rumbling noise; it was *Tim-me-la-le* the Thunder. The elder tried but failed. The younger told him to try again. He did so and in a short time made thunder all right. Then they went through the hole and up above the sky into the *Yel'-lo-kin* country.

When wintertime came the younger said, "Come, let us go back." So they came down through the hole in the sky and traveled south and saw that people were there already. Then they shouted and made thunder and rain. After that they returned home through the north hole in the sky. And every winter even to this day they come back and thunder and make rain to make things grow for the people.

## *Che-ha-lum'-che,* the Rock Giant of Calaveras County

Source: *The Dawn of the World–Myths and Tales of the Miwok Indians of California,* by C. Hart Merriam, 1910. Lincoln: University of Nebraska Press, p. 231.

The Northern Mewuk say: *Che-ha-lum'-che* the Rock Giant carries on his back a big burden basket [*che'-ka-la*] which, like himself, is a rock. He lives in caves, of which there are two near Mountain Ranch or El Dorado in Calaveras County, one at Murphys, and one on Stanislaus River.

*Che-ha-lum'-che* comes out only at night and wanders about seeking Mewuk [people] to eat. He prefers women; of these he catches and carries off all he can find. Sometimes he makes a crying noise, *hoo-oo'-oo,* like a baby, to lure them. If they come he seizes them and tosses them into his big pack basket and carries them to his cave, where he eats them. In the basket is a long spike which pierces their bodies when they are thrown in, so they can not escape.

In his caves are the remains of his victims–horns of deer and bones of people and different kinds of animals.

Indians never throw their dead into caves. If they did, *Che-ha-lum'-che* would get them. Any man who would put a dead person in a cave would be killed by other Indians.

## *Oo'-le,* the Rock Giant of the Chowchilla Foothills

Source: *The Dawn of the World–Myths and Tales of the Miwok Indians of California,* by C. Hart Merriam, 1910. Lincoln: University of Nebraska Press, p. 232.

The Southern Mewuk say: Far away in the west, in the place where the sun goes down, lived *Oo'-le* the Rock Giant. At night he used to come up into the foothills to catch people and eat them.

## *Loo-poo-oi'-yes,* the Rock Giant of Tamalpais

Source: *The Dawn of the World–Myths and Tales of the Miwok Indians of California,* by C. Hart Merriam, 1910. Lincoln: University of Nebraska Press, pp. 232-233.

The *Hookooeko* of *Nicasio* and San Rafael say: A woman had a husband and two boy babies–twins. The woman's brother killed her husband and the little boys did not know that they ever had a father. When they were big enough they went off every day to play by a big rock in the woods. They went always to the same place; they liked this place and always went there. This was the very place where their father, when he was alive, used to go every day to sing, but the little boys did not know that they had ever had a father.

One day the boys heard somebody say: "You come here every day just as your father used to do." The voice came from the rock; it was the voice of *Loo'-poo-oi'-yes* the Rock Giant. Then the boys knew that had had a father. They went to the rock and saw long hairs sticking up. These hairs grew out of the nostrils of *Loo'-poo-oi'-yes;* the boys took hold of them and pulled them out.

This made *Loo'-poo-oi'-yes* angry and he took a long hooked stick and tried to catch the boys to kill them. He was all rock except a place on his throat where he wore an abalone shell. The boys saw this and shot their arrows through it and killed him. When he died he fell to pieces; the pieces were rocks and scattered over the ground. Inside he was flesh like other people, but outside he was rock, except the place on his throat where the abalone shell was.

### La'-lum-ee, the Rock Giant of Wennok Valley

Source: *The Dawn of the World–Myths and Tales of the Miwok Indians of California,* by C. Hart Merriam, 1910. Lincoln: University of Nebraska Press, p. 236.

The Olayome of Putah Creek say: In a cave under the cliff on the east face of *Oo'-tel-tal-lah pow'-we*, a small mountain southwest of the south end of Wennok Lake in Lake County, dwells *La'-lum-me,* the Rock Giant. He used to roam about nights, catching Indians and carrying them off to his cave to eat. He has not done this for some time.

### Sachacha, the Ogre

Source: *The North American Indian,* Vol. 14, by Edward S. Curtis, 1930. Massachusetts: The Plimpton Press, p. 176.

*Sachacha* lived among the cliffs along the river. His food was human beings. He would come to a village and take his choice of the women. Nothing could harm him. One day he went to a village and selected a fine, fat young woman, whom he took home; and afterward she gave birth to two children. Still he kept bringing home people for food, and nothing else. His wife had nothing to eat. She had two brothers, who came now to find her.

The younger said, "Where is our brother-in-law's weakest spot?"

She told them that his left ankle was the most tender spot.

When *Sachacha* came home, the brothers proposed a contest with arrows. So they set up a mark. *Sachacha* entered the contest, but gave them no chance to touch his left ankle. After a while they proposed a visit to the spring, and there while he kneeled down to drink, they began to shoot at his ankle. The arrows that struck his body simply glanced off, but one that struck the ankle killed him. Then they threw his two sons into the cave where he had slept on a bed of human hair, and with their sister they returned home.

### Yalali, the Giant

Source: *The North American Indian,* Vol. 14, by Edward S. Curtis, 1930. Massachusetts: The Plimpton Press, p. 177.

A man and his wife and his mother-in-law, and their little baby still in its basket, lived a short distance from the village. It was a season of famine, and the man remained out hunting late into the night. One night the two women with the baby were down beside the stream cooking buckeye soup. It was so late that the night was too cold for the baby, and the young woman decided to

carry it to the camp and leave it with her husband. For she thought he must have returned, because a fire had just been kindled in the hut.

A voice in the house said, "Give the baby to me."

She handed the infant in, and a hand took it. But a long, claw-like nail scratched her, and in fright she ran back to her mother and told about the adventure.

The infant meanwhile had begun a frightened wailing, and the mother ran back and said: "Give me the baby. He will not stay here."

The child was handed to her, and with her daughter she ran to the village. Untended, their cooking fire died down, and *Yalali*, the monster in the house, perceiving that they were escaping from him, gave chase and almost caught them just as they dashed into the door of the ceremonial house. In the morning the people made a plan for getting rid of *Yalali*. They trailed him to his home and found him in a tree gathering cones. For when he had no human flesh he ate pine-nuts.

They gathered brush and wood, and piled it around the tree, saying to him: "Gather here all the cones you can find, and we will bring the wood on which to roast them. We will pile up this brush, so that if you should fall you will not be hurt." When they had enough wood piled up, they set fire to it.

Then *Yalali* came down quickly, and in desperation tried to leap over the fire. But he fell into it and was roasted to death. His body was obsidian [volcanic glass], and when the flesh was burned off the obsidian burst and flew about in all directions, and was scattered among the tribes for the use of all.

## *Yayali,* the Giant

Source: *Miwok Myths,* by E. W. Gifford, 1917. Berkeley: University of California Publications in American Archaeology and Ethnology, Vol. 12, No. 8, p. 334.

"Where are you, grandchild? Where are you, grandchild? Where are you? Where are you? Yes. Yes. I am lost. Where are you? This way. Where are you, grandchild? Someone comes. Look out. Get ready. Prepare yourself, for *Yayali* comes."

The people broke cones from the tops of the pine trees and bundled these together. As *Yayali* started to climb the declivity where the people had taken refuge, they set fire to the bundles of pinecones and threw them into *Yayali's* burden basket. They threw the burning cones into the basket. *Yayali* became so hot that he tumbled. "Which way shall I fall?" he asked. They told him to fall to the north. [The Giant met his death near Columbia, Tuolumne County. The informant has seen white rocks near Columbia, reputed to be the bleached bones of the Giant.]

## *Yayali,* the Giant

Source: *Miwok Myths*, by E. W. Gifford, 1917. Berkeley: University of California Publications in American Archaeology and Ethnology, Vol. 12, No. 8, pp. 292–302.

The Giant walked from below. He shouted as he journeyed up the mountain, shouted all of the way. He shouted to the people as he searched for them, shouted all around the hills.

Chipmunk answered him. Chipmunk told the people that someone was coming up the mountain shouting. "Perhaps he comes to tell us something," said Chipmunk. "I shall meet him."

Chipmunk said to his wife, "I think your brother comes. I shall meet him, for I think he comes." It was raining heavily when Chipmunk went to meet the newcomer. Chipmunk called to him, "Come, tell us who you are."

The Giant answered Chipmunk by saying, "There is my meat."

Chipmunk again answered the Giant's call, for he thought that his brother-in-law was coming. Chipmunk at last realized that the newcomer was not his brother-in-law, and he said to himself, "I have found someone. I have met someone. He is not my brother-in-law." When Chipmunk saw the burden basket on the back of the Giant, he knew that he was not his brother-in-law.

Chipmunk said to himself, "I do not think I will go anywhere now. I do not think I will be able to reach home."

Just then the Giant approached him and asked him where he was going. Chipmunk replied, "My assembly house is over there." The Giant said, "Go ahead and I will go with you."

Upon arriving at the house, Chipmunk told the Giant to enter ahead of him, while he obtained wood and built a fire. The Giant insisted, however, that Chipmunk take the lead, saying that he was not a member of the family.

"You are the owner of the house," said the Giant. "You lead into your own house. I am not the owner of it."

Chipmunk demurred and asked the Giant to go ahead. "Take the lead, or you will freeze," he said to the Giant. "You have been in the rain and have become wet. I will build a fire for you."

Chipmunk's insistence was of no avail.

Again the Giant said, "You take the lead. You are the owner of the house."

Then Chipmunk, to save further argument, led the way into the house. The Giant followed him. As they approached the door, the Giant reached into his basket, securing a stone. He threw the stone at Chipmunk, striking him on the back and killing him.

After he had killed Chipmunk, the Giant told Chipmunk's wife to help him bring in the meat. He then made himself at home and married Chipmunk's widow. He cooked Chipmunk, the owner of the house, whom he had killed. He told his new wife to eat of Chipmunk's flesh after he had cooked it.

She said, "You eat it."

The Giant insisted, "You eat it, you eat it."

After the Giant left the house, his wife [Chipmunk's widow] dug a hole in the ground. She placed in the hole her daughter by Chipmunk. She fed the little girl with deer meat.

The Giant returned at sundown. He had in his basket many people, whom he had killed. When he entered the house, he said to his wife, "We will not starve. We have plenty of meat." The woman told the Giant to eat the human flesh himself. She cooked deer meat for herself. She ate the deer meat. The Giant ate the people whom he had killed.

The Giant's wife cooked deer meat, with which she fed her daughter, whom she had hidden in the pit. She did not wish the Giant to see her daughter; for fear that he might eat her.

As the Giant departed the next morning, he said to his wife, "You have a better husband than you had before. He obtains more meat than your former husband, Chipmunk. I go now to get you more meat."

He proceeded into the hills in search of more people. He told his wife before he left, that he would be back at sundown. As he departed he rolled a big boulder against the door, so that his wife might not escape. He rolled

large boulders against both ends of the assembly house, and also one over the smoke hole at the top of the assembly house, where the smoke emerges. He closed the doors tightly with large boulders. After he had closed the doors, he went into the hills, to capture more victims. He returned with a load of people in his basket. He had captured many large, fat people for his wife. He rolled the boulders aside, and entered the house.

While he was away, his wife had cooked deer meat. The Giant wished to feed his wife upon fat people. He told her to eat the flesh of fat people.

She said, "Yes," but instead she ate deer meat. The Giant thought that she ate the fat people, but instead she ate deer meat.

He threw away some of the human flesh, because he could not eat it all.

Again he obtained more fat people and cooked them. He told his wife to eat the flesh of the fat people. He said, "If you do not eat them, I will kill you." He said, "I think you have a very good husband. He always obtains plenty of meat, when he hunts. He never misses a person with his stone." Again he returned with a large load of victims, whom he cooked for his wife. He cooked, and he cooked, and he cooked. When it became dark he danced. He was so tall that his head projected through the smoke hole of the assembly house.

The Giant's wife gave birth to two boy babies. Both of them were little giants. She wished to kill them, but she feared that the Giant would avenge their deaths. She fed them and they grew. All the while she kept Chipmunk's daughter in the pit. She fed her continually with deer meet.

When the Giant departed for the day, she took her daughter from the pit, and held her in her lap, while the two little giants slept. She cried all day,

when the Giant was away. She mourned for poor Chipmunk. She feared the Giant, but she could not escape, because the boulders, which the Giant put against the doors, were too heavy for her to push away. So each day she sat in the house and cried.

When the Giant returned with more fat people in his basket, he told his wife, "You eat them. This is the meat which I cooked for you. You eat them. This is the best one. I selected it for you."

The woman replied, "Yes."

Then the Giant danced. He danced. He danced. His head went through the smoke hole, when he danced. When he felt happy he danced, his head going through the smoke hole.

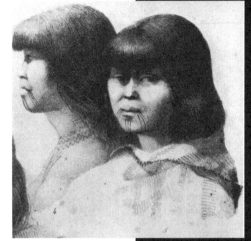

He told his wife, "Care for my sons. Don't lose them. Care for my sons. Do not fear hunger, for I will always bring you plenty of meat. I am always sure to obtain meat when I hunt."

He went into the hills again in the morning to capture more women and boys and men. He killed everybody, old people, young people, girls, and men. He killed so many that he filled his basket in a very short time. His wife, however, had plenty of deer meat, which Chipmunk had obtained for her.

Every night, when the Giant came home, he danced. After he had danced, he cooked the meat for his wife, giving her old men and old women. He took for himself the young people. When he came home, he brought pine nuts with his victims.

The old white-shelled pine nuts, that were worthless, he cracked and gave to his wife, "Eat these pine nuts. Here are plenty of pine nuts. You will not become hungry, if you stay with me.

Thus he spoke to his wife, when he came home each night. He said to her, "Eat these pine nuts, for I perceive that you are hungry."

His wife said, "Yes." However, she deceived him, for she did not eat the pine nuts. When he was not looking, she threw them away. She threw them away, when he was not looking. At the same time, she made believe that she ate the pine nuts. She ate only pine nuts which Chipmunk had obtained for her. She did not eat those which the Giant brought to her. Each time that the Giant went away, she ate from her own stock of pine nuts, which Chipmunk had collected for her.

The old women and the fat women that the Giant obtained, he brought to his wife; also those women who were pregnant. He said to his wife, "Eat. Eat well."

His wife replied, "Yes, I am eating them." Yet all the time she deceived him.

Again he went into the hills to hunt people. He traveled all over the country in his search. When he returned, he brought a large load of people. Upon his arrival, he cooked the old women for his wife. Then he danced outside of the assembly house. Afterwards he danced inside. His wife did not eat the old women whom he cooked for her.

She said, "Yes, I am eating," but she always deceived him. She worried every day; for fear that the Giant would kill her. That which he cooked for her she put into a hole, making believe, however, that she ate it. Instead, she ate deer meat. The Giant thought that she ate the persons whom he cooked for her.

The deer meat, which she cooked each day while the Giant was absent, she fed to her daughter in the pit. Each day, when she took her daughter from the pit, she cried. She felt sorry for the girl, because her father had been cooked in the fire. The thought of Chipmunk's sad end depressed her and

made her cry all day, while the Giant was away. When the Giant returned in
the evening, she hid her daughter in the pit. She herself lay over the pit, so
that the Giant would not find her daughter. She sat over the pit, so that the
Giant would not take the girl. The two sons of the Giant lay in the corners of
the house. The Giant changed them from corner to corner, when he came
home. The boys never cried. They laughed all the time. That is all that they
did.

Chipmunk's brothers below dreamed about him. One of them said, "I
think I will visit him. I will see how he fares. I dreamed that he was sick." So
spoke one of Chipmunk's brothers after he dreamed about him. He told no
one that he was leaving, but proceeded secretly into the mountains. He did not
follow the regular trail, but went through the brush, passing through the high
mountains. He spoke to no one of his proposed visit. He did not hasten, but
traveled slowly toward his brother's home.

At last he arrived at Chipmunk's assembly-house, he said to his sister-in-
law, "I am coming. Why are these large boulders against the door?"

Then his sister-in-law answered him from within, saying, "Come in. The
Giant killed your brother. He closes the door with those large boulders each
time he goes out."

Then Chipmunk's brother rolled aside the boulders at each end of the
house.

His sister-in-law said to him after he entered, "The Giant killed your
brother. Just see us. There are the Giant's two sons."

Her brother-in-law then inquired about her daughter. "Where is my brother's girl?" he said.

The woman replied, "She is in this hole. I did not want the Giant to see
her."

Chipmunk's brother asked his sister-in-law when the Giant would return. She said, "Sometimes he returns after sundown, sometimes before sundown. Today he went far and will not return until tomorrow morning."

Then her brother-in-law told her to crush some obsidian. He said, "You can go home. The Giant has many brothers. If they overtake you, and try to catch you, while you are on your way home, throw the crushed obsidian in their faces. I shall not go. I shall remain here."

She crushed obsidian and placed it on a deer hide. After she crushed it, her brother-in-law told her to start for home.

He warned her especially not to lose the obsidian. "If they catch you," he said, "you can use it. Throw it in their eyes." He then proceeded to dig holes in different directions.

Following his advice she started. Meanwhile he dug holes, one, toward the south, one toward the east, one toward the north, and one toward the west, He dug them so that he might conceal himself and dodge from one to the other in case he were pursued. He made holes all around the assembly house, both inside and outside. After he had finished digging the holes, he did nothing. He rested and walked about outside of the assembly house.

He thought about the Giant and wondered when he would return. He went into the hills and cut a manzanita stick, sharpening one edge of it. He worked upon it all day, making it sharp. His sister-in-law told him to be careful with it. He asked her what the Giant did when he came home. She told him that the Giant always danced, and that every time he danced, his head projected through the smoke hole, his head projected through the smoke hole at the top of the house.

He finally finished sharpening the manzanita stick, making it very sharp. Then he walked around, he walked around. While he watched the Giant came over the hill. He said to himself, "I think that is he coming now." He stood outside and watched the Giant. As the Giant approached the house, Chipmunk's brother stepped inside.

The Giant saw him and said, "There is another victim. There is another victim." The Giant was glad that he had another person to kill. The Giant followed close behind him into the house.

Chipmunk's brother had killed the two young giants. He gouged out their eyes after he killed them and threw their eyes into the fire, putting one in each corner. Before his sister-in-law had left, he had asked her where the young giants kept their hearts. She had told him it was in their ankles and that is where he hit them with the stick, when he killed them. After he had thrown their eyes into the fire, he went outside. The young giants were in each corner beside the fire. The two young giants were dead.

Chipmunk's brother now talked to the Giant. He asked him, "What do you do first, when you come home?" The Giant replied, "I dance. Just watch me dance."

Then Chipmunk's brother went into his holes and came forth in different places. The Giant tried to catch him and followed him about, but Chipmunk's brother was too quick for him and dodged into the holes. The Giant chased him around the assembly house. Every time that the Giant neared him, he jumped into a hole, appearing again in another part of the house.

He told the Giant, "You cannot catch me unless you dance. After you dance, I will let you catch me. I want to see you dance first."

Chipmunk's brother stayed outside, while the Giant danced. He shouted at the Giant and said, "Dance more. Jump higher through that smoke hole. I like to see you dance."

The Giant did as Chipmunk's brother told him. While he danced, Chipmunk's brother with his manzanita stick climbed on top of the assembly house. Suddenly he struck the Giant across the neck, decapitating him. The head rolled down close to the spring near the house and the body of the Giant collapsed inside of the house.

Chipmunk's brother then cut the Giant to pieces and scattered the flesh over the trees, on top of the rocks, and inside of the assembly house.

One of the Giant's brothers dreamed. He dreamed that his brother was obtaining plenty of meat. He said to the other brothers of the Giant, "Let us visit our brother. He is married now and obtains plenty of meat every day."

Then a large number of the Giant's brothers proceeded to the Giant's assembly house. When they arrived at the house, they saw the meat hanging on the trees. "Plenty of meat, plenty of meat, plenty of meat. Our brother is quite expert with his stone," they said.

Then they cooked the meat which they found on the trees, not knowing it was their brother's flesh. They thought that it was the flesh of various people whom he had killed. Each of them ate a piece. They had all that they wished.

The brother desired a drink, so they searched for the spring, which they found. Just as the youngest one was about to drink, he noticed the head lying beside the spring.

"We ate our brother," he said to his older brothers. Then they all returned to the house. The youngest one said, "Someone killed our brother."

"What shall we cry?" the youngest one said.

One of the others answered, "Well, we will cry 'oak.' I do not know who killed our brother. We do not know whence the murderer came. Let us sleep and dream about it."

After sleeping, they arose. The one who had proposed that they sleep pointed to the south. The others did not believe that the slayer of their brother came from that direction.

Each of the others said, "I have not dreamed about him yet. Let us sleep again." Again they awoke and the one who had dreamed said, "A man from the north killed our brother."

Again they slept, for they did not believe each other. One of them awoke and awakened the rest. "A man from the east killed our brother," he said. But they did not believe him.

The youngest brother, who found the head near the spring, started to cry. The others tried to stop him. He went again to the spring and thrust his head into the water. When he returned to his brothers, he pretended that he had cried more than they. They thought that the water on him was a tear. They said, "He is the only one who really mourns for his murdered brother." Then they said, "Let's sleep again."

The youngest brother dreamed and awakened the others. He told them that he dreamed that a man from the west had killed their brother. He said, too, "Our sister-in-law is on the way to her father's house. I surely dreamed it."

They all said, "Let's cry." The youngest one objected, saying, "Let's sleep before we cry." Then he dreamed again. He dreamed that his sister-in-law was on the way to her father's house.

"Well, let's arise," said the youngest brother. "Let's try to catch our sister-in-law before she reaches her father's home." Thus spoke the youngest brother. "We must hurry," he said. "After we have made a good start, we can slacken our pace." They all proceeded on their way shouting.

Chipmunk's brother laughed after he killed the Giant. The Giant's brothers all ran and Chipmunk's brother laughed. Before their sister-in-law reached her father's house, the Giants overtook her.

One of them said, "Here is our sister-in-law. You catch her," he said to one of his brothers. As one of them seized her, she threw a handful of crushed obsidian into their faces. They shouted, for she had thrown it into their eyes.

Each one said, "Something is in my eyes. Hurry, remove it. Hurry, remove it. Hurry, remove it. Hurry, remove it." They examined each other's eyes for the obsidian. They looked and looked and looked. While they were examining each other's eyes, their sister-in-law left them. Again they pursued her and overtook her before she reached her father's house. They said to each other, "Catch her, catch her, catch her."

One of them caught her. Again she threw the crushed obsidian. She threw it into his face before he caught her. "I have something in my eye," he said. "I have something in my eye. I have something in my eye. I have something in my eye." Again they examined each other's eyes to remove the crushed obsidian. They looked and looked and looked.

Again they followed her. They said, "Let's hurry. Let's catch her before she reaches home. Hurry. She has her daughter on her back." Then they ran. They ran to catch her. Just as they were about to seize her, she threw the crushed obsidian in their faces again. Each of them said, "She has thrown something into my eyes." Then while they examined each other's eyes, she escaped.

After they had removed the obsidian from their eyes, they said, "Hurry. Let's catch her." Then they ran. "Catch our sister-in-law. Hurry," they said. When they attempted to capture her again, she threw the obsidian in their eyes. "Something has come into my eyes. Something has come into my eyes. Something has come into my eyes. Hurry, remove it," each one said. "Hurry, so that we may catch her."

They ran after her again. Every time they ran they shouted. Once more she threw the obsidian in their faces and one of them got it in his eyes. Again she ran and they pursued her. They said, "We will catch her and hold her this time. She will soon exhaust her obsidian," Again she threw the obsidian in their faces, when they tried to lay hands on her. She threw it into their eyes. Then they looked into each other's eyes and removed the pieces.

"Hurry," they said, "so that we may catch our sister-in-law." Then they ran. Once more she threw obsidian in their eyes, when they were about to seize her. Again she ran and this time they were close behind her. They shouted continually, while they ran. When they attempted to seize her again, she threw the crushed obsidian in their eyes. They looked in each other's eyes and removed the obsidian. This delayed them and prevented them from capturing her. Again they said, "Hurry, so that we may catch our sister-in-law." Once more they caught her and she threw the obsidian in their eyes.

"She approaches her father's home. Hurry, that we may catch our sister-in-law," they said. They ran. The woman had not lost her daughter, while she was running. When the giants overtook her again, she once more threw obsidian in their eyes.

The woman said to her daughter, "We will reach home safely. We will reach your grandfather's. Hurry and do not become tired. Hurry or they will catch us."

In the meantime the Giant's brothers were drawing closer to her. When they went to catch her, she again threw the obsidian into their eyes. They examined each other's eyes and removed the crushed obsidian. She escaped from them again, while they were removing it. She had very little obsidian left, but she was nearing her father's house. She was approaching it, while the Giants picked the obsidian from each other's eyes.

"We are nearing home," she told her daughter, "so do not be frightened. Your grandfather [Lizard] will save us when we arrive there."

The Giants ran close behind her, shouting as they ran. They stopped frequently to dance and to sing. Then they would run after her to catch her. When they were about to catch her, she threw the crushed obsidian at them.

She drew near her father's house. The Giants ran after her, saying to each other, "We must catch her before she reaches home."

When they had nearly captured her, she threw the crushed obsidian in their eyes. That was the only way she could escape from them. At last she reached the house.

She called to her father to open the door. She said, "A Giant killed your son-in-law. Hurry, open the door. The Giant ate your son-in-law."

Her father opened the door, which was a large rock. After his daughter had stepped inside, he spat on the door so that the Giant's brothers could not open it. The assembly house turned into rock, when be spat upon the door, turned into rock all around.

The Giants encircled the house several times inquiring for the door. Lizard did not answer them. They finally became tired and sat down. Then they began to sing and dance.

The old man asked his daughter, "Who are they? Who are they?"

She replied, "They are the Giant's brothers."

The old man, her father, said, "Let the wind blow them away. Let the wind blow them away. Throw them away. I do not want them here." Then a great wind came, but the Giant's brothers turned and blew the great wind back.

Then the old man in the assembly house called a great snow. The great snow came and covered everything. "Come and cover everything," said the old man, when he called the snow.

After the snow had covered the Giants, they shouted and it melted. They shouted and the snow melted.

After the snow melted, the old man said, "It is strange that they do not mind me. What is the matter with them? It is strange that they do not mind."

Then he called the hail. He called the hail to try and force them to go away. He hoped that the hail would chase them away. Thus spoke Lizard, when he called the hail. When the hail started, the Giant's brothers shouted. The hail ceased immediately.

Then Lizard, the woman's father, called for a flood. He wished the water to wash away the Giant's brothers. Thus spoke Lizard, when he called for the flood to help him. The flood came suddenly and washed away the Giant's brothers, before they had an opportunity to shout. They did not return, for the water drowned them.

Then the woman told Lizard, her father, "The Giant killed my daughter's father. He killed him. The Giant killed him. He ate him after he killed him. When the Giant came, we thought that it was Chipmunk's brother coming to tell us something. I told Chipmunk to go and meet him, when he shouted. I did not know that it was a Giant coming. Then Chipmunk went to meet the Giant. When Chipmunk approached the Giant, he shouted to him and asked who he was. The Giant replied, 'Come here. I am here.' Thus spoke the Giant, when Chipmunk met him. Then the Giant said, 'That is my meat over there. I caught him, caught him, meat.' Thus spoke the Giant. We knew nothing about the Giant, but thought that it was Chipmunk's brother coming for a visit. Then Chipmunk brought the Giant home, brought the Giant home. He feared the Giant and tried to leave him in the hills, but the Giant followed him. Chipmunk's brother is there now. He has taken his dead brother's place. I do not know how he fares. He said to me, 'You go to your father. I will stay here. I will stay here and take my brother's place. I am ready for another Giant.'" [The Giant made his home on Table Mountain, near Jamestown, Tuolumne County.]

### *Yayali* the Giant

Source: *The Central Sierra Miwok Dictionary,* by L.S. Freeland and Sylvia M. Broadbent, 1960. Berkeley: University of California Publication in Linguistics Vol. 23, p. 58.

Two women are spreading out buckeye-nuts. To *Lymylymyla* from *Wakimy,* the women have come up. He, then, *Yayali* the giant appears to the east of them. While they are in the midst of spreading their buckeye nuts, he has reached the other side [of the valley] shouting as he comes, shouting! "A monster is coming!" say the two women.

The elder of the women has a child with her. "Give me the boy, let me take him on my lap!" says *Yayali.* "He always cries, you mustn't try to take him on your lap," says the woman.

"So I've found some wives for myself!" says *Yayali,* and he roasts meat for them, human meat, meat of the pregnant women he has brought in from hunting.

When this is finished, then says *Yayali*: "I'm going out after diggerpine nuts." It is almost dark when he appears again, coming from far away. [In the meantime the women] make a long torch. When it is almost dark they light it near where the buckeye is spread out, and after they have lit it they run away, west the women go, home to where they live in an earth-covered house. Away down in the west when they're almost home, they hear him.

"Run! He's coming!" says the older one to her little sister. He's close behind, he almost catches them. As they come near home, they've tossed the baby to an old woman, and have gone inside the earth-covered house. Tarantula has closed the entrance with a rock, and sealed it over with his nasal secretions.

"Give me the boy!" says *Yayali* to the old woman. He's tossed the baby in his burden basket and brought him to *Sewiya*. He threw the baby against a tree and the baby was transformed into tree.

Some people went out hunting deer after he had left. Over on the other side the hunters found *Yayali* [up in a tree], crushing pine cones with a rock to get the pinenuts out. "Why here's our grandfather, getting pinenuts!" they said. Two of them climbed up after him and began throwing pinecones in his burden basket. The people are gathering brush together at the bottom, while he is still up in the tree. He looks about wildly up there, as he feels the load of pine cones growing heavy. The fire has blazed up at the bottom of the tree, and the people have climbed down.

Then *Yayali* begins to cry out. "In what direction am I to die?" he says.

"To the west!" they say. They point it out to him. "To the west you're to die!" they say. He doesn't want to. "Die to the south!" they say. He doesn't want to. "Die to the north!" But that way he doesn't want to. "Die to the east!"

And as they say it he falls that way, east. His head rolls away east, and there it turns into obsidian, turns into arrowpoint rock over in the east. His dead body, that turns into rock. They named it *Kulto*, the place that used to be his body. That is the place where he died. [This is Table Mountain, a rock-covered mesa close to the Rancheria where these Indians live].

## *Yayali*, the Man-eating Giant

Source: Unknown.

And now we are telling a different story; this girl is sitting listening. Long ago, this *Yayali* was finishing off the people. He carried them off all the time, he used to kill them all and finish them off. Then he raised two little children, he brought them up. Then those children used to play with the skulls of their mother and their relatives, they used to roll them. They would roll them to the bottom from on top over a flat, sloping rock, then they would get them and take them back on top. They used to do that every day; the two little ones kept on playing. Then one day Coyote went to visit them and saw them. He stayed there who knows how long. He watched which way [*Yayali*] went, where he came out.

"Goodbye," *Yayali* said.

"Yes," he said; "I'll take care of the children here," he said. He asked the children, "Where does your grandfather come out?"

"Right there he'll always come out; he comes out there all the time," said the children.

In the evening, [*Yayali*] came, and they ate supper. But [Coyote] cooked this meat that he had put in the bottom of the pack basket and ate it himself, he ate this jackrabbit hidden here in his pack basket. Then it was night, and they went to sleep. When [*Yayali*] was snoring hard, [Coyote] looked for where his heart was. Then he found it in the middle of his foot. Then he stretched his feet out. When he stretched out his legs, this is the way he went when [Coyote] touched him in the middle of his foot: "Grunt, grunt, grunt," he said.

Then, "Oh, it's right there, your heart," [Coyote] said.

He went to sleep again. He did the same thing again, he stretched out, stretched himself out. Right in the middle of his foot, in the middle of it, he did the same thing that way. "Grunt, grunt, grunt," he said. "Oh, it's right there," said this Coyote. He went to sleep.

They got up the next day, and he went out the next day again. Just the same when he came back he came out in exactly the same place again. [Coyote] was watching carefully whether he would come out in the same or a different place. He didn't come out any other place, only in that very same place. The next day he went again, and the same way he watched where he went.

Then he asked the children again, "Will he come out the same place?" he said.

"Yes," they said.

"Does he always come out in the same place?"

"Yes," they said.

In the evening for supper he cooked the meat. Then Coyote would hide it in the pack basket and eat his own meat, not what he was given, he wouldn't eat that at all. Then they went to sleep at night.

Then early in the morning, "I'm going hunting again," [*Yayali*] said, and went. He went the same way he always went. Then Old Lady Coyote went out next.

"I'm going to get some wood," [Coyote] said to his grandchildren. Then he went on the other side of this high mountain, where he came out. He stuck his bone awls all around. Then when [*Yayali*] came back [Coyote] watched him.

"Oh, you just came out, coming back again," Coyote said. Coyote watched him. [*Yayali*] stepped on one [bone awl] and sat down to pull it out; [another one] stuck him right there in the buttocks. He rolled all around, and got stuck all over then, everywhere he went, where he rolled, then he got stuck all around in his ribs. Then he died.

Then [Coyote] told all these nations, "I killed this one, the one who was finishing off us people," he said. Then next they burned up this one that he killed.

"All of you watch well, you with good eyes. All watch this one. If we don't find his eyes, he'll finish us all off again," he said. "Keep looking, watch for his eyes to pop out," he said. So they burned him.

Then a little later, when [*Yayali*] got cooked, his eyes popped out. Everybody looked up. These two, Spotted Towhee and Brown Towhee, "You had better stay far off, you can't see, you've got too much matter in your eyes," they said to these two.

They stayed far off and watched again. Everybody failed to see it pop. So then, "Did you see it?" they asked these two with matter in their eyes.

"How could we see it?" they said; "Our eyes are no good. Look for it yourselves, you who have good eyes," they said.

"Please," they said. "He'll finish us all up if you don't tell us; maybe you saw where his eyes landed. But if we don't find them, he'll eat all of us," they said.

"Yes, under that thing, it looks like his eyes, [under] those leaves." Then they got them.

"Yes, that's it," they said. They got them, and mashed them all up. Then everything was all right. That's all.

# The Shasta

Historically, the Shasta occupied the northern most part of California in Siskyou County, where their reservation is today. Their language is part of the Hokan family. The Shasta have two names for a bigfoot-like creature, *Itssuruqai* (cannibal monster) and *Tah tah kle'ah* (Owl Woman Monster), a word that is shared with their close neighbors, the Yakama.

### The *Tah-tah-kle'-ah* (Owl-Woman Monster)

Source: *Ghost Voices–Yakima Indian Myths, Legends, Humor, and Hunting Stories,* by Donald M. Hines, 1992. Issaquah: Great Eagle Publishing, Inc., pp. 63-64.

Before the tribes lived peaceably in this country, before the last creation, there were certain people who ate Indians whenever they could get them. They preferred and hunted children, as better eating. These people, the *Tah-tah kle'-ah*, were taller and larger than the common human. They ate every bad thing known such as frogs, lizards, snakes, and other things that Indians do not eat. They talked the Indian language, and in that way might fool the Indians. There were five of them, all sisters. But at the last creation they came up only in California. Two were seen there. They were women, tall big women, who lived in a cave.

One time the Shastas were digging roots and camped. They knew that the two *Tah-tah kle'-ah* were about, were in that place. They were careful, but the *Tah-tah kle'-ah* caught one little boy, not to eat, but to raise up and live with them. The boy thought he would be killed, but he was not. The *Tah-tah kle'-ah* had him several days. Every day the big women went out to gather stuff for food. Each had a big basket on her back and would come home with it filled with everything bad–frogs and snakes. These they would throw in the fire alive to cook. Then, with a stick, they pitched them from the fire to the boy to eat. But he would not eat them. He went out and looked for his own food, roots and other things he liked. He did not try to escape, to get away. He was afraid to being overtaken and killed. The *Tah-tah kle'-ah* might roast him and eat him.

Often at night after the *Tah-tah kle'-ah* had eaten, there would be left in the baskets some objects the boy could not see. These he believed to be human beings. They were roasted and eaten after he had gone to bed. He was allowed to see everything brought in the basket, all but these particular beings, whatever they were.

Each day the boy would go farther and farther from the *Tah-tah kle'-ah's*

cave. He went in search of food and to play. At last he began searching to find his way back to his people. He kept looking for a way to reach them, but each night he would return to the cave.

One day the little boy had all plans laid. He was going to run away from the rock-den of the Monster-women, leave them and their bad, poisonous things. The *Tah-tah kle'-ah* left in the morning with the big baskets over their backs. When they were out of sight, they boy hurried away. He ran fast, traveled over rough, wild places, and at last reached his own people. They were glad, for they had supposed him dead. He was now safe.

## Owl-Woman Monster

Source*: Ghost Voices–Yakima Indian Myths, Legends, Humor, and Hunting Stories*, by Donald M. Hines, 1992. Issaquah: Great Eagle Publishing, Inc., p. 65.

Owl [*Sho-pow'-tan*] was the man. He was a big chief who lived at *Po-ye-koosen*. He went up the Naches to hunt deer. Many men went with him. They hunted all one sun, and when evening came, Owl did not return to camp. The hunters called to each other, "Owl is not here! Owl is away! Owl is lost!"

*Tah-tah-kle'-ah*, the evil old woman with her basket, heard that call in the twilight, "Owl is lost!" And she said to her four sisters, "We must go hunt Owl who is lost from his people. We will get him for ourselves."

Owl knew that *Tah-tah-kle'-ah* was coming for him; so he went up to a hollow place in the *Tic-te'ah*. You can see the trail that he traveled up the face of the rock to the cave high up in the wall of *Tic-te'ah*. Grass is growing along the narrow trail. You can see it when you are out from the rock where it winds up the cliff."

Owl had killed a deer. He filled the tripe with the blood of the deer. He heard *Tah-tah-kle'-ah* coming, and he knew she would kill him. He knew, and he placed the blood filled tripe in front of him. *Tah-tah-kle'-ah* entered the mouth of the cave. She looked. It was dark, but she saw it, the strange thing lying there. She did not know. She was afraid. She called to Owl, "Take it away! I do not like it!"

Owl said, "No! That is something powerful, step over it." *Tah-tah-kle'-ah* did as told, stepped her foot over the tripe. Owl was ready. He did not get up. He sat there; and when the *Tah-tah-kle'-ah* stepped, he punched the tripe with his stick. He punched it often and it went, "Kloup! kloup! kloup!"

*Tah-tah-kle'-ah* was scared! She screamed, threw up her hands, and fell from the cliff. The *wana* [river] ran by the base of the cliff, deep and swift. *Tah-tah-kle'-ah* fell into the water and was killed."

## How Rabbit Killed *Tah-tah kle'-ah*

Source: *Ghost Voices–Yakima Indian Myths, Legends, Humor, and Hunting Stories,* by Donald M. Hines, 1992. Issaquah: Great Eagle Publishing, Inc., pp. 191-192.

*Tah-tah kle'-ah* wanted to eat Cottontail Rabbit, *Iques*, but Rabbit always got away from her. Rabbit was too quick, too smart for *Tah-tah kle'-ah*. They were along a river; Rabbit made it cold. He called the blue ice to come on the water. *Tah-tah kle'-ah* wanted to cross the river. Rabbit found a place in the night where the ice was thin, where the water was swift and strong. He placed his dung all across on the ice, made them to look like rocks. Rabbit told *Tah-tah kle'-ah* that he had found a good place where she could cross. He showed her the "stones" all laid on the ice. Rabbit said to her, "Look! See how strong the ice is. It holds up ten rocks. You can walk across on the ice here."

*Tah-tah kle'-ah* started out on the ice. It began to crack, to break with her. She came back scared, afraid! Rabbit than took up dung which looked like a stone and threw it hard out on the ice. The stone struck and bounced along the ice. Rabbit instructed *Tah-tah kle'-ah*, "Fill your leggings with rocks. They will help you to go on the ice." Rabbit helped *Tah-tah kle'-ah* fill her leggings with real stones. She walked out on the ice. It began to break again; she stopped. Rabbit called to her, "Go on! There is no danger."

*Tah-tah kle'-ah* walked out to about the middle of the river. The ice broke. *Tah-tah kle'-ah* dropped through into the cold, swift water. She drowned. Rabbit was now no longer afraid of her catching him and eating him.

54

## How Coyote Tricked the People (Devouring *Tah-tah kle'-ah*)

Source: *Ghost Voices–Yakima Indian Myths, Legends, Humor, and Hunting Stories,* by Donald M. Hines, 1992. Issaquah: Great Eagle Publishing, Inc., pp. 215-216.

Coyote [*Speel-yi'*] was traveling along the mountain slope on the north side of the *n-Che'-wana* above [what is now] Fall Bridge. He looked ahead on the trail. Something was coming, something to meet him on the trail. It was big, something bad! It looked frightful! Coyote stopped and looked again, took a good look. Yes, he knew what it was, knew what he was going to meet. It was *Tah-tah kle'-ah*, the monster who devoured everybody she met. It was too late to run. He could not escape by running. Coyote had to act quickly or he was gone. He knew what he would do. The great leaning wallrock in the mountain side hung over as if it would fall down. Coyote hurried, placed his hands against the face of the ancient cliff. He braced and pushed hard! *Tah-tah kle'-ah* came up to him. She looked at him and said, "What are you doing? Why do you do that?"

Coyote answered, "Do you not see that the rock is falling from its place? Come hold it while I go bring a pole-brace to prop it. Push hard! Do not let it fall from its place."

*Tah-tah kle'-ah* put her hands against the cliff and bore with all her mighty strength. Coyote ran away looking for a timber-brace, a big pole of some kind. He went fast, looking everywhere along the trail. There was no *ilquis* [timber] growing there. Coyote knew this. He went faster. He wanted to get away from the *Tah-tah kle'-ah*. When Coyote stayed long, when he did not come back, *Tah-tah kle'-ah* grew tired. She slacked pushing. The rock did not fall! It stood there firm and fast; nothing could pull it down. The *Tah-tah kle'-ah* knew. She said to herself, "That was Coyote! He tricked me and got away."

## Destruction of the *Itssuruqai* Monsters

Source: *The North American Indian,* Vol. 13, by Edward S. Curtis, 1930. Massachusetts: The Plimpton Press, pp. 204-212.

*Itssuruqai* was coming up Klamath River, devouring people. As his name indicates, he was extremely emaciated. The people fled when they knew of his approach; for whenever he reached a village, he would go into the houses, and any whom he found he would eat. Coyote, hearing of this, laid a great pile of firewood, put cooking stones among the sticks, and then covered his body thickly with white pitch. The next morning *Itssuruqai* was seen approaching. He came to Coyote and spoke in a hoarse whisper, like a man whose lungs are not good: "I would like to taste your meat."

"Well, we will make a fire outside," said Coyote.

"I will take you first."

Coyote sat near the fire, and *Itssuruqai* cut a piece from his breast. But it was only the white pitch that he cut off. He held it before the fire, roasted it, and ate it. He said, "Your meat is too strong."

"Well, many people everywhere talk about me," replied Coyote. "That is what makes my meat sour. I would like to taste your meat."

"All right," said *Itssuruqai*. Coyote made ready to cut off a piece; but he

cut out the lungs and the liver and the heart, and ran away with them, pursued by *Itssuruqai*, who cried: "My heart, my heart! Give back my heart!" Coyote ran swiftly, and after a time he doubled back to the fire, which was now a great bed of coals. The people had raked a hollow in them, and therein Coyote threw the heart and lungs and liver of *Itssuruqai*. There was a great explosion, and *Itssuruqai* himself fell dead. Then all the people in the country, hearing the noise, said, "Oh, Coyote has killed *Itssuruqai*!"

In the high western mountains lived *Itssuruqai* with his grandson and ten Chipmunks, his slaves. When he came home at night, he would order one of them in his husky whisper, "Go, get water!" But the slave would refuse, and he would say then: "Oh, you are bad I will hang you!" So he had hanged nine slaves on nine successive days, and only the youngest Chipmunk was left. He piled up a great quantity of brush like a woodrat's nest, and in the bottom he spread cattail down. He went hunting and killed a small squirrel, which he laid in the ashes undrawn. When it was cooked, Chipmunk opened it and took out the steaming entrails. He said, "Oh, see what a fat squirrel!" *Itssuruqai*, who always sat with his back to the fire, looked about, and Chipmunk dashed the hot entrails in his eyes, and ran. Blinded with the heat, *Itssuruqai* could not see to pursue his slave, but he took his little grandson on his back and gave chase as best he could. Chipmunk led them out into the brush and into the midst of the pile which he had arranged, and when they were in the very center of it, he put fire to the cattail down. Then *Itssuruqai* exploded with a great noise, and the people in all the land knew that he had been killed.

There were ten brothers, and one was married. His mother-in-law was always warning them, "Do not go to the top of yonder mountain." One day the eldest brother thought: "Why does she tell us not to go to that mountain? I think I will go and see." So he went to the mountaintop and sat down. A man came. He was very thin, and had red leggings, a red shirt, and a red hat. His clothing was the red summer coat of a deer. He sat down in front of the young man and said in a hoarse whisper, "Fill it up!" The young man filled his pipe and handed it to the stranger, who smoked. Almost at once the pipe burst. The young man thought, "Well, he is going to kill me." The stranger whispered, "Try my pipe!" He filled it, and the young man tried to smoke, but was not strong enough to draw through the stem. The other said, "Let me see your bow!" He took the bow, drew it, and the bow snapped. "Let us wrestle!" he said. The young man thought, "This is the time he is going to kill me." So they wrestled. The knoll on which they stood fell away in a precipice, and at the bottom was a lake. Soon the young man was thrown down into the water.

When the eldest brother did not come home, the next eldest went to search for him, and, following his tracks, came to where he had sat on the mountaintop. He sat down in the same spot, facing the same direction, with his feet in his brother's tracks; and soon he saw the red-clothed man coming. First they smoked, then they drew the bows, and last they wrestled; and the second brother was hurled into the lake. In this way nine brothers were destroyed.

Then the youngest took up the search. He was very small. When the stranger commanded, "Fill it up!" he filled his pipe and handed it to him, saying: "I think your father never had a pipe like this. For I am very poor." His pipe was tightly bound with deerskin, and though the stranger drew as powerfully as he could, he was unable to break it. He gave the youth his own pipe, which broke when the youth smoked. The stranger failed also to break the young man's bow, but his own was broken by the youth. Then they wrestled, and the youth hurled his opponent into the air, and he fell with a great noise into the lake. When the people in the country round about heard the noise, they knew that *Itssuruqai* had been killed. Then the youth went down to the lake, and gathering up the bones of his brothers, took them home and laid them in the sweat-house, and built a fire therein. Whenever he went in to replenish the fire, he did not look at the bones. After a while he heard sounds in the sweat-house, "*Hu, hu, hu!*" All day the sounds grew louder, and at sunset there was a voice, imploring: "Please, brother, let us come out! It is very hot." He opened the door, and his nine brothers stepped forth and went to swim in the river.

# The Wintu

T he Wintu historically occupied the northwestern portion of the Sacramento Valley, California. Their language is part of the Penutian group. The traditional Wintu word for giant man is *Supchet*.

## Story of *Wineepoko* and *Supchet*

Source: *A Bag of Bones–Legends of the Wintu Indians of Northern California,* by Marcelle Masson, 1966. Happy Camp: Naturegraph Publishers, pp. 84-91.

Long, long ago there lived at Flume creek about three miles below Castella lots of Indians. Some lived in common houses, some in earth lodges. There was one man who had twelve sons. The Indian men hunted for deer and some went fishing for salmon, while the womenfolk gathered berries, potatoes and greens, the season being summertime. They hunted north, south and east across the Sacramento River. They killed plenty game and caught plenty fish, so they always had plenty to eat.

As the time went by the people were increasing, so game was getting scarce in those directions where they had been hunting most; so some went hunting toward west, following Flume creek.

This one man, *Wineepoko*, who had twelve sons, was chief of people and also was bow and arrow maker who had superhuman strength for a little man, for he was short in his make-up.

While the other men would go out hunting he and his twelve sons stay at home making bows and arrows with good flint points on the arrows. He was teaching his sons to follow his trade for a living.

Pretty soon his oldest son got married and they lived by themselves.

One day when they went hunting westward one went farther west up hill. He saw a large deer way west nearly to the top of mountain and finally caught up with it and killed it. It happened to be on ridge east down hill toward Flume creek. While he was skinning the deer he saw a nice large grouse on a limb of fir tree near him. Instead of finishing skinning his deer he goes shooting at the grouse until he shot all his arrows away. Still the grouse sat on the limb, never moved. Just then he looked westward. He saw a large tall man coming towards him. Nearer he came. He looked terrible in his face, but he waited for him, to see who he was. Finally the tall man comes up to him, says, "hello, my good man. What a nice deer you have killed. Have you shot at my dear pet grouse? One is sitting there on limb on tree." *Wineepoko's* son said, "yes, but I could not hit it."

This tall big man that he is talking to is *Supchet* who lives west of big rock mountain, west of Castella, head of south fork of Castella creek. This grouse that sits on limb of fir tree is a magic grouse put there by *Supchet* to fool Indian people. So now after talking a while, *Supchet* says to *Wineepoko's* son, "you look young and strong, what say let's wrestle?"

Other fellows say no, but *Supchet* begged him to wrestle. He caught hold of his arm and told him to come on, get up. But *Wineepoko's* son said, "no, I don't want to wrestle."

*Supchet*, being much bigger man, pull him up on his feet; then they wrestle and fight for a while until *Wineepoko's* son gave out. Then *Supchet* threw him down hard on ground, took his heart out, took it home, going west.

All other men have gone home with their game by now, but this one man has not come home yet. Night coming on and he still hasn't showed up. His father and mother and brothers are getting worried.

Next morning they all got up early, went down to river, took bath, came to the house and ate breakfast. One of *Wineepoko's* sons says, I will go out and look for my brother while others are hunting for game. All right, said old *Wineepoko*. The other sons stayed with their father at home making bows and arrows.

After going up westward, the one that is looking for his brother comes to a ridge going west up hill, finds his brother's tracks, follows the track up the ridge. He sees where his brother had sat down to rest. While standing and looking around he saw a nice large grouse sitting on a limb of a fir tree. Not hunting for deer, he thought he had better shoot at grouse, so he shoots at it. He shot and shot until he shot all his arrows away. He looks at the grouse, thinking what a poor shot he was. While looking around he looked towards west and saw a tall man coming toward him. He waited to see who he was and where he came from, for he was total stranger to him. He saw he was very rough looking and ugly.

The tall man comes to *Wineepoko's* son and says "hello, my good man. Where have you come from? Very far?"

It seems *Wineepoko's* son did not find his brother's body so he asked *Supchet* if he had seen anybody the day before.

"No," said *Supchet*, "you are only one I have met so far." So they talked awhile. Finally *Supchet* says to *Wineepoko's* son, "you seem to be young and strong, what say let's wrestle?"

*Wineepoko's* son said, "no, I cannot wrestle; I am not strong enough for that game."

"Oh, come on," said *Supchet*, "I show you how."

So he grabs hold of one arm, pulls *Wineepoko's* son up and grabs him around the waist. They start to wrestle. Finally comes to fighting. They fight and fight until *Wineepoko's* son gave out and fell to ground. Then *Supchet* killed him, cut his chest open, took out his heart, took it home to west.

Meantime, like day before, other hunters are already going home with their game. After sunset, and *Wineepoko's* son has not come home yet. Finally night comes on. He has not showed up. Now all the people are worried and say to old *Wineepoko*, let's go in your big earth lodge, hold meeting what to do. So they all went into the earth lodge, menfolk only, and decide old *Wineepoko* and his ten remaining sons go look for his two lost sons, one son every day until all ten sons not come; then old *Wineepoko*, the father, go last.

All agreed. So every day these ten remaining sons go out to look for their brothers. Each day no one come home to tell their father and mother where they been. Finally, all the sons were gone.

When the last son, who was the oldest, was gone, old *Wineepoko* calls the rest of his people to come in his big earth lodge and hold another meeting. Old *Wineepoko* told his people he would go out look for his lost sons and if he did not come home for them all to look for him next day. All agreed.

Old *Wineepoko*, for first time, got up earlier than others. He went down to river, took a bath, came back to his big earth lodge, ate his breakfast. Then he gathers up all the tools he uses for making bows and arrows and put them in his best otter quiver. He also took his smoking pipe and strongest tobacco he had. He says to his wife and all his people, "I am going. If I don't come back tonight all you men look for me together. Not few; all of you, mind you."

So old *Wineepoko* went west, up Flume creek, and came to ridge leading up west. He saw his lost sons' footprints. When he saw those tracks he commenced to sing "*Wini, wini, wini, wini*," his mournful song as he went along. He kept up his singing until he saw a nice large grouse sitting on fir limb just ahead of him. When he got near the tree he stopped and looked at it a while. Finally he thought he had better shoot at it. So old *Wineepoko* got his bow and arrow out of his quiver and shot at the grouse. He only knocked the feathers off of it. The grouse flew away. It was the first time it ever got touched by anybody.

Old *Wineepoko* sat down on a rock and looked around. He found that he was sitting where someone had been fighting. He saw the ground was pretty well worn down. While sitting there singing his mournful song he looked to the west and saw a tall man coming toward him. He came slowly, taking his time.

Old *Wineepoko*, looking at him all time never takes his eyes off of him; he saw he was very mean looking and ugly. The tall man comes to him and says, "hello, old man. Are you taking rest here? You found good place to rest."

This was *Supchet*, a giant. Instead of answering him old *Wineepoko* sings his mournful song, "*Wini, wini, wini, wini*."

*Supchet* says, "I am talking to you; answer me. Where have you come from? Tell me, quick."

Old *Wineepoko* kept on singing, "*Wini, wini, wini, wini*."

"Don't '*wini, wini*' me. Come, old man, talk to me like man," says *Supchet*.

Old *Wineepoko* stopped and looked at him sharp and said, "when you get old and feeble as I am you'll talk to your chiefs."

*Supchet* says, "old man, fill your pipe with tobacco. Let's smoke."

Old *Wineepoko* said, "when you get old and feeble as I am you'll fill your pipe and give it to your chiefs to smoke."

Finally *Supchet* said, "I'll fill my pipe. We'll have a smoke." So he filled his pipe with poison tobacco, lighted it, and handed it to old *Wineepoko*. He got hold of it but the pipe fell to the ground and got broken.

*Supchet* said, "now you have broken my pipe! What you do that for?" He was getting angry now.

"It did not like my hand so it broke," old *Wineepoko* said.

*Supchet* said, now you fill your pipe with your tobacco. Let's smoke yours.

So old *Wineepoko* filled his pipe with strongest tobacco he had, lighted it, took couple puffs and handed it to *Supchet*. He smoked. After three or four puffs he choked. He almost fainted. He threw pipe down on top of rock, hard as he could, but it did not break. *Supchet* said to old *Wineepoko*, "your tobacco is no good; it pretty near choke me. What kind of tobacco is it?"

"It is good tobacco. Finest I got," old *Wineepoko* said.

After sitting down a while *Supchet* said, "let's wrestle, old man."

Old *Wineepoko* said, "when you get old and feeble as I am you will wrestle with your chiefs."

"Oh, come on, old man." *Supchet* was getting desperate now. "Come on, I said, old man, come on!" He gets hold of one of *Wineepoko's* arms and pulls him up; being young and big and powerful, he pulls him up on his feet.

"Now you grab me 'round my waist," *Supchet* says to him.

"I can't," says the old man, "I'll grab hold here." And he grabs around *Supchet's* legs. "No, no, old man, up higher." He takes hold of old *Wineepoko's* arms and puts them around his waist.

"All right," says old *Wineepoko*. He squeezed *Supchet* hard. They fought for a long time. Finally old man was getting tired. He tells his tools that he had sacked in his net bag to come out and help fight this man. So all the tools jumped out of net bag, went to pound and drill into *Supchet's* legs and finally got *Supchet* begging for mercy. But old *Wineepoko* would not listen to him; he finally knocks him down and kills him.

Old *Wineepoko* now takes out his flint dagger, cuts *Supchet's* chest wide open and takes his heart out. He also cut scalp off *Supchet's* head and ties both on a stick. He goes west, following trail where *Supchet* came. He got to *Supchet's* earth lodge, found *Supchet's* wife and daughter, killed them both, cut out their hearts and scalped them and tied them on stick with *Supchet's* heart. He looked around in the earth lodge. He saw twelve hearts hung up, pretty well up in the earth lodge. It was his twelve lost sons' hearts. He takes them down, goes back to his home. On way he comes to a lake; here he washes his twelve sons' hearts, making them look fresh. He goes on down east and the day was getting pretty much in afternoon.

Just before he got to his earth lodge he leaves his sons' hearts in a deep hole in Flume creek, then goes.

His wife and all the other people were glad to see him home. They saw he had killed the *Supchet*; he had three hearts and three scalps tied on a stick.

That night they dance war and scalp dance. About toward daylight all twelve *Wineepoko's* sons came home alive.

So this ends this story. I finish.

# The Basket Woman

Source: Unknown.

Long ago when the children would gather around the fire, the elders spoke of a terrible one who walked among us in the shadows of the night. This is that story for all of our people, whether they are young or old.

"Don't go out there in the dark," the young father warned his children. "Stay here close by the fire where we can see you," he added. The children had heard this before, but there seemed to be an air of urgency in their father's voice. "We'll stay close," they replied. "We will stay close" was the standard answer, and the one the adults wanted to hear. But some of the more adventurous children would soon steal away into the dark.

On this evening, as the people of the encampment prepared to sleep, a young boy convinced two of his cousins to follow him into the dark. "We'll only be gone for a few minutes at most," he said. "We can stay within the light of the camp fire and still be safe. Anyway, there is nothing to be afraid of." This last statement came across with more of a tremble than the boy would have wanted, but nonetheless the three boys stole away.

"Look, we are within sight of the light and there is no sound in the night so we can play a little longer if you want." The other boys were not too keen about this new plan but agreed anyway, neither wanting to be the one who gave up to his own fear. The boys played and grew louder, but did not think anything of it. They were playing hide and seek, and tag and their laughter grew louder and louder until the youngest of the three said "We've gone too far!" "No we haven't," was the reply, but they had gone too far. They had played and chased themselves all the way from the camp meadow to the river–over a mile away!

As the thought of this settled in their minds, each boy whispered, "I'm afraid." Their whispers came too late, though. You see, people learn from a very young age to walk and act respectfully among their relations when they are out in the darkness, away from the safety of the campfire. They must also beware of the Basket Lady. The boys, being boys, had been too loud while cavorting in the darkness, for just as they said they were afraid, a figure stepped into their view. Before they knew what was happening, the Basket Lady threw them into the air and into a very, very large burden basket.

Tumbling over each other and clawing and scratching to get out, the three heard a young girl's voice say, "Relax, there are others in here too. We were grabbed shortly after the sun went down and the sky became dark. Is it still night time? Where are we?" The oldest boy found the strength to answer. "It was night when we were captured. I think we are down by the Sucker Pool. What is this we are in, do you know?" he asked. "We have stopped several times as more children fall in, but I'm not sure what this is. My eyes were covered with pitch a while ago and I can't see anything. The walls feel like a basket, though," she added. "But it would be impossible for such a basket to be woven, don't you think? And if it was, to carry such a load, the carrier would have to be very big and very strong," replied the boy.

With that, the basket thumped to the ground and the children tumbled out, collecting bruises and cuts as they fell to the ground. Since the boys had just been dropped in the basket, their eyes were still clear, at least for a while. As they cleared their heads, they saw the ground around them in the glowing light of a very large but dormant fire pit. On the ground, within a few feet of where they were, lay hundreds and hundreds of bones and skulls, clothing and

moccasins. They also saw the outline of a very big person tending to another very large basket, stirring it as though stirring acorn soup.

"Do not move, boy," the coarse voice said. "I know what you boys think you can do, but I won't let you." With that, the huge woman spun on her heels and swiped hot pitch across the eyes of the three, bound their hands like the others and turned back to the embers of the fire. "All of you hold hands and form a line," the Basket Lady said. She took the small hand of the first child and led her with the others, attached like a long string of frog eggs, around the embers and sat them down. Having done this, she went back to her work, stirring baskets and their contents and singing a song. The oldest boy heard this and knew they were in even bigger trouble: it was an eating song. Stunned, he sank back and prepared to meet his fate. The others, over fifty in number, sat huddled in this circle of despair and sobbed, though their eyes would not tear because of the pitch.

As the oldest of the three measured his last thoughts, the girl who had first spoken to him pressed his shoulder with hers. "We will be all right. My papa told me to sing this song whenever I needed strength to ward off bad things. I have been singing to myself and I know we will get away," she whispered. This made the boy recoil as he, a brave boy, could not see how that was possible.

The Basket Lady came back to the circle and began to dance. As she did, she threw her hand at the fire repeatedly. Each time, the fire would spark and spark until, with a mighty effort, it sprang to life and quickly became very hot. The young girl felt the heat and remembered something her grandmother had shown her. Pitch, when hot, was used as a sealant on their water baskets. They would coat the outside with the pitch to seal in the water so they would not leak. "Maybe..." she thought, and leaned closer to the warmth. Nothing happened, so she leaned even closer, as close as she dared, not knowing where the Basket Lady was. She whispered, "Boy, help me move closer to the fire." "No, you will get burned, the fire is too hot," he answered, "I know that, I'm counting on it," she said. "Look, do not argue with me, just help me move." And so, with that, he did, and she did, and luckily the Basket Lady did not notice.

"Psst, I think this will work. I can feel the heat, but the pitch is melting from my eyes. If I just, yes that is it. I can see again. The pitch is still there but I can see," she almost screamed. Just then the Basket Lady brought an even larger pot close to the fire and started heating stones to heat the water. She was still singing her songs, but she had not noticed the children as they spread the word and one by one heated the pitch from their eyes. As they were better able to see, they began to silently unwrap the milkweed ropes that bound their hands behind them.

The Basket Lady came back singing and dancing toward the children to check on the stones she was heating when, as a group, they arose and pushed her into the fire, She immediately became consumed in the flames, and the children started to cry in thanks for their salvation. Their parents from all parts of the north had been searching through the night and saw the flames rising higher and higher and began running to this secluded area, where they saw their children in the glow of the fire.

The children, who had faced their own early demise, ran towards their parents, each vowing to never leave the safety of the circle of their family's light. As they gathered together, the flames from the Basket Lady's fire began to shower the sky with hundreds and hundreds of sparks that flew and flew in all directions, setting down in hundreds of unknown locations. The parents, and those who had searched, took their children home, but to this day they still tell of the Basket Lady who now lives on in the many different places those sparks landed.

Do not stray too far from the light of your family fire, or go off into the dark of night making a lot of noise, because we cannot be sure of where all the sparks went.

# The Yokuts

The Yokuts speak a language within the Penutian language stock that includes over ten tribes in the west. Their traditional homelands included the central San Joaquin Valley and foothills in California, where the tribe still lives today. One of the few tribes to use a term that translates to "bigfoot" (*Shoonshoonootr!*), he is also known as *Mayak datat* (Hairy Man).

### How People Were Made

Source: *Mayak datat: An Archaeological Viewpoint of the Hairy Man Pictographs*, by Kathy Moskowitz Strain, 2003.

All the birds and animals of the mountains went to *Hocheu* [Painted Rock] to make People. Eagle, chief of all the animals, asked each animal how they wanted People to be. Each animal took a turn and said what they had to say.

Fish said, "People should know how to swim, like me, so let them be able to hold their breath and swim very deep."

Hummingbird said, "People should be fast, like me, so let them have good feet and endurance."

Eagle said "People should be wise, wiser than me, so People will help animals and take care of the Earth."

Turtle said "People should be able to protect themselves, like me, so lets give them courage and strength."

Lizard said, "People should have fingers, like me, so that People can make baskets, bows and arrows."

Owl said "People should be good hunters, like me, so give them knowledge and cunning."

Condor said, "People should be different from us, so give them hair, not feathers or fur to keep warm."

Then Coyote said, "People should be just like me, because I am smart and tricky, so have them walk on all fours."

Hairy Man, who had not said anything yet, shook his head and said, "No, People should walk on two legs, like me."

All the other animals agreed with Hairy Man, and Coyote became very angry. He challenged Hairy Man to a race, and they agreed who ever won could decide how People should walk.

They gathered at the waterfall, below *Hocheu*, to begin the race. Coyote started and took a shortcut. Hairy Man was wiser than Coyote and knew that Coyote would cheat to win and People would have to walk on all fours, so Hairy Man stayed behind and helped Eagle, Condor, and the others to make People. They went back to the rock and drew People, on two legs, on the ground. The animals breathed on them, and People came out of the ground.

Hairy Man was very pleased and went to People, but when they saw Hairy Man, they were scared and ran away. That made Hairy Man sad.

When Coyote came back and saw what they had done, he was very angry and drew himself on the rock eating the moon (he is called *Su! Su! Na*). All the other animals drew their pictures on the rock as well, so People would remember them. Hairy Man was sad because People were afraid of him, so he drew himself sad. That is why Hairy Man's picture is crying to this day. That is how people were made.

# When People Took Over

Source: *Mayak datat: An Archaeological Viewpoint of the Hairy Man. Pictographs,* by Kathy Moskowitz Strain, 2003.

People spread out all over the mountains, taking all the land and eating all the food. Animals didn't have anyplace to go. Eagle, chief of all the animals, told the animals that they could not remain in their traditional places, because people had taken them. He asked them where they wished to go.

Eagle said, "What are you going to become? What will you be? I myself am going to fly high up in the air and live on squirrels and sometimes on deer."

Hairy Man said, "I will go live among the big trees [Giant Sequoias] and hunt only at night when people are asleep."

Dog said, "I will stay with people and be their friend, I will follow them, and perhaps I will get something to eat in that way."

Buzzard said, "When something dies I will smell it. I will go there and eat it."

Crow said, "When I see something lying dead, I will pick out its eyes."

Coyote said, "I will go about killing grasshoppers. That is how I will live."

Hummingbird said, "I will go to the flowers and get my food from them."

Condor said, "I will not stay here. I will go far off into the mountains. Perhaps I will find something to eat there."

Woodpecker said, "I will get acorns and make holes in the trees [to store them in]."

Bluejay said, "I am going to make trees grow over the hills. I will work."

Rat said, "I will go where there are old trees and make my house in them."

Mouse said, "I will run here, there, and everywhere. I shall have holes, and perhaps I can live in that way."

Trout said, "I will live in the water and perhaps I can find something to eat there."

That was the time when animals stopped being like us and scattered.

# Food Stealing

Source: *Mayak datat: An Archaeological Viewpoint of the Hairy Man. Pictographs,* by Kathy Moskowitz Strain, 2003.

In the old days, women learned never to leave their acorn meal unattended. They would spend all day pounding on the big rocks near the river, making the acorn meal, and then take it down to the river to leech it. They would then leave it in the sun to dry, but they would come back and it would be gone. They would find big footprints in the sand where they left the meal and they would know that Hairy Man took it. He likes Indian food and knows to wait until the acorn is leeched of its bitterness before taking it. We always wondered if he liked the sound of women pounding acorn and knew when to come and get food.

## Bigfoot, the Hairy Man

Source: *Big foot and other stories,* by E. Johnstone, 1975. Tulare: Tulare County Board of Education.

Big Foot was a creature that was like a great big giant with long, shaggy hair. His long shaggy hair made him look like a big animal. He was good in a way, because he ate the animals that might harm people. He kept the Grizzly Bear, Mountain Lion, Wolf, and other larger animals away. During hot summer nights all the animals would come out together down from the hills to drink out of the Tule River. Big Foot liked to catch animals down by the river. He would eat them up bones and all.

It was pleasant and cool down by the river on hot summer nights. That is when grown ups liked to take a swim. Even though people feared that Big Foot, the hairy man, might come to the river, people still liked to take a swim at night.

Parents always warned their children, "Don't go near the river at night. You may run into Big Foot."

Now Big Foot usually eats animals, but parents said, "If he can't find any animals and he is very hungry, he will eat you. Big Foot, the hairy man, doesn't leave a speck or trace. He eats you up bones and all. We won't know where you have gone or what has happened to you."

Some people say Big Foot, the hairy man, still roams around the hills near Tule River. He comes along the trail at night and scares a lot of people. When you hear him you know it is something very big because he makes a big sound, not a little sound.

Children are cautioned not to make fun of his picture on the painted rock or play around that place because he would hear you and come after you.

Parents warned their children, "You are going to meet him on the road if you stay out too late at night." The children have learned always to come home early.

*The images seen in the lower row in this basket depict the "Hairy Man."*

# The Yurok

The Yurok live, both now and in prehistoric times, along the Klamath River in northwestern California. Their language is a part of the very rare Algic family group. Their traditional word for bigfoot is *Omah*.

## Yurok Story

Source: *The Field Notes of John P. Harrington,* Vol. 2, Reel 002, Frames 070b-073b.

There was one Bluff [Creek] Boy and he was out hunting. The folks used to teach the son what the old man learned not to do. So they taught the son there is a woman [on] the other side of the big bluff there at Bluff [Creek] who will pick you up and this [young man] was a fast runner so he [thought] I'll go and see this woman. They were going out hunting, they were going through there. They met a big woman and she said: "Oh I am glad to meet you, my husband!" [She] had a basket on her back. "Come in my basket, I'll pack you!"

So she went home with that boy in the basket on her back. She took the boy into her house. And the boy look[ed] around and saw deerskins all over that she had killed–she was a fast runner, just overtook deer and picked them up. Her sister was living with her–there were two of them. Then when she went out hunting, she put the [young man] in her packbasket. So when they went out, she went under a tree, and he grasped a limb and was hanging there, and she didn't know it, she went by and the [young] fellow then ran for home.

And when he got home, he said to his father: "A woman was getting me." "I told you not to go there." They heard a hollering up on the hill: "Husband, come back! You can't get away from me." So when he came to K'enik, California, he went across the river, and then the woman up on the hillside back of Martins Ferry hollered again: "Come back husband, you can't get away from me!" And when he got to bald Hills she hollered again: "Come back, husband, you can't get away from me." And when he reached Ossigyen, California [this is on the coast], she hollered again: "Husband, come back! You can't get away." At Ossigyen this boy got a canoe and went out in the ocean, going south. And when he got to in front of Orick she hollered from Orick Mt. "Husband, come back, I'll throw this pestle at you [she was going to hit him, going to drown him]." She threw it. And that rock is a pestle. She just missed the canoe.

The [young] man landed at *s/·owmme/·y* [village at point on the coast]. (Everywhere he had landed came to {sic} he had hollered: "Ye help me.") But they were everywhere afraid of him. And the man at *s/·owmme/·y*, said, you stay right here, I can stand them off. He told him to come in and shut the door and live under the rock. The house was under the rock. And shortly they heard a jump on top of that rock and a holler: "Come out my husband, I am [going]

to kill you if you don't come." She was dancing there trying to break that rock on top. They kept a hearing it. And finally the head man he got scared for the woman was so powerful that she almost broke thru the rock dancing on top of it. Then this man prayed to the ocean telling the breakers: "Come ge[t it] over, I am getting scared." Then when the breakers came over the rock, it washed the woman back inland again. Then the man said: "There are enough bad things in this world, better be drowned so there will not be such a thing." So she drowned. That was the last of her. But it left that rock out there–that's Redding's Rock. The [young] fellow got away.

*Note: Redding's Rock is out in the ocean about four miles west of Orick. The Yurok word for Redding's Rock is the same word for pestle.*

# THE GREAT BASIN CULTURE

# Great Basin Cultural Area

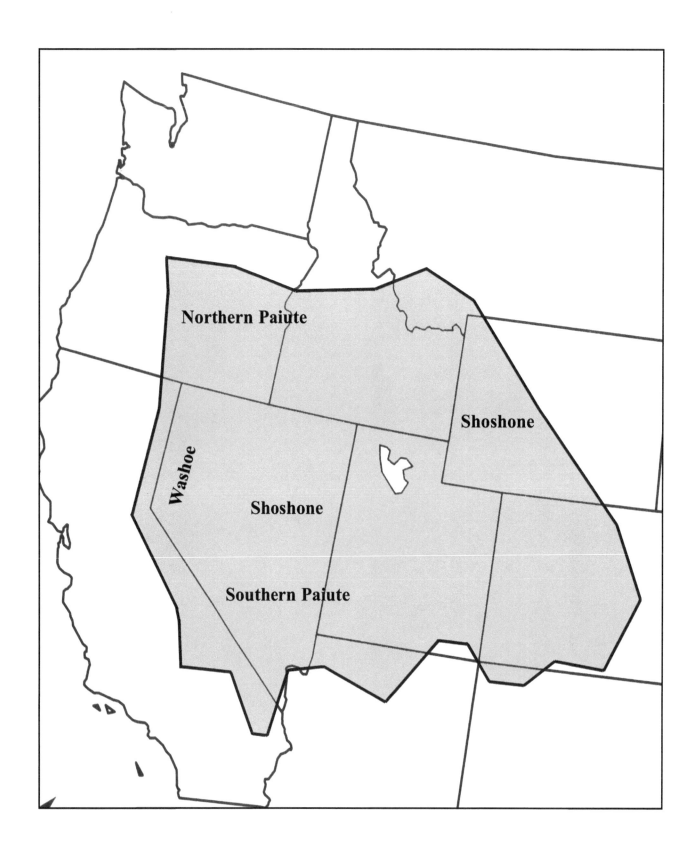

Northern Paiute

Shoshone

Washoe

Shoshone

Southern Paiute

# The Northern Paiute

The Northern Paiute (also known as the Numa) lived in parts of California, Idaho, Nevada, and Oregon. Today, the tribe maintains reservation lands in all of these states. Their language is part of the Uto-Aztecan family. The traditional Northern Paiute word for a bigfoot-like animal is *Si-Te-Cah*, which translates as "people eater."

### The Creation of the Indian

Source: *Myths of Idaho Indians,* by Deward E. Walker, 1980. Moscow: University of Idaho, pp. 165-170.

Coyote's children were playing the hand game indoors. A woman outside warned them, "Boys, listen, something is coming." However, they paid no attention to her. She said again, "Boys, an ogre is coming." Still they paid no attention to her. Her husband was inside and she asked him to keep her child there while she jumped into a pit and covered it up. The ogre came and killed all of the boys. Then he said, "I have killed them all." The woman heard him say this. He sang as he went away.

She crawled out of the pit about sunrise and heard her boy crying indoors. "You had better come to me, my child," she said. She stretched out her hand and he took it and came out. They found some food growing on the mountains and the woman dug it up and ate. She made the child sleep there, then left him. A second ogre met her and asked, "Where is your home?" She replied, "Over there on that knoll. A man like you is there." She was pointing out the place where her boy was.

The ogre went there and swallowed him but wanted more to eat, so he returned for the woman. When she saw him coming back, she dug a hole and crawled into it. The ogre tracked her all over but failed to find her. At last he scraped away the earth with his hand and almost uncovered her hiding place, but just before he got to her he said, "It is nearly sunset time. I'll stop now and get her tomorrow." The woman knew that in a little more time he would have unearthed her. She was crying for he would have swallowed her.

She got out and ran away. The ogre came the next day and continued digging, but he only found the empty hole. Meanwhile, the woman met an old woman who said, "You can hide there, but I don't know what to do with you. My grandchildren are no good. They will eat you up when they get home." The old woman dug a hole before her grandchildren's return, put the woman in it and covered the opening with willows.

One grandchild came and said, "Coming here I saw someone's tracks." "I have not seen anyone today," the old woman answered. "Well, I saw tracks there," "I was over there, I think you saw my tracks," said the old woman. The rest of the grandchildren came carrying cottontails, birds, and other food.

They cooked the food, but the old woman did not eat. "Why don't you eat?" they asked. "I'll eat tomorrow. Tomorrow I shall not have any food, so I am leaving it till then." The hidden woman watched them through the willow covering. All the grandchildren were lying around the fire without their blankets.

Before sunrise they went hunting and then the old woman said to her guest, "You had better get up and go. Eat what I have here and go to your destination. There are many dangerous things on the road and you had better not touch them when you pass by. There are heads by the road. Don't touch any head on the road or it will hurt you." The woman went on and found the heads just like the old woman said. She touched one head, and it began to pursue her. She became frightened and ran on as fast as she could.

She arrived at a camp where a man asked her, "Well, have you touched a head on the road?" "Yes, one on this side," she replied. "Then it is coming," the man said and shut up his house. He stuck some sticks on the roof and told the woman to sit down under them. They heard the head coming before they saw it. It struck the ground as it came along and bounced backward and forward. When it tried to climb up after the woman, the sticks got stuck in the orbits of its eyes and the head stayed there. The man went outside, looked at it, took it down and gave it to the woman saying, "Take this head back to where it belongs and put it back exactly like it was before." She did as he said. Then he told her, "If you wish to go, go. There are two camps on the road. The people of the first camp eat nothing, but those of the second eat all kinds of fruit."

The woman arrived at the first house and its owner said, "I eat bad food that is not suitable for you. Find another man on the road and stay with him." At the second house a man asked her, "Where do you come from?" "From over there," she said. "Tell me all about it. Then I'll give you something to eat." She told him she was looking for a certain man and he gave her food. She was close to her destination and the man told her, "You have only a short distance to go. From the summit you can see the house you are looking for."

She went to that house and that is how she got to Job's peak. There was plenty to eat there, so she picked up some food and ate it sitting outside on the south side of the house. The owner of the house said, "There is enough to eat here. Come in and sew my moccasins." She opened the door and entered. The man sat on one side of the house and she on the other. He prepared some food and gave it to her. When she had eaten, she went outdoors and gave the man some of her food. He ate some and returned the remainder to her. And so they were married.

The next day the man went hunting and in the evening he returned with an antelope. On his way home he saw a boy and a girl who said, "Our father has got something to eat." The next day he went hunting again. When he came back home, he saw two more children. The boys and girls ran up to him saying, "Our father seems to have something to eat." In this way he made four children in two days. The man and woman were the Paviotso.

The boys always shot at each other under their father's legs and the girls also fought. When they grew up, they made arrow points and used them in their fights. Their father said, "Don't do that, you are brothers," but the boys paid no attention to him. "If you don't stop fighting, I'll send you to different places and I'll go elsewhere myself, and then people will only be able to come to me when they die. If you don't stop, I'll send one pair of you to Stillwater and the other to Lovelocks." The boys went down to the valley and returned before sunset, but one was bleeding because he had been hurt by the other's arrow. The father lost all patience and sent one pair to Stillwater and he other to Lovelocks saying, "Now if you want to continue fighting, keep on as long as you wish."

One boy and one girl went to Stillwater Valley and made a fire with a light smoke. In Lovelocks the smoke was darker. The father saw it and after a while he began to go that way by walking under the rocks. He and his wife were crying because they felt sorry for the children. The man cried aloud and broke a rock making a cleft that is still visible east of Job's Peak. They were crying and their marks are still to be seen, because their tears turned into springs. Where there was plenty of water the father took out his bow and arrows and shot at the rocks, and the arrows are still on the rock. He made Chalk Mountain there.

On the other side, at Westgate, they camped and cried, making another spring. At Middlegate he said, "My children, whenever you come for pine-nuts, come here and drink this water." They went on farther and got to Eastgate and he made a big rock there. "Whenever my boys come here, let them rub their foreheads against those rocks." He went on and camped on the other side of Eastgate. The impression of his feet can be seen by the springs on the north side. On the other side there was another spring and there he piled up some rocks. "Whenever my boys suffer from disease, let them come here and give beads to the rock and ask it to cure them."

His wife, said, "Which way are you going? We'll never find a better place. We might as well go back to our boys, I am sorry for them." The man said, "Don't say that. We might find a better country." He went on and then stopped. The woman said, "I'd like to go back to our boys." He answered, "We are pretty near our destination. We'll get there soon."

He came to a body of water and walked over to it as though it were land. On the other side he found a white mountain where he stopped and sat down for a while. The woman did not say a word. Farther on he found a spot and while sitting there, he opened the clouds and told his wife to look through. "Perhaps you will find another country." She looked and saw a beautiful valley which was green all over. He said, "I think we had better go through the clouds to the beautiful country. Don't grieve too much. Perhaps some day the boys will die and come to us. Whenever anyone dies, he'll come to us." They went there but no mountain was to be seen there at all except in the east, where there was only a little one. "We ought to go and find some timber so that we can live under it." They looked until they found some and then they made camp there.

The man went hunting as before and they lived very well. One day he went to the little mountain and found seed there like ours. He told his wife, "This is our fruit. You had better get some so we can live on it. Be careful if you go to the mountain every day, or our children may catch some disease and die. Then they may come here and you may find them."

Once she found something that looked as if it had been used. When her husband returned from the hunt she gave him some food and told him about her find. "It looks like fire," she said and showed it to him. He said, "This might come from our old home. I don't know what to do with it." He pulled it back. "We might spoil it, but we'll know pretty soon. Perhaps our children are coming back this way. If people die and we do our part, they will come here." They did not know what do and were crying, when the woman looked round and saw somebody far off.

She did not tell her husband immediately, but sat down. Soon after this she rose and looked again and saw that it looked like someone moving. Then she told the man, "It looks like somebody is coming." "Well, it may be some people," he said. "There was no one living before we came here. Be quiet." She looked again. "It looks like a person." The man said, "Long ago I saw one person here, maybe he has come back." The woman looked again and saw that it was a person. Her husband said, "You had better prepare food for him. He may be hungry."

He arrived and the man knew who he was. The man said to his wife, "Perhaps you know what we are going to do. He comes from your old home." The stranger said, "I thought you were no better than I. You had better fix it properly so that dying persons may come here. Make some basket-jugs, one big one and one small one, and put your find in there. See what will happen." The woman obeyed, put some water in the jugs, and threw in their find. They found little babies in the water. "Keep them in there a while," the stranger said.

They looked again, and one child was already old enough to walk. They washed it with water. "Take the children to the little mountain," said the newcomer. "Let them go through one hole the first time, then they will grow a little more. Let them come through the second hole, then they will be of the same age as you." They gave them something to eat and then they sent them out. As they left the man said, "There is a good place for you and there you have to be, go and stay there. Perhaps more will come and I'll send them over to you."

## The *Si-Te-Cah*

Source: *Life Among the Piutes–Their Wrongs and Claims* by Sarah Winnemucca Hopkins, 1883. Boston: G.P. Putman's Sons, p. 75.

Among the traditions of our people is one of a small tribe of barbarians who used to live along the Humboldt River. It was many hundred years ago. They used to waylay my people and kill and eat them. They would dig large holes in our trails at night, and if any of our people traveled at night, which they did, for they were afraid of these barbarous people, they would oftentimes fall into these holes. That tribe would even eat their own dead— yes, they would even come and dig up our dead after they were buried, and would carry them off and eat them. Now and then they would come and make war on my people. They would fight, and as fast as they killed one another on either side, the women would carry off those who were killed. My people say they were very brave. When they were fighting they would jump up in the air after the arrows that went over their heads, and shoot the same arrows back again. My people took some of them into their families, but they could not make them like themselves. So at last they made war on them.

This war lasted a long time. Their number was about twenty-six hundred (2600). The war lasted some three years. My people killed them in great numbers, and what few were left went into the thick bush. My people set the bush on fire. This was right above Humboldt Lake. Then they went to work and made tuly or bulrush boats, and went into Humboldt Lake. They could not live there very long without fire. They were nearly starving. My people were watching them all round the lake, and would kill them as fast as they would come on land. At last one night they all landed on the east side of the lake, and went into a cave near the mountains. It was a most horrible place, for my

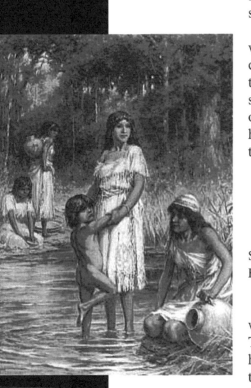

people watched at the mouth of the cave, and would kill them as they came out to get water. My people would ask them if they would be like us, and not eat people like coyotes or beasts. They talked the same language, but they would not give up. At last my people were tired, and they went to work and gathered wood, and began to fill up the mouth of the cave. Then the poor fools began to pull the wood inside till the cave was full. At last my people set it on fire; at the same time they cried out to them, "Will you give up and he like men, and not eat people like beasts? Say quick—we will put out the fire." No answer came from them. My people said they thought the cave must be very deep or far into the mountain. They had never seen the cave nor known it was there until then. They called out to them as loud as they could, "Will you give up? Say so, or you will all die." But no answer came. Then they all left the place. In ten days some went back to see if the fire had gone out. They went back to my third or fifth great-grandfather and told him they must all be dead, there was such a horrible smell. This tribe was called people-eaters, and after my people had killed them all, the people round us called us *Say-do-carah*. It means conqueror; it also means "enemy." I do not know how we came by the name of Piutes. It is not an Indian word. I think it is misinterpreted. Sometimes we are called Pine-nut eaters, for we are the only tribe that lives in the country where Pine-nuts grow. My people say that the tribe we exterminated had reddish hair. I have some of their hair, which has been handed down from father to son. I have a dress which has been in our family a great many years, trimmed with this reddish hair. I am going to wear it some time when I lecture. It is called the mourning dress, and no one has such a dress but my family.

*Note: The cave that is described is thought to be Lovelock Cave, a well-known archaeological site.*

# The Shoshone

The Shoshone still inhabit their traditional homelands of Idaho, Nevada, Oregon, Utah, and Wyoming. Broken into two bands, Eastern and Western, their language is part of the Uto-Aztecan linguistic family. The Shoshone have two words for a cannibal giant, *Dzo'avits* and *Tso'apittse*. Hairy man is called *Zoe'ah'vich*. A man eater is a *Nuwa'deca*.

### *Dzo'avits* and the Weasels

Source: *Myths of Idaho Indians,* by Deward E. Walker Jr., 1980. Moscow: University of Idaho Press, pp. 150-152.

Weasel was living in his lodge. In the evening, he began to long for his brother. He grew sleepy and his wife told him to go to bed, but he still thought of his older brother. "A giant is eating my older brother," he said. He cried and continued to cry all night. His wife asked him to keep still but he did not cease wailing. "My brother is being eaten by the giant, *Dzo'avits*." At last he fell asleep, but he began to cry again when he woke up in the morning. His wife said, "Keep quiet! Perhaps your brother will be back soon."

Weasel, however, went away crying. He knew where the giant's tent was situated, so he went to it and looked in. He had his obsidian knife with him. A woman was sitting there, weaving a willow cup. Weasel entered and sat down. He saw a large knife covered with blood hanging in the lodge. "Let me have that cup," said Weasel to the woman. She cleaned the bottom of the cup and then gave it to him. Weasel hung the cup around his neck, even though it was very greasy. He sat down and remained seated for a long time. At last he heard the giant coming home. The giant dropped his bundle outside and entered the lodge.

As soon as he came in, he told the woman to prepare some food. "I have brought some Indians home." The wife arose, took the large, bloody knife and went outside where her husband had left his Indian captives, but she could not find any in his bag. "There are none here," she said. "You must have lost them. Where are they?" "There are not many of them," the giant answered. "There are only a few. They may be in the bottom of the bag." He looked in, but the Indians were gone. He began to cry. At last he stopped crying and sat down.

He looked at Weasel and noticed that he was very fat, so the giant thought he would be good to eat. He proposed that they should try to cut each other's throats. Weasel agreed and the giant took his big knife. "I'll try to cut yours first," said Weasel. The giant put his head in position and Weasel tried to cut his neck. The giant laughed and said to his wife, "You must not look at us two." The woman lay down and covered herself up. The giant again told her she must not watch them.

Weasel began to cut once more, and then he drew out his obsidian knife. He was going to use it and the woman noticed it. "What kind of a stone has that boy got? What is the boy doing there?" she asked. The giant pulled away. "Where is that knife?" "Nowhere," said Weasel. "I spat it out, I threw it away. I don't have it any more." Then he began to cut the giant's neck. *Dzo'avits* again warned his wife not to watch them, so she lay down and covered her face. Weasel placed his knife against the giant's throat and the giant fell asleep. Then Weasel took out his obsidian and cut off the giant's head. He carried it outside and threw it away. The woman arose and the boy struck her with the knife and killed her. Thus he killed them both.

Then Weasel sat down and wept for a long time. Finally, he stopped, picked up the head of an Indian, looked at it and threw it away again. He could not find his older brother's gray hair, though he searched for it everywhere. He picked up one Indian head after another, but could not find his brother's gray hair. He sat down and cried for a long time. At last he picked up the giant's head. Then he examined the giant's body. At last he pulled off the giant's teeth and looked between his jaws. There between the giant's big teeth, he found his brother's gray hair. He took it out and in the night he brought it home crying.

At home he tied it to his fire-drill and stuck it in the ground until morning. His wife was there. In the morning, his brother came to life and called Weasel, "Get up, younger brother." Weasel said, "My older brother is talking, listen to him." The older brother said, "Get up and eat." Weasel looked at his brother, threw his arms about him and kissed him. "Let me alone and eat," said the older brother. Both of them laughed. The older brother was well again, but he could not lie down comfortably.

# The Weasel Brothers

Source: *Myths of Idaho Indians,* by Deward E. Walker Jr., 1980. Moscow: University of Idaho Press, pp. 152-153.

A giant was walking and pulling along some wood. Weasel tracked him until he caught sight of him. When Weasel got close enough, he hit the giant. "What is this?" asked the giant. "That boy has hit me." They built a fire, and the giant proposed a wrestling-match. "Whoever loses shall be thrown into the fire." Weasel won and, throwing his opponent into the fire, killed him with a fire-stick.

Then Weasel started off toward the giant's lodge. "Take care," said Weasel's older brother. "Another powerful giant will kill you. Don't go over there." Weasel was not afraid, and did not believe what his brother told him. As he was going along, he saw another giant looking down from a cliff. Weasel hit that giant, too, making him bark like a dog. "What is that?" he shouted. "That Weasel has struck me." Then the giant tried to trick Weasel. "Come, younger brother," he cried, "look down at these girls." When Weasel approached him, the giant tried to hurl him down, but Weasel evaded him, and stole up behind him. The giant looked down. "Have I killed him?" he asked. Weasel, who by then was standing behind the giant, pushed him over and killed him.

Weasel went on his way again. "Take care," said his brother.

"Strong bear will kill you. Don't go in that direction. There is a bear with two cubs who kills strangers in a swinging-game. They will kill you immediately." "My older brother," said Weasel, "I am going to look for them." He arrived at their home. They put him down but he jumped in time and was not hurt. Then he told the bears to get into the swing. He threw them all down and killed them. He scraped off the old bear's flesh, and put on her skin. In the meantime, the old Weasel had tracked him, thinking he might have been killed by the bear. At sunrise, he caught up to him and saw the bear's tracks. He peeped through the willows, took aim at the supposed bear and shot at it. He missed it by a trifle. Weasel jumped up and laughed at his brother. Then the older Weasel also laughed. "What is the matter with you? You frightened me." "Oh, it was only a joke," Weasel answered.

The older Weasel wanted to hunt water-elk. They went to the bank of the stream, and the older brother took off his clothing. "I am going into the water," he said. "I am going to hunt water-elk. You must not get frightened, because you will die of thirst if you run away." He went in further and the water came up to his eyes. At last he was entirely beneath the water. The water-elk were standing up and jumping around. The younger Weasel suddenly became frightened and ran away, shooting off his arrows.

He famished with thirst. The old Weasel had killed an elk and was skinning it. "Perhaps my younger brother ran away," he thought, "and died of thirst." He left the elk entrails in the water and tracked his brother. At last he found him, gave him water to drink, and made his younger brother wake up again.

# Cannibal Giant

Source: *Shoshone Tales,* by Anne M. Smith, 1993. Salt Lake City: University of Utah Press, p. 37.

Once there lived an old woman and her granddaughter. They went out every day to gather pitch from pine trees. One day the Cannibal Giant found them. He chased them around. He can run fast. He chased them around a big tree. The grandmother and her granddaughter thought it was fun to have the giant chase them. They laughed. Soon they tired. Then he caught them. He flicked his fingers at their nipples. Their breasts swelled up. Then he killed them and took them home. He ate their bodies, all except their breasts, which he cut off and hung up to dry. The grandfather went out to look for his wife and granddaughter when they didn't come home. He found the giant's tracks and followed them to his cave where he found the giant asleep. He had his bow and arrows with him but he could not kill the giant. So he shot at his penis and that is how he killed the giant. The giant is like a rock.

## *Tso'apittse*

Source: *Shoshone Tales,* by Anne M. Smith, 1993. Salt Lake City: University of Utah Press, pp. 62-65.

*Tso'apittse* was a rocky giant with pitchy hands. When children are naughty their parents tell them the giant will come down from the mountain: "*Zo a wi zo ho ho ho.*"

A young man and his wife went up in the mountains. He wanted to hunt deer. He had traveled up to that place before he was married and he knew the country better than his young wife did. She didn't know all the superstitions of this place. When they were to camp that night, her husband told her, "This is a place were we used to camp. There is a good spring near here where you can get water. There is something about that spring. It is a very pretty spring, wide and round. If you go there be careful, because that is *Tso'apittse's* spring. It is where the giant and his family get their water. When you get your water, don't look in the spring. Don't let your face be reflected in the water." She believed him. He said, "Don't stay at the spring, don't sit down, be quick about getting your water."

He went hunting every day and she had to stay at camp alone. Every day she went for water and did just as her husband told her. Then one day she got to thinking, "I wonder what is wrong, why I can't stay by the water." She thought about how her hair needed washing. Why not wash her hair in the spring? So she went down. First she made a brush out of low sagebrush, she was going to wash her hair. She got to the spring, filled her jug, set it down, and started undoing her hair. She started washing her hair. She sat down to do this. When she finished, she leaned over and looked into the water. She could see her face very clear and she sat and admired herself. Then she began to brush her hair, using the water as a mirror. This was the first time she had seen herself and she thought how pretty she was, how beautiful her hair was. Then finally, she braided her hair and was ready to go home. To her surprise she couldn't get up. She was glued to the ground. Evening came, the sun was almost down. She kept trying to get up, but couldn't.

Meantime, the giant's children, who lived in the mountain, looked at the spring. One ran to her mother and said, "There is something in our spring. I saw something moving there." The mother went out and looked and saw it. Then *Tso'apittse* came home and they told him. He was happy. He warmed up his pitchy basket (he had pitchy hands, too) and put it on his back and ran to the spring. The girl heard his heavy footsteps and his breathing, "*wi wi wi*." When he was near the earth shook. The girl tried to get up but couldn't. *Tso'apittse* got to the spring. He kept hitting her on the breast with a flat club till her breasts all swelled up. Then he hit her head with his hands and scalped her. He killed her and slung her into his pitchy basket and took her home. His children came to meet him and were so glad he had brought something to eat.

The husband knew something must be wrong when he came to camp, for there was no fire there. It was too dark for him to track anything that night so he stayed there. He was very miserable. Next morning he got up very early. He was so nervous he couldn't sleep. He made a big fire and stood by it until the sun came up. When it was light he went down to the spring. He saw tracks where *Tso'apittse* had stood. He knew where the *Tso'apittse* family lived but he knew he could do nothing if he went there. So he went back to his parents' house to see if his father could help him. He told his father what had happened. So he and his father started making lots of arrows. So when he went back to the place he had lots of arrows. His father said, "You can't hit these *Tso'apittses*, their bodies are made of rock. Their only vulnerable place is in the anus. You go at night. Don't go in the daytime, for *Tso'apittse* is not home in the daytime. At night *Tso'apittse* will be lying down. Hanging above him will be your wife's breast. His legs will be crossed and he will be kicking at your wife's breast. When his anus is exposed, shoot at it."

So the young man went to his wickiup in the mountains and got ready to go see *Tso'apittse* at night. He went there. The *Tso'apittse* family lived in a great cave. The young man looked in. It was dark outside. His father had told him to try to not make any tracks *Tso'apittse* could track him and kill him, too. The young man was afraid to do anything that night. He looked around to see what he could do the next night.

The next night he went back there. He took some of his arrows with him. He got very close. He shot but his arrow didn't hit the anus. It tickled the giant and he grabbed it and it broke. The young man kept shooting but he couldn't hit the anus and kill him. So he went back to his wickiup. Next night he took more arrows and went back. He saw *Tso'apittse* kicking at his wife's breast hanging up there and it made him so mad. The third day he had looked over his arrows very carefully. One arrow had a longer point than the others, about four inches long. He thought his father must have put it in. It was an obsidian point. He went back that evening. He thought he would get him tonight. He shot a couple of ordinary arrows at *Tso'apittse*. *Tso'apittse* said, "So straws are tickling me." Then the young man took the arrow with the obsidian point and shot and it hit *Tso'apittse's* anus. *Tso'apittse* said, "Ooooh," and squirmed around. His children didn't know what was the matter. The young man watched *Tso'apittse* squirm and die.

# Cannibal Giant (2)

Source: *Shoshone Tales,* by Anne M. Smith, 1993. Salt Lake City: University of Utah Press, p. 75.

He had a house to which he would invite people. The first time they came, everything would be all right. Then, next time there would be a big feast and lots of people would come. He had a big thorny sickle that cuts for miles around and when the people were coming in great numbers he would swing his sickle and kill all the people. His hands stayed clean that way and the people died far off and the survivors didn't suspect him.

Then, one time a family came who had a wise little son. He hunted all the time, he was a good hunter. He found lots of skulls, skulls of the people who had been killed by the giant. He went home and told his parents about it. They went away and came back with some more people. Then they went to visit the giant. The little boy was with them. The boy met an old man there. He did not live with the giant but near there. The old man told him to warn his parents to leave because the man they came to visit was a cannibal. He never pitied anyone. He killed people for miles around. The boy said, "Oh, one time when I was out hunting I found lots of skulls. That must have been it."

The giant's name was *Naahpaihtem Parnbi*, Six Heads.

## Tso'apittse (2)

Source: *Shoshone Tales,* by Anne M. Smith, 1993. Salt Lake City: University of Utah Press, pp. 82-83.

*Tso'apittse* started from his house to hunt for people. When he walked, the mountains shook. He sang, "I wonder if there are any Pine Nut Wood people here." He was walking in the forest to look for people to eat. As he came through the trees he saw a couple of fresh human tracks. The people were hunting cottontails. *Tso'apittse* said, "Ah, human cottontails have been here," and he looked to see which way the tracks went. He started at a trot to trail them. The people heard *Tso'apittse* coming and saying, "*Whi, whi, whi, whi.*" That scared them. The only way they could get away was to climb up. So they started to climb up the hill and down the other side. When they got to the foot of the hill, there was an old woman camping there and they made for her house. The old woman said, "You keep going, I'll use my club on him." She dreamed that she was a monster-fighter.

*Tso'apittse* was already coming down, still hot on the tracks. The old woman was in the back of the house. *Tso'apittse* sat down and said, "*Hudu.*" Then he got up and the old woman jumped up too and they had a hand-to-hand fight. *Tso'apittse* had a conical basket for packing things in. It was lined with pitch. He threw people inside and they stuck and couldn't escape. He tried to put the old woman in but he failed. The old woman finally threw *Tso'apittse* on his behind. He got up and saw the print of his behind on the ground. He got up crying and went home because he wasn't allowed to have the print of his behind on the ground.

So afterward, *Tso'apittse* tried to make another hunt. He looked for more human tracks. As he went over the saddle of mountain he came near a man who was traveling. The man stood still and froze with his arms outstretched like a tree. *Tso'apittse* walked right by him. *Tso'apittse* looked at the man then went on. He stopped again and looked. He was suspicious. He would go away and look back to see if it moved. The man was still there. *Tso'apittse* said, "What is it? A burnt stump?" He went back a way and looked again. He couldn't make up his mind what it was. *Tso'apittse* came right up close. The man just froze and he didn't dare breathe. *Tso'apittse* said, "He has a penis and a nose." He tickled him but the man didn't move. *Tso'apittse* pushed him over and the man fell with his arms out and he didn't move. *Tso'apittse* went away and said, "Oh, it's just a burned stump." The man didn't get up until *Tso'apittse* was gone. *Tso'apittse* kept going on down to the valley.

Near a big pine a couple of boys ran into him. *Tso'apittse* said, "Young human cottontails." He chased them around the junipers panting, "*Tsoa whi whi, tsoa whi whi.*" They kept on chasing around in the junipers. He said, "I'm going to have a feast." They kept on running and the two boys hid behind a tree. When *Tso'apittse* wasn't looking they ran to another tree. They got up to the summit and looked back and saw *Tso'apittse* still running around the tree saying, "*Whi, whi, whi.*" After a while when they were a long way off he started trailing them again. They went down the other side of the mountain and came to an old man's house and said to the old man and his wife, "*Tso'apittse* is chasing us." The old man was a doctor and he sat down and started singing and said, "You'd better go along home." The old man was calling on all his spirit helpers. He was calling the last one when *Tso'apittse* came in at a trot. *Tso'apittse* had big red eyes and he popped them out to look fierce. *Tso'apittse* sat down and said, "*Hudu.*" The old man's wife was hiding back of the house. The doctor had all his spirit helpers. *Tso'apittse* was looking back the way he had come. The doctor made some waving motions with his hands over *Tso'apittse's* head and took out *Tso'apittse's* spirit and threw it back up the trail. *Tso'apittse* saw his spirit going up the trail and he jumped up and chased it back up the mountain.

Around Eureka on the hillside is a big rock that looks like a person. They say that is *Tso'apittse's* body where he died chasing his spirit.

### Another Tso'apittse Tale

Source: *Shoshone Tales,* by Anne M. Smith, 1993. Salt Lake City: University of Utah Press, pp. 83-84.

A man and his wife had one child. They kept telling him, "Don't cry or *Tso'apittse* will hear." He was an unruly child. Afterward they heard *Tso'apittse* coming. The mother and father went to the back of the house and hid. They were mad at the child. *Tso'apittse* came in and said, "Oh, my little granddaughter, here is some rat liver for you." He had some pitch and he warmed it in his hands and said, "*Tsoawet,*" [deathly] and put his hands on her head. When he pulled them away her scalp came off with them. He took her home with him.

(When *Tso'apittse* comes, the children are held there by some power and the parents get away alone.)

So *Tso'apittse* went hunting again to find the father of the little girl. He came upon him and chased him and finally caught him and put him in his basket. *Tso'apittse* was going through the pine trees. The man reached up and grabbed a limb, and *Tso'apittse* went on without knowing the man had gotten

away, and went home. *Tso'apittse* got home to his children and said, "There is one human cottontail in my basket, go and look for it." They looked and said, "There's nothing here." *Tso'apittse* jumped up to see for himself. Then he started back to where he had caught the man. The man heard him coming and hid and watched him. A big blizzard came. The man started for *Tso'apittse's* house and cut a big pine club on the way. At the cave the man killed all *Tso'apittse's* children. Pretty soon he heard *Tso'apittse* coming and he blocked the door with trees and branches. *Tso'apittse* said, "What has grown in my door?" He shook it and could not get it out. Just as the trees were about to give, *Tso'apittse* gave up. He said, "It's cold." He tried again, but had to give up. He couldn't move. Toward morning the man heard *Tso'apittse* cease whining. He was frozen. The man leaped out and saw *Tso'apittse* lying down, frozen to death. So he went off without making a sound. He thought *Tso'apittse* might just be sleeping. The man was never bothered anymore so he thought he must have killed him.

### *Tso'apittse* (3)

Source: *Shoshone Tales,* by Anne M. Smith, 1993. Salt Lake City: University of Utah Press, pp. 137-139.

People had a camp. There were a lot of women there. One woman had a baby, a baby boy. *Tso'apittse* came and said, "Give me that little boy, I want to hold him. You're my friend, I want to pet the baby." So the woman gave

*Tso'apittse* the baby to hold. When she got it, she ran away with the baby. She stole the baby. *Tso'apittse* started for her camp.

The boy grew bigger. He ate drippings from his own nose, which he blew into a cup. He added water to it and made gravy of it. That is all he had to eat. He kept growing bigger. *Tso'apittse* kept pulling the boy's penis. It grows long. Then the boy is grown, and *Tso'apittse* marries him. Every time *Tso'apittse* comes home she wanted to have intercourse with him. She says, "Come now, take out your penis." The boy is a man now. He goes to hunt mountain sheep. One day while he is out he meets someone up there [on the mountain] who says to him, "Do you know you are living with *Tso'apittse*? That stuff you eat isn't real food, it's no good." This person gives him mountain sheep to eat. There is never any fire or light at *Tso'apittse*'s house. This man the boy meets makes fire and light. He tells the boy to make a fire when he got home. The boy says, "How do you make a fire?"

The boy puts the mountain sheep meat up in a tall tree and cuts off the lower limbs so there is a long smooth trunk. He brings home only the mountain sheep heart, lungs, and liver. He comes home.

When he gets home he make a fire. It's dark now and *Tso'apittse* comes home. She looks at the fire and says, "What are you doing? Put out that fire." The boy gives the mountain sheep heart to *Tso'apittse* but she throws it away. *Tso'apittse* said, "You must have met somebody who told you to do this." *Tso'apittse* never eats the heart. She hits the ground with it all night. *Tso'apittse* doesn't want any fire or any light.

Daylight comes. The boy says, "I killed a sheep up there. You go get it and pack it." *Tso'apittse* goes to get the meat. The boy goes away in the opposite direction. *Tso'apittse* goes to where the meat is, but she can't reach it. She wants the wind to blow, she wants a South Wind. A big wind comes but it doesn't break the tree where the meat is as *Tso'apittse* wanted it to. The tree is too strong. Then *Tso'apittse* wishes for another wind, the West Wind. It comes. It breaks the tree and *Tso'apittse* gets the meat and then goes home. *Tso'apittse* goes fast, she runs. When she gets there, she finds the boy is gone. She tracks him.

As the boy goes, he meets a woman gathering seeds for food. The woman hides him in her gathering basket and covers it with a smaller one. *Tso'apittse* comes and says, "Where's my man?" The woman says, "I haven't seen him." *Tso'apittse* says, "Look, that little basket is crooked." The woman says, "Look up that way." When *Tso'apittse* looks, the boy gets out and runs away. The boy goes up a mountain. When he is near the summit, *Tso'apittse* looks up and sees him there on the mountain. The boy runs. He meets a man hunting jackrabbits. It is Coyote who is hunting jackrabbits. *Tso'apittse* comes and says to Coyote, "Where is my man?" Coyote is making an arrow, putting the foreshaft into the butt. *Tso'apittse* says, "What's the matter with your arrow? It's crooked." Coyote says, "*Tso'apittse*, you look the other way." Then *Tso'apittse* looks the other way and Coyote takes the boy out of the butt of the arrow and the boy runs away.

The boy runs to another hill. *Tso'apittse* sees him up near the summit. *Tso'apittse* runs after him. The boy comes to a man's camp. The man is a rock wren, a bird who lives in rocks on top of the rocks. He is a small bird with a long nose. The bird hides the boy. The bird is going to make an arrow. He cuts a stick, heats a stone arrow-straightener to rub the stick on to make it straight. He has a stone pestle and puts it between his legs so that it looks like a penis. Soon *Tso'apittse* comes and says, "Where's my man?" The bird says, "I haven't seen him." Then *Tso'apittse* looks at the bird, sees what she thinks is

his penis, and says, "I want that." The bird says, "All right, I'll give it to you." This bird had a cave for a house. He says, "Come, let's go into the cave." So he and *Tso'apittse* go into the cave and he gives it to *Tso'apittse*. The cave begins to get small and *Tso'apittse* says, "What is happening to the cave?" The bird says, "When I have intercourse with my wife, the cave always does this." Then the cave got smaller and smaller and the little bird got out the tiny hole that was left. When he gets out, the entrance shuts up tight.

The bird saw the boy's long penis and said, "That's no good, let's cut it off." So he cut it off.

*Tso'apittse* became echo.

### *Tso'apittse* (4)

Source: *Shoshone Tales,* by Anne M. Smith, 1993. Salt Lake City: University of Utah Press, p. 154.

Two men were hunting cottontail rabbits in the mountains. There was snow. Cottontail was hiding under brush. *Tso'apittse* tracked the two men. They didn't see *Tso'apittse*. *Tso'apittse* came near them and the men saw him and ran away. *Tso'apittse* was crying up there. The men ran and ran and ran and they got home. Tso'apittse ran after them. When the men got home they told an old man, "*Tso'apittse* is tracking us." The old man is a doctor. He sings and sings. Then *Tso'apittse* comes but because the doctor sang he couldn't catch the men. So *Tso'apittse* went home.

### Another *Tso'apittse* Tale (2)

Source: *Shoshone Tales,* by Anne M. Smith, 1993. Salt Lake City: University of Utah Press, pp. 154-155.

There was a man who fought with his wife. Soon *Tso'apittse* came to this man because he fought with his wife. *Tso'apittse* carried him off in his basket. When they went under a tree, the man caught on a limb and climbed out of the basket.

*Tso'apittse* went home. His children came out to meet him. *Tso'apittse* said, "Go look in my basket and cook what's there for my supper. We will kill him." The children look and say, "There is nothing in there."

"Go and look again. He must be someplace."

"No, there is nothing there." *Tso'apittse* went and looked but there was nothing in the basket.

By this time the man was home. He had a big stone knife.

*Tso'apittse* tracked him to his home but the young man took his stone knife and slit his hands down from his fingers. *Tso'apittse* stayed there at the man's house all night. It was cold. He waited outside for the young man to come out. He fell down, it was cold, he died. The young man came out and saw him. He got a stick and poked *Tso'apittse's* eyes out with it. *Tso'apittse* died. Next morning the man went to *Tso'apittse's* home looking for the *Tso'apittse* children. They were crying from hunger. He killed them.

# Jarbidge

Source: Unknown.

The name "Jarbidge" is a white version of our [Shoshone] word *Tso'apittse*. *Tso'apittse* is a cannibal giant who lives in the Jarbidge Canyon. The giant preys on Indians, tossing them into a basket slung across his back. He takes them to his home to cook and eat his victims. Because *Tso'apittse* is a hairy devil, we don't go to the canyon for fear of being captured and eaten. My people say, "to get away from *Tso'apittse* run uphill because his eyes can only look down. So if you run uphill ahead of him, he can't see you."

# The Southern Paiute

The Southern Paiute (also known as the Nuwuvi) inhabited southeastern California, and parts of Arizona, Nevada, and Utah. Today, the tribe maintains reservations in all four states. Their language is part of the Uto-Aztecan family. Their traditional word for a hairy giant is *Nu'numic*, not to be mistaken for personal names of giants *Tse'nahaha* and *Pu'wihi*.

### *Nu'numic* the Giant

Source: *Myths of the Owens Valley Paiute,* by Julian H. Steward, 1936. Berkeley: University of California Publications in American Archaelogy and Ethnology, Vol. 34, No. 5.

*Nu'numic* and his wife lived in a large cave near Fish springs. He was the enemy of the Indians and used to prey on them. The Indians came to Fish springs daily to bathe or to get fish to eat.

*Nu'numic* would go down through the Black Rock country and visit people at the different springs. Once, several women were at Black Rock springs, gathering Indian sugar. They saw the giant coming and the younger women ran away. One woman, who was too old to get away from *Nu'numic*, stayed where she was. She took some of the sugar cane and covered herself. She stayed there, quiet as a 'possum, under the grass.

But the giant had seen her already and knew where she was. He went to the place and sat on her. After a while he became so heavy that she had to move. The giant knew all the time that there was somebody under him. When she had to move, he said, "What is there under me, anyway?" He knew all the time what was under him. He uncovered her, and said, "Well, there is somebody under me!" He captured her and took her to his home. At his rock cave, he ground her up, cooked her, and ate her for a meal.

Another time, he went down from his home to Hine's spring, and there he found a little baby, *Pau'ha*, lying on top of a rock. The baby's body left an impression on the rock which may be seen today. *Nu'numic* said, "Who could have left you here, and what are you doing here?" While he was wondering, he thought he would have fun with *Pau'ha* before he killed him. With his little finger, he thumped *Pau'ha* on the forehead to see if it would wake him up. He said, "You poor little thing. Whoever left you here?" And he placed his forefinger in the palm of the baby's hand. The *Pau'ha* took a grip on his finger.

Then the little baby got up on his feet and dragged *Nu'numic* toward the spring where he lived. The giant tried to take hold of brush to stop himself, but nothing would help him. When the little baby came to the spring he said, "This is my water. Now feel good." He picked the great man up and threw him into the lake. Then he swam after *Nu'numic* and took him down under the water. That was the end of the giant. He had lived to about seventy-five years of age.

## *Nu'numic* the Giant

Source*: Myths of the Owens Valley Paiute,* by Julian H. Steward, 1936. Berkeley: University of California Publications in American Archaelogy and Ethnology, Vol. 34, No. 5.

*Nu'numic* was a great giant who lived near Black Rock. He used to walk up and down Owens Valley. He was so large that he could walk the whole length of the valley in a short time. The *Patsuan'was* were tiny water babies. They lived in the sloughs throughout the valley.

The *Patsuan'was* decided that they wanted to get rid of *Nu'numic*. One day, one of them came out of the water and lay in the road to wait for *Nu'numic. Nu'numic* came walking along with his big strides, and saw the *Patsuan'wa.* He looked down at the little creature, and said, "My, but this is cute." He reached down at the little creature, and said, "Here, little thing, take hold of my finger." He wanted to play with the baby. The *Patsuan'wa* grabbed the giant's large finger in his small hand. His hand was so little that it would hardly go around *Nu'numic's* finger.

After a while, *Nu'numic* said, "Let go, now. I want to go on." But the *Patsuan'wa* kept hold of his finger. *Nu'numic* said, "Let go." But the little creature clung to him. Then he tried to shake it off, but could not. The *Patsuan'wa* began to walk, pulling *Nu'numic* behind him. *Nu'numic* tried to get loose. He said, "I want you to let me go. I want to be free." But the baby paid no attention to him. He dragged the giant to the water. Then he went into the water and pulled *Nu'numic* under and drowned him. That was the end of *Nu'numic.*

## The Woman and the Giants

Source: *Myths of the Owens Valley Paiute,* by Julian H. Steward, 1936. Berkeley: University of California Publications in American Archaelogy and Ethnology, Vol. 34, No. 5.

Once there lived a giant named *Tse'nahaha* who killed people by looking at them. He always carried a big basket of thorns on his back. When he caught anyone, he threw him over his back into the basket.

A group of Indians were playing the hand game in a certain house, and were having a good time. They had stationed a woman outside to watch for *Tse'nahaha*. After a while, she heard *Tse'nahaha* coming. He was talking to himself and singing. The woman tried to warn the people that the giant was coming, but they did not hear her. *Tse'nahaha* was getting closer. The woman became frightened, and jumped into a little pit and pulled a basket over herself.

She heard *Tse'nahaha* come up and stop. He stooped down and crawled into the doorway of the house and looked around. Twice he made a sucking noise with his lips. When he looked at anyone in the house, that person died at once. The others noticed the dead ones staring and said, "What are you people looking at? What is there worth looking at?" Then they too looked at *Tse'-nahaha* and died. Soon they were all dead. Only a little baby was left inside, sleeping. *Tse'nahaha* went away.

The baby commenced to cry. It was almost daylight now. The baby crawled over to the people and pushed them over. Then the woman left the pit

and went inside, but she did not look at the dead people. She called the baby, and said, "Let's go away." She set the house on fire, took the baby, and went away. With her digging-stick, she dug *kani'd* while the baby slept and ate.

As she was living this way, another giant, *Pu'wihi* came along. *Pu'wihi* picked up the baby, holding his head between his second and third fingers, and carried him over to the woman. He said to her, "Where are you from?" She answered, "I am from that house over there–the one with the smoke coming out. There are many men in it." The giant went toward the house. The woman was very frightened and tried to hide. She set her digging-stick in a clump of wild oats and vaulted as far as she could.

When the giant came back from the house he did not see her. He looked all around. He was furious and twisted his nose in anger. He found the wild oats and saw the mark of her stick. This showed in which direction she had jumped, and he went to a big flat rock. She had gone under this rock, and was crying.

The giant took the rock away and uncovered her, but it was dark by this time. He said, "I'll get her in the morning. Now I'll make a fire and grind up this baby." He found a large flat rock, ground up the baby, and ate him. He was having a fine time and lay there, singing. The woman could hear him. After a while he went to sleep. Then the woman got up and made another jump toward the east, to the house of her aunt.

When the woman came to her aunt's house, she was safe. The giant could not see the mark of her stick to find out which way she had jumped because this time she had jumped from a rock. The Paiute Indians come from this woman.

# The Washoe

The Washoe currently occupy their traditional homelands around Lake Tahoe in California and Nevada. Their language is in the Hokan family. The Washoe name for a female giant is *Suskia*.

## *Suskia*, the Giantess

Source: *The North American Indian,* Vol. 15, by Edward S. Curtis, 1930. Massachusetts: The Plimpton Press, p. 103-105.

A woman was preparing acorn meal at the spring. It was evening. In the house her baby was crying, but she gave no heed. Then *Suskia*, assuming the likeness of the woman, entered the house and bore the crying baby away. She carried him home and kept him until he grew to boyhood.

One day Gopher Woman, always weaving baskets, told the boy that *Suskia* was not his mother. In a distant village, she said, lived his real mother. "When there is a fire on the mountain where your people live," she said, "I will point out the place to you, and you can go home."

So when there happened to be a fire on the mountain, Gopher Woman prepared chia meal for the boy, and she gave him also a flat basket. "Roll this basket ahead of you," she said, "and it will lead you home. Follow wherever it leads."

So the boy started, following the rolling tray. When *Suskia* returned and asked where her son was, Gopher Woman replied, "He was here a short time ago." Then *Suskia* was angry, and they quarreled. *Suskia* tried to harm Gopher Woman, but the little woman ran into her burrow, and when *Suskia* kicked at her, she dodged back, only to reappear at some other hole. Then *Suskia* seized a tray, rolled it off, and followed it.

In the village the people saw, far away, two persons running toward them, each following a rolling tray. When the first reached them, they recognized him as the lost infant, and quickly concealed him in a roll of matting, which they stood in a corner of the house. The strong shamans gathered in the house and closed the door. When *Suskia* approached, they exerted their power and tried to prevent her from coming farther, but she was too strong. She came, and forced open the door.

"Give me my son!" she demanded.

"We have no son of yours," they said.

"But here are his tracks coming into the house," she declared.

So they had to agree to give up the boy. They said, "Close your eyes, and we will place him in your mouth." She closed her eyes, and they threw a red-

hot stone into her gullet. She leaped up, rushed out of the house, and disgorged the stone. Then she ran back into the house and gave a kick at the bundle of matting, and the boy fell dead. Suskia also fell dead on the floor, and her body became that of an owl.

The people warned their children not to approach the body. But one day some of them plucked the owl's feathers and placed them on their heads. Soon their heads felt lifeless, and they could not move from the place. So they lay there, crying and calling for help. When their parents heard them, they did not dare to approach lest they also be unable to stir from the spot. Then the eldest of the children thought of something. He said he would arrange his fingers, one on another, and his toes in the same way, and he would put feathers between them. The others were to do the same thing, and then he would sing, and when the song reached its highest pitch, they would straighten their fingers and toes and would fly away. So this they did, and the boy sang, "*Wichukanomovo, kanonoe-e, numa* [twist on the leg, feet, my hand]!" The pitch constantly rose, and at the highest point they straightened out their fingers and toes, and flew away, meadowlarks.

# THE
# GREAT PLAINS
# CULTURE

# Great Plain Cultural Area

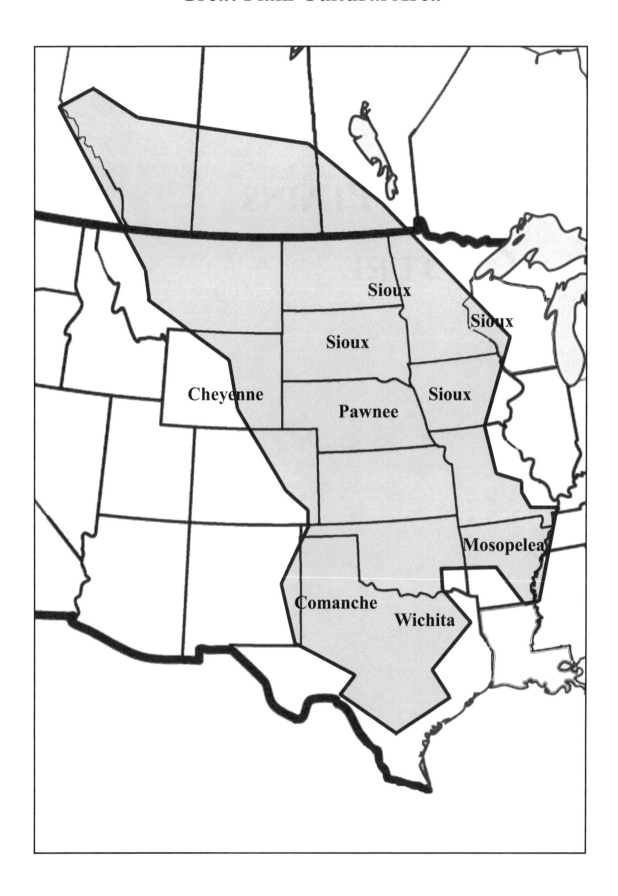

# The Cheyenne

Original residents of the Plains, the Cheyenne are now broken into two groups, the Northern Cheyenne living in Montana and the Southern Cheyenne in Oklahoma. Their language is a part of the Algonquian linguistic stock.

### Hairy Clan

Source: *The Life of George Bent,* by George Hyde, 1890.

Part of the Cheyenne's began to move south of the Platte River to live. They were led by the *Hevhaitanio* clan or Hairy Men. The Hairy Man clan was a large group and had many famous warriors in its camp. The clan was closely tied to a hairy beast that is said to have great strength and courage.

# The Comanche

Along with the Cherokee, the Comanche (also known as the Numunuu) were one of the largest tribes in the United States prior to the European arrival. Their traditional homelands included eastern New Mexico, southern Colorado, southern Kansas, all of Oklahoma, and most of northern and southern Texas. Today, the Comanche government is located in Lawton, Oklahoma. In the Comanche traditional language (in the Uto-Aztecan stock), a bigfoot-like creature has two names, *Mu pitz* and *Piamupits*, both which mean "cannibal monster."

### *Piamupits* or *Mu pitz*

Source: *Fossil Legends of the First Americans,* by Adrienne Mayor, 2005. New Jersey: Princeton University Press, pp. 196-197.

*Piamupits* or *Mu pitz* is a cannibal monster who was a terrifying cave dwelling ogre, about 12-feet tall and covered in hair. *Sanapia*, a Comanche medicine woman, described *Mu pitz* as a very tall, hairy giant with big feet. He is huge and has a foul smell. He is a fur-covered man like Bigfoot. Comanche elders put out food for the *Mu pitz* because he still roams Oklahoma. Comanche grind *Mu pitz* bones into a power and use it to treat sprains and bone problems. They tested the bones first to see if it had special power by putting the bone on their tongues.

### The Boy Who Escaped from the Giant

Source: *The North American Indian,* Vol. 19, by Edward S. Curtis, 1930. Massachusetts: The Plimpton Press, p. 194.

One day a small boy was playing alone at quite a distance from the camp. A Giant came by, picked him up, and put him in a bag which he carried on his shoulders.

The boy tried in every way to get out, but the mouth of the bag was drawn tightly, and it was too strong to tear. After trying many times to escape, he had to give up. As the Giant walked along, a little Bird came and perched on the bag. When the boy heard the Bird, hope returned, and he asked his feathered friend for help.

The Bird flew away and returned with a fire-drill, which he gave to the boy, saying, "Set the bag on fire and burn up the Giant!" The boy set fire to the bag, and when a hole had been burned through, he jumped out. While the Giant was fighting the fire, the boy escaped.

## Peah-Moopitz Kahnik (Pia Moopitsi Kahni)

Source:  Daniel A. Becker, May 1940.

A giant lived in a cave located on the southern slope of Elk Mountain in the early days before the white man came. Exacting two buffaloes every fortnight from the Indians living south of the mountain, he was a constant and fearful menace. As the years went by and the buffalo became more scarce because of the frequent buffalo hunts of the many different tribes of Indians, the fulfilling of the giant's request was made increasingly difficult. Slowly the white men came in. They also organized buffalo hunts.

Finally, when the Indians found it almost impossible to furnish the required number of buffalo, they held a council. A young brave was designated to confer with the giant concerning their problem. Cattle were to be suggested as a substitute.

Approaching the entrance of the cave, the brave called, "Great Giant, I come before you to ask an important question."

"What is it you want?" said the giant.

"There are not enough buffalo on the prairies or in the mountains. Will you accept the beef of cattle instead? We have been eating it for years and find it very delicious."

"Cattle are very small, but I shall be satisfied if your tribe will bring me twenty," replied the giant.

Cattle were thus substituted for buffalo, but the change of the diet did not agree with the giant. He became increasingly irritable and nervous and menacing. The coming of so many white men, bringing confusion to the quiet mountain country, was also disquieting to the giant. The Indians, trying to appease his wrath, brought him forty beeves.

Finding his new diet more and more disagreeable, and the encroachment of the white man unbearable, the giant left his cave for a more secluded spot in the larger mountain range farther west.

## The Woman and the Dwarf

Source: *The North American Indian,* Vol. 19, by Edward S. Curtis, 1930. Massachusetts: The Plimpton Press, p. 195-196.

There was once a woman who was returning home through the hills. Her husband had accompanied her, but he had been killed on the way. It was fast growing dark, and as she went along, she heard some one calling to her, but she saw nobody whichever way she looked. Finally she looked down at her feet and saw a Dwarf standing in the doorway of his house. He had a quiver full of arrows over his shoulder. He said to her: "You get in this house and stay there. It is growing dark, and there is a Giant who is on your trail. If he ever finds you, he will eat you.

The woman hid, and soon a Giant came along.

He asked the Dwarf: "Have you seen any one come along this trail? I am following a woman, and I want something to eat."

"No, I have seen no one tonight."

"Her tracks lead up to your door."

"There is no one here. If you do not believe me, lift up the house and look in. There is no one around."

The Giant lifted up the house and looked in. As he bent over, the Dwarf cut his head off and threw it away.

He called the woman out, and told her: "The Giant is dead. Start home now, because your camp is a long way off. You would have been eaten that time, but I saved you."

## The Woman Who Married a Giant

Source: *The North American Indian,* Vol. 19, by Edward S. Curtis, 1930. Massachusetts: The Plimpton Press, p. 196.

One day a young mother went down to the creek to bathe, taking her little son with her. When they were about ready to go home, a handsome young man came by who asked the woman to go home with him. She agreed at last, and they started; but as it was a long way, they married first. After much traveling they reached his home, late in the evening, and by moonlight she saw that it was made of silver.

When she awoke in the morning, she found that her husband beside her had become a Giant, which frightened her greatly. She thought over many plans to escape and make her way back to her own camp, but none seemed suitable. After several days the thought came to her to go down to the creek, so she said to him, "I am going down to the creek to wash clothes for my boy." The Giant saw nothing wrong with this plan, and let her go.

Once there, she saw a large Bullfrog on the bank, to which she spoke: "Brother Bullfrog, the Giant will call us in a little while, and I am afraid of him. When he calls, say that we are still washing."

Frog said: "Sister, I shall help you," and he gave them a bag of medicine to aid in their escape–a downy feather and a piece of buffalo cow's stomach–saying, "The Giant will pursue you, and when he does, throw down these things."

After they had fled, every time Giant called, Frog answered, "We are still washing."

Finally Giant became suspicious and went down to the creek to see why they were staying there so long, but he found no one. In a rage he pursued, gaining rapidly upon them. When they looked back they could see him coming up fast, and the woman in alarm threw down what Frog had first given her, the downy feather. Immediately a dense fog rose behind her, in which Giant became lost and groped about for a long time. Finally he emerged and picked up the trail again. When he came near a second time, the woman threw behind her the stomach of the buffalo cow, which turned into canyons and draws behind her. The Giant became entangled in this rough country and found his way out with great difficulty, but at last he followed the trail again and began to overtake them.

They reached a river, with no means of getting across, and followed along the bank until they came to where Crane was standing, of whom they begged: "Brother Crane, the Giant is following us to eat us! Help us!"

"Here is a louse from my head; crack it in your teeth on your way across," Crane instructed.

He planted his long legs on both banks, and they crossed in safety over his body. Soon Giant came long; he could see that his victims had crossed safely. He angrily ordered Crane: "Put me across! If you do not, I shall kill you!"

Crane stretched out his legs for Giant, but when he reached midway, Crane folded his legs and Giant fell in the water. The last the woman saw of him he was floundering about in the stream.

# The Mosopelea

The Mosopelea once inhabitant regions that stretched from the lower Mississippi to Ohio. They speak a language within the Siouan language stock. The traditional Mosopelea name for bigfoot is *Yeahoh*, which means "monster" and is directly related to the sound the animal made.

### The *Yeahoh*

Source: *Interview of Lee Maggard, Putney, Harlan County, Kentucky, 1950.* Western Folklore–Volume XVI, January 1957, No.1.

Once they was man out huntin', he got lost, and after a while he begin to get hungry. He come to a big hole in the ground and he thought he would venture down into it. He went down in there and he found that the old *Yeahoh* lived in there and had deer meat hangin' up and other foods piled around the walls. The man was afraid at first, but *Yeahoh* didn't bother him and he went toward that meat to get him some. The Yeahoh walked over and looked at the knife and said, "*Yeahoh, Yeahoh,*" a time or two. He cut it off a piece of the meat and it started eatin' it.

Well, the man stepped over to the middle of the pit and took out his flint and built him up a fire. And the *Yeahoh* watched him and looked at the fire and at the flint and said, "*Yeahoh, Yeahoh*" again. The man put his meat on a stick and br'iled him a nice piece and started eatin' it. The *Yeahoh* watched him and acted like it wanted a piece. The man cut it off a piece of the br'iled meat and reached it over, and the *Yeahoh* commenced to eatin' it up and smackin' its lips and saying, "*Yeahoh, Yeahoh.*"

Well, the man lived there with it a long time and they got along all right. After so long they was a young'un born to 'em, and it was half-man and half-*Yeahoh*. And the *Yeahoh* took such a liking to the man it wouldn't let him leave. He got to wanting to get away and go back home. One day he slipped off and the *Yeahoh* follered him and made him go back. Went on that way for a good while, but he picked him a good time and slipped away. This time he got to the shore where there was a ship ready to set sail.

He got on this ship and he looked and saw the *Yeahoh* comin' with the young'un. It screamed and hollered for him to come back and when it saw he wasn't goin' to come, why, it just tore the baby in two and held it out one-half to him and said, "*Yeahoh, Yeahoh.*" He sailed on off and left it standing there.

# The Pawnee

In pre-contact times, the Pawnee inhabited a large area from South Dakota to Texas and Louisiana. The tribe is currently located in Nebraska and Oklahoma. Their language is in the Caddoan family.

### Drowned Giants

Source: *Fossil Legends of the First Americans,* by Adrienne Mayor, 2005. New Jersey: Princeton University Press, pp. 192.

The first men who lived on earth were very large Indians. These giants were very big and very strong [and] used to hunt the buffalo on foot. They were so swift and strong that he could run down a buffalo, and kill it with a great stone, or a club, or even with his flint knife. A giant could throw a bull buffalo over his back as a hunter today carries an antelope, and he would tuck a yearling in his belt like a rabbit. But these giants did not believe in *Tirawa*, the Creator. Nowadays, all people, wherever they live–all Indians, all white men, all Mexicans and all black men–speak to [*Tirawa*] and ask that he will give them the right kind of a mind, and that he will bless them.

But the giants of the old days did not respect the Creator, thinking that nothing could overcome them, they grew worse and worse. At last, *Tirawa* got angry and made the waters rise. The ground became soppy mud. These great people sank down in the mud and were drowned. The great bones found on the prairie are the bones of these people.

# The Sioux

Made up of three major bands, the Dako-ta, Lakota, and Nakota Sioux historical-ly occupied North and South Dakota, Mon-tana, Nebraska, and Wyoming. Today, the tribe is mainly concentrated in South Dakota, although there are populations in other states. Their language is in the Siouan family. The traditional Sioux words for a bigfoot-like creature are *Chiye-tanka* (big man) and *Iktomi* ("The Trickster" or "Double Face").

### *Chiye-tanka*

Source: *The Spirit of Crazy Horse,* by Peter Mathiessen, 1980. Minnesota: Viking Press.

*Chiye-tanka* or Big Man is a kind of husband of *Unk-ksa*, the earth, who is wise in the way of anything with its own natural wisdom. Sometimes we say that this one is a kind of animal from the ancient times who can take a big hairy form; I also think he can change into a coyote. Some of the people who saw him did not respect what they were seeing, and they are already gone.

They exist in another dimension from us, but can appear in this dimension whenever they have a reason to. See, it's like there are many levels, many dimensions. When our time in this one is finished, we move on to the next, but the Big Man can go between. The Big Man comes from God. He's our big brother, kind of looks out for us.

### Manstin, the Rabbit

Source: *Iktomi and the Ducks and other Sioux Stories,* by Zitkala-Sa, 1901 (reprint 1985). Lincoln: University of Nebraska Press, pp. 143-156.

Manstin was an adventurous brave, but very kind-hearted. Stamping a moccasined foot as he drew on his buckskin leggins, he said: "Grandmother, beware of *Iktomi*! Do not let him lure you into some cunning trap. I am going to the North country on a long hunt."

With these words of caution to the bent old rabbit grandmother with whom he had lived since he was a tiny babe, Manstin started off toward the north. He was scarce over the great high hills when he heard the shrieking of a human child.

"*Wan*!" he ejaculated, pointing his long ears toward the direction of the sound; "*Wan*! That is the work of cruel Double Face. Shameless coward! He delights in torturing helpless creatures!"

Muttering indistinct words, Manstin ran up the last hill and lo! In the

ravine beyond stood the terrible monster with a face in front and one in the back of his head!

This brown hairy giant was without clothes save for a wild-cat-skin about his loins. With a wicked gleaming eye, he watched the little black-haired baby he held in his strong arm. In a laughing voice he hummed an Indian mother's lullaby, "*A-boo! A-boo!*" and at the same time he switched the naked baby with a thorny wild-rose bush.

Quickly Manstin jumped behind a large sage bush on the brow of the hill. He bent his bow and the sinewy string twanged. Now an arrow stuck above the ear of Double Face. It was a poisoned arrow, and the giant fell dead. Then Manstin took the little brown baby and hurried away from the ravine. Soon he came to a teepee from whence loud wailing voices broke. It was the teepee of the stolen baby and the mourners were its heartbroken parents.

When gallant Manstin returned the child to the eager arms of the mother there came a sudden terror into the eyes of both the Dakotas. They feared lest it was Double Face come in a new guise to torture them. The rabbit understood their fear and said: "I am Manstin, the kind-hearted, Manstin, the noted huntsman. I am your friend. Do not fear."

## White Feather the Giant Killer

Source: *North American Indians Myths and Legends,* by Lewis Spence, 1914. New York: George G. Harrap and Co., pp. 296-301.

There once dwelt in the heart of a great forest an old man and his grandchild. So far as he could remember, the boy had never seen any human being but his grandfather, and though he frequently questioned the latter on the subject of his relatives he could elicit no information from him. The truth was that they had perished at the hands of six great giants. The nation to which the

boy belonged had wagered their children against those of the giants that they would beat the latter in a race. Unfortunately the giants won, the children of the rash Indians were forfeited, and all were slain with the exception of little *Chacopee*, whose grandfather had taken charge of him. The child learned to hunt and fish, and seemed quite contented and happy.

One day the boy wandered away to the edge of a prairie, where he found traces of an encampment. Returning, he told his grandfather of the ashes and tent-poles he had seen, and asked for an explanation. Had his grandfather set them there? The old man responded brusquely that there were no ashes or tent poles, he had merely imagined them. The boy was sorely puzzled, but he let the matter drop, and next day he followed a different path. Quite suddenly he heard a voice addressing him as "Wearer of the White Feather." Now there had been a tradition in his tribe that a mighty man would arise among them wearing a white feather and performing prodigies of valor. But of this *Chacopee* as yet knew nothing, so he could only look about him in a startled way. Close by him stood a man, which fact was in itself sufficiently astonishing to the boy, who had never seen anyone but his grandfather; but to his further bewilderment he perceived that the man was made of wood from the breast downward, only the head being of flesh.

"You do not wear the white feather yet," the curious stranger resumed, "but you will by and by. Go home and sleep. You will dream of a pipe, a sack, and a large white feather. When you wake you will see these things by your side. Put the feather on your head and you will become a very great warrior. If you want proof, smoke the pipe and you will see the smoke turn into pigeons."

He then proceeded to tell him who his parents were, and of the manner in which they had perished, and bade him avenge their death on the giants. To aid him in the accomplishment of this feat he gave him a magic vine which would be invisible to the giants, and with which he must trip them up when they ran a race with him.

*Chacopee* returned home, and everything happened as the Man of Wood had predicted. The old grandfather was greatly surprised to see a flock of pigeons issuing from the lodge, from which *Chacopee* also shortly emerged, wearing on his head a white feather. Remembering the prophecy, the old man wept to think that he might lose his grandchild.

Next morning *Chacopee* set off in search of the giants, whom he found in a very large lodge in the center of the forest. The giants had learned of his approach from the 'little spirits who carry the news.' Among themselves they mocked and scoffed at him, but outwardly they greeted him with much civility, which, however, in nowise deceived him as to their true feelings. Without loss of time they arranged a race between *Chacopee* and the youngest giant, the winner of which was to cut off the head of the other. *Chacopee* won, with the help of his magic vine, and killed his opponent. Next morning he appeared again, and decapitated another of his foes. This happened on five mornings. On the sixth he set out as usual, but was met by the Man of Wood, who informed him that on his way to the giants' lodge he would encounter the most beautiful woman in the world.

"Pay no attention to her," he said earnestly. "She is there for your destruction. When you see her turn yourself into an elk, and you will be safe from her wiles."

*Chacopee* proceeded on his way, and sure enough before long he met the most beautiful woman in the world. Mindful of the advice he had received, he turned himself into an elk, but, instead of passing by, the woman, who was really the sixth giant, came up to him and reproached him with tears for taking the form of an elk when she had traveled so far to become his wife. *Chacopee* was so touched by her grief and beauty that he resumed his own shape and endeavored to console her with gentle words and caresses. At last he fell asleep with his head in her lap. The beautiful woman once more became the cruel giant, and, seizing his axe, the monster broke *Chacopee's* back; then, turning him into a dog, he bade him rise and follow him. The white feather he stuck in his own head, fancying that magic powers accompanied the wearing of it.

In the path of the travelers there lay a certain village in which dwelt two young girls, the daughters of a chief. Having heard the prophecy concerning the wearer of the white feather, each made up her mind that she would marry him when he should appear. Therefore, when they saw a man approaching with a white feather in his hair the elder ran to meet him, invited him into her lodge, and soon after married him. The younger, who was gentle and timid, took the dog into her home and treated him with great kindness.

One day while the giant was out hunting he saw the dog casting a stone into the water. Immediately the stone became a beaver, which the dog caught and killed. The giant strove to emulate this feat, and was successful, but when he went home and ordered his wife to go outside and fetch the beaver only a stone lay by the door. Next day he saw the dog plucking a withered branch and throwing it on the ground, where it became a deer, which the dog slew. The Giant performed this magic feat also, but when his wife went to the door of the lodge to fetch the deer she saw only a piece of rotten wood. Nevertheless the giant had some success in the chase, and his wife repaired to the home of her father to tell him what a skillful hunter her husband was. She also spoke of the dog that lived with her sister, and his skill in the chase.

The old chief suspected magic, and sent a deputation of youths and maidens to invite his younger daughter and her dog to visit him. To the surprise of the deputation, no dog was there, but an exceedingly handsome warrior. But alas! *Chacopee* could not speak. The party set off for the home of the old chief, where they were warmly welcomed.

It was arranged to hold a general meeting, so that the wearer of the white feather might show his prowess and magical powers. First of all they took the giant's pipe (which had belonged to *Chacopee*), and the warriors smoked it one after the other. When it came to *Chacopee's* turn he signified that the giant should precede him. The giant smoked, but to the disappointment of the assembly nothing unusual happened. Then *Chacopee* took the pipe, and as the smoke ascended it became a flock of pigeons. At the same moment he recovered his speech, and recounted his strange adventures to the astounded listeners. Their indignation against the giant was unbounded, and the chief ordered that he should be given the form of a dog and stoned to death by the people.

*Chacopee* gave a further proof of his right to wear the white feather. Calling for a buffalo hide, he cut it into little pieces and strewed it on the prairie. Next day he summoned the braves of the tribe to a buffalo hunt, and at no great distance they found a magnificent herd. The pieces of hide had become buffaloes. The people greeted this exhibition of magic art with loud acclamations, and *Chacopee's* reputation was firmly established with the tribe.

*Chacopee* begged the chief's permission to take his wife on a visit to his grandfather, which was readily granted, and the old man's gratitude and delight more than repaid them for the perils of their journey.

# The Wichita

The Wichita originally inhabited areas of Kansas and Oklahoma. Today, their reservation lands are located in Oklahoma. The Wichita language is part of the Caddoan linguistic family.

## The Deluge

Source: *The North American Indian,* Vol. 19, by Edward S. Curtis, 1930. Massachusetts: The Plimpton Press, pp. 50-52.

It was told from father to son, from generation to generation, that some day something was going to happen to the people; that there would come a time, no one knew how far off, when there would be continuous rain and all the world would be covered with water. The people knew in their hearts that this flood was coming and their minds were prepared for it. But they were worried because it might happen tomorrow, or this summer or in the following year; they were anxious because they did not know when it would occur. They ever cautioned the children not to wander off, because they might be caught in the flood if they were too far from home. Then came a time when it commenced to rain. The people were not sure whether or not this was the time of the deluge, but they were afraid, and all remained indoors. So great was the downpour that at the end of three days the people felt that this must be the promised flood, so they began to talk of what to do and where to go. The women cried and wailed in fright.

An old man spoke, saying: "What is the matter? What are you thinking of; why are you uneasy?" He called together the old men. "I have something to tell you men. I feel sorry for the people who are crying." To the young men he ordered, "Go to the forest; cut dead cottonwoods and bring them to me, for they are light." The young men brought back long stout logs, which the old man ordered cut into even lengths. "Now go back and cut three more," he directed. With the first logs he made a foundation for a raft by laying them side by side. The three brought in last he notched at intervals and laid across his raft foundation, one at each end and one in the middle. He lashed these to the logs with withes.

A young man asked, "Why do you notch the logs?"

"To secure them firmly by making them fit closely together. These logs are dry; they will never sink," he answered.

All the time the rain fell. The young men brought armfuls of osiers which the old man used to bind the timbers together. He used also the soapweed which he made into rope. The raft was so large that it took many men to interweave the willows and the soapweed rope. The young men were sent to fetch willow poles. One of these was set upright on each corner, notched, and lashed firmly in place. Two more were set up in similar manner on each side of the raft near the middle. Others were laid horizontally, one on top of the other, the ends lashed to the corner and middle poles, to form walls for the raft.

The work proceeded rapidly because it still rained. The old man directed that branches be brought, such as are used for making arbors; these were spread on the bottom of the raft. He went about the village, saying to the women, "You women commence to prepare food that the children will have something to eat, because something is happening."

All over the village could be heard the pounding of corn. Other people brought enough leaves and brush to cover the bottom of the raft. People began to be greatly frightened, standing about and talking in groups. One of them cried: "Look over there! Something is happening!"

They saw a dark wall of water rising. The old man directed the women to bring the seed of the corn, which he placed in the joints of cane and planted them firmly in the earth. The water came up higher; they asked one another, "What is going to happen?" The old man called the people to the raft, but they were terrified and cried, "This thing will sink!"

When the water rose still higher the people went aboard the raft. Its walls had been built so high that there was no danger of its occupants falling overboard. As it rose in the water many people were frightened because they did not know what was to happen. There was a motion to the raft; it rocked and was whirled about by the swirling currents.

Now they noticed that the flood was up to the necks of the "four things standing in the water" [monsters]. They were gradually sinking out of sight as the water rose.

The people became hungry; first the children were provided for, then the adults. The older ones talked, trying to encourage the others. One very old man said: "Do not be frightened; be contented. Remember that long ago a certain person told us that it would rain twelve days. It is getting near the end of that time now. Soon the rain will cease."

The water rose higher and closer to the heads of the four huge beasts. One of the four declared, "I have got to give up; I am going to fall to the south." Soon another said, "I must give up; I am going to fall to the west." The third announced, "I am going to fall toward where the cold wind comes from." The fourth said, "Some time when our bones dry out and people find them, they will keep pieces of bone for their medicine.

Before this time the people did not know the four directions. From the last words of the monsters the people learned them.

After twelve days and nights the rain ceased and the waters receded. The people felt glad, for they knew that some one had cared for them. They saw that the joints of cane with the corn seed were still standing. If these had been lost, the people would not have had the corn which they now have. Soon the raft grounded, but no one dared to get off because of the deep mud. Though the wind blew continuously, twelve more days and twelve nights passed before it dried the earth firmly enough to walk on. There was no village left when the people finally landed. The old man said: "Do not be sad because you have lost your homes. One good thing has happened; you are still living." He took up the canes with the corn from the ground. He gave the corn seed to the older women, the good workers. Then they searched for the sites of their former homes; they could barely see where their houses had been.

## The Deluge 2

Source: *The North American Indian,* Vol. 19, by Edward S. Curtis, 1930. Massachusetts: The Plimpton Press, pp. 53-54.

In the old days there were many Wichita villages. One, where lived the chief-over-all, was larger than the others. This chief had a wife, but no children. His heart longed for sons, but his wife refused to be a mother. Many years passed with no children in the lodge of the chief, then the wife gave birth to four uncouth creatures, which rapidly grew into monsters.

The chief was troubled, and called a council of his men to ask what should be done with these strange beings. Many urged that they be killed, but their mother begged that they be spared. When very young these creatures did no harm, but as they grew older they became vicious, killing children and wrecking the village. The chief and his council then decided to move the monsters outside the village. Their bodies grew rapidly, but their legs did not grow. All of the men of the tribe joined in moving them from the village. They were placed on high ground, all four in a group, with their rumps together and their heads facing toward the four directions. By this time their bodies had become so large that their legs would not carry them. Their necks extended to great length. They continued to grow very huge and tall and wicked. They reached out and snatched people or animals who journeyed forth, so that the villagers came under the complete control of the monsters. The people starved, for if they went out for food, the monsters would get them. The headman did not like this, so he went to the turtle, saying, "I need

help, even if everyone is destroyed. I want you to do something to these monsters."

The huge turtle went underground until he was beneath the feet of the monsters. Then the rain came; but the birds flew over before the rain commenced, as a sign that a flood was approaching, which was the arrangement the chief had made with the turtle. After the birds had been seen, the sky grew black with great clouds, and the rain poured. As the water rose, the monsters stuck up long necks, holding their mouths to the sky and moving their feet as if to stretch them long.

The people had been told that when the birds flew over, something would happen, so they became frightened, trying to escape as the water swallowed them up. The turtle moved under the feet of the huge beasts, making the ground soft, and the water came so high that nothing but their heads was above water. Then the monster in the south said, "I am falling south; I can not stand on my legs any longer." The one in the west cried, "I am giving out and falling to the west." The monster in the north said, "My turn has come; I am falling." The monster in the east declared, "My turn has come; I am falling east."

The rain continued until there was a great flood which destroyed all the people. There was nothing left but land floating in water.

# The
# Northeast
# Culture

# The Northeast Cultural Area

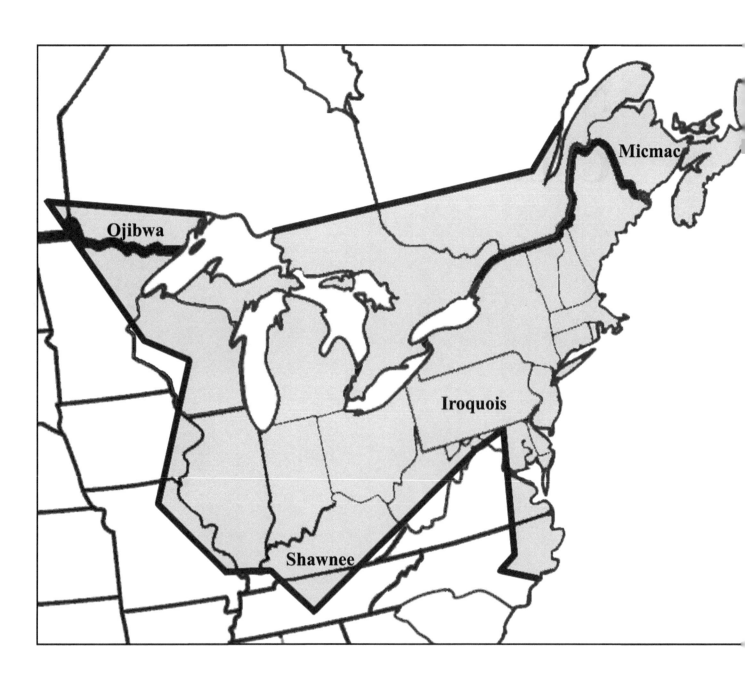

# The Iroquois

The Iroquois are a confederacy of six different tribes, the Mohawk, the Oneida, the Onondaga, the Cayuga, the Seneca, and the Tuscarora. They all speak a language within the Iroquoian family group. At the time of the arrival of Europeans, the six tribes occupied upstate New York and parts of Pennsylvania, Ontario, and Quebec. The tribes today are spread out throughout Canada, New York, and Wisconsin. Because the six tribes were so closely united, ethnographers often failed to differentiate between them when recording their traditional stories. As a result, stories from each tribe are lumped together under the heading of "Iroquois." The traditional words for bigfoot-like creatures are *Ot-ne-yar-hed* (stonish giant), *Tarhuhyiawahku* (giant monster), and *Ge no sqwa* (stone giants).

**The *Ot-ne-yar-hed***

Source: *Iroquois Folk Lore Gathered from the Six Nations of New York*, by Rev. William Beauchamp, 1965. New York: Ira J. Friedman Co.

The *Ot-ne-yar-hed* or Stonish Giants, had overran the country. They fought a great battle, and held the people in subjection for a long time. The Stonish Giants were so ravenous that they devoured the people of almost every town in the country. At the Mississippi they had separated from all others and gone to the northwest. The family was left to seek its habitation, and the rules of humanity were forgotten, and afterwards eat raw flesh of the animals. At length they practiced rolling themselves on the sand, by this means their bodies were covered with hard skin; these people became giants and were dreadful invaders of the country. The Holder of the Heavens led them into a deep ravine near Onondaga, and rolled great stones on them in the night. But one escaped, and since then the Stonish Giants left the country and seeks an asylum in the regions of the north.

The Onondagas say that a Stone Giant lived near Cardiff. He was once like other men, but was a great eater, becoming a cannibal, and increased in size. His skin became hard and changed into scales, which alone would turn an arrow. Every day he came through the valley, caught and devoured an Onondaga, a fearful toll. The people were dismayed but formed a plan. They made a road in the marsh with a covered pitfall, decoyed the giant through the path and down he went and was killed. Of course when the Giant was found, it did not astonish the Onondagas that he was of stone.

The Onondagas have also a story of a Stone Giant's race with a man near Jamesville. He ran the man into the hollow at Green Pond, west of that village, where the rocks rise 200 feet above the water on three sides. On the south side the precipice can be ascended by a natural stairway at one spot, and the man was far enough ahead to reach the top before the other. He lay down and looked from the rocks to see what the other would do. The latter came and looked around. Not seeing the man he took out of his pouch what seemed a finger, but was really a pointer of bone. By means of this he could find any object he wished, and so it was always useful in hunting. As he climbed the rocks the man reached down and took away the pointer before the other saw him. The giant begged him to restore it. If he would do this he was promised good luck and long life for himself and friends. Though he begged so piteously the man ran home with it to show his friends, leaving him there helpless, unable to find his way. His friends interceded, telling him to accept the giant's good offer and not incur his enmity. So they went back and found him still at the lake. He received his pointer, promising to eat men no more, and good luck followed the man.

## The Stone Giantess

Source: *North American Indians Myths and Legends,* by Lewis Spence, 1914. New York: George G. Harrap and Co., pp. 254-257.

In bygone times it was customary for a hunter's wife to accompany her husband when he sought the chase. A dutiful wife on these occasions would carry home the game killed by the hunter and dress and cook it for him.

There was once a chief among the Iroquois who was a very skillful hunter. In all his expeditions his wife was his companion and helper. On one excursion he found such large quantities of game that he built a wigwam at the place, and settled there for a time with his wife and child. One day he struck out on a new track, while his wife followed the path they had taken on the previous day, in order to gather the game killed then. As the woman turned her steps homeward after a hard day's work she heard the sound of another woman's voice inside the hut. Filled with surprise, she entered, but found to her consternation that her visitor was no other than a Stone Giantess. To add to her alarm, she saw that the creature had in her arms the chief's baby. While the mother stood in the doorway, wondering how she could rescue her child from the clutches of the giantess, the latter said in a gentle and soothing voice: "Do not be afraid: come inside."

The hunter's wife hesitated no longer, but boldly entered the wigwam. Once inside, her fear changed to pity, for the giantess was evidently much worn with trouble and fatigue. She told the hunter's wife, who was kindly and sympathetic, how she had traveled from the land of the Stone Giants, fleeing from her cruel husband, who had sought to kill her, and how she had finally taken shelter in the solitary wigwam. She besought the young woman to let her remain for a while, promising to assist her in her daily tasks. She also said she was very hungry, but warned her hostess that she must be exceedingly careful about the food she gave her. It must not be raw or at all underdone, for if once she tasted blood she might wish to kill the hunter and his wife and child.

So the wife prepared some food for her, taking care that it was thoroughly cooked, and the two sat down to dine together. The Stone Giantess knew

that the woman was in the habit of carrying home the game, and she now declared that she would do it in her stead. Moreover, she said she already knew where it was to be found, and insisted on setting out for it at once. She very shortly returned, bearing in one hand a load of game which four men could scarcely have carried, and the woman recognized in her a very valuable assistant.

The time of the hunter's return drew near, and the Stone Giantess bade the wife go out and meet her husband and tell him of her visitor. The man was very well pleased to learn how the new-comer had helped his wife, and he gave her a hearty welcome. In the morning he went out hunting as usual. When he had disappeared from sight in the forest the giantess turned quickly to the woman and said:

"I have a secret to tell you. My cruel husband is after me, and in three days he will arrive here. On the third day your husband must remain at home and help me to slay him."

When the third day came round the hunter remained at home, obedient to the instructions of his guest.

"Now," said the giantess at last, "I hear him coming. You must both help me to hold him. Strike him where I bid you, and we shall certainly kill him."

The hunter and his wife were seized with terror when a great commotion outside announced the arrival of the Stone Giant, but the firmness and courage of the giantess reassured them, and with something like calmness they awaited the monster's approach. Directly he came in sight the giantess rushed forward, grappled with him and threw him to the ground.

"Strike him on the arms!" she cried to the others. "Now on the nape of the neck!" The trembling couple obeyed, and very shortly they had succeeded in killing the huge creature.

"I will go and bury him," said the giantess. And that was the end of the Stone Giant.

The strange guest stayed on in the wigwam till the time came for the hunter and his family to go back to the settlement, when she announced her intention of returning to her own people.

"My husband is dead," she said, "I have no longer anything to fear." Thus, having bade them farewell, she departed.

# The Micmac

The Micmac (also known as the Mi'kmaq) historically inhabited the Canadian Maritimes including Nova Scotia, the Gaspé Peninsula in Quebec, Prince Edward Island, and the eastern half of New Brunswick. The tribe still occupies the same areas, as well as a reserve in Maine. Their language is part of the Algonquin language stock, and their traditional words for a bigfoot-like creature are *Chenoo* (devil cannibal) and *Gougou*.

### The Story of the Great *Chenoo*

Source: *The Algonquin Legends of New England,* by Charles G. Leland, 1884. Boston: Houghton, Mifflin, and Company, pp. 233-244.

An Indian, with his wife and their little boy, went one autumn far away to hunt in the northwest. And having found a fit place to pass the winter, they built a wigwam. The man brought home the game, the woman dressed and dried the meat, and the small boy played at shooting birds with bow and arrow; in Indian–all went well.

One afternoon, when the man was away and the wife gathering wood, she heard a rustling in the bushes, as though some beast were brushing through them, and, looking up, she saw with horror something worse than the worst she had feared. It was an awful face glaring at her–a something made of devil, man and beast in their most dreadful forms. It was like a haggard old man with wolfish eyes; he was stark naked; his shoulders and lips were gnawed away, as if, when made with hunger, he had eaten his own flesh. He carried a bundle on his back. The woman had heard of the terrible *Chenoo*, the being who comes from the far, icy north, a creature who is a man grown to be both devil and cannibal, and saw at once that this was one of them.

Truly she was in trouble; but dire need gives quick wit, as it was with this woman, who, instead of showing fear, ran up and addressed him with fair words, as 'My dear father', pretending surprise and joy, and, telling him how glad her heart was, asked where he had been so long. The *Chenoo* was amazed beyond measure at such a greeting where he expected yells and prayers, and in mute wonder let himself be led into the wigwam.

She was a wise and good woman. She took him in; she said she was sorry to see him so woebegone; she pitied his sad state; she brought a suit of her husband's clothes; she told him to dress himself and be cleaned. He did as she bade. He sat by the side of the wigwam, and looked surly and sad, but kept quite. It was all a new thing to him.

She arose and went out. She kept gathering sticks. The *Chenoo* rose and followed her. She was in great fear. "Now," she thought, "my death is near; now he will kill and devour me."

The *Chenoo* came to her. He said, "Give me the axe!" She gave it, and he began to cut down the trees. Man never saw such chopping. The great pines fell right and left, like summer saplings; the boughs were hewed and split as if by a tempest. She cried out, "*Noo, tabeagul boohsoogul!*–My father, there is enough!" He laid down the axe; he walked into the wigwam and sat down, always in grim silence. The woman gathered her wood, and remained as silent on the opposite side.

She heard her husband coming. She ran out and told him all. She asked him to do as she was doing. He thought it well. He went in and spoke kindly. He said, "*N'chilch*-My father-in-law," and asked where he had been so long. The *Chenoo* stared in amazement, but when he heard the man talk of all that had happened for years his fierce face grew gentler.

They had their meal; they offered him food, but he hardly touched it. He lay down to sleep. The man and his wife kept awake in terror. When the fire burned up and it became warm, the *Chenoo* asked that a screen should be placed before him. He was from the ice; he could not endure heat.

For three days he stayed in the wigwam; for three days he was sullen and grim; he hardly ate. Then he seemed to change. He spoke to the woman; he asked her if she had any tallow. She told him they had much. He filled a large kettle; there was a gallon in it. He put it on the fire. When it was scalding hot, he drank it all off at a draught.

He became sick; he grew pale. He cast up all the horrors and abominations of earth, things appalling to every sense. When all was over he seemed changed. He lay down and slept. When he awoke he asked for food and ate much. From that time he was kind and good. They feared him no more.

They lived on meat such as Indians prepare. The *Chenoo* was tired of it. One day he said, "*N'toos* [my daughter], have you no *peZaweoos* [fresh meat]?" She said, "No." When her husband returned the *Chenoo* saw that there was black mud on his snowshoes. He asked him if there was a spring of water near. The friend said there was one half a day's journey distant. "We must go there tomorrow," said the *Chenoo*.

And they went together, very early. The Indian was fleet in such running. But the old man, who seemed so wasted and worn, went on his snow-shoes like the wind. They came to the spring. It was large and beautiful; the snow was all melted away around it; the border was flat and green.

Then the *Chenoo* stripped himself and danced around the spring his magic dance; and soon the water began to foam, and anon to rise and fall, as if some monster below were heaving in accord with the steps and the song. The *Chenoo* danced faster and wilder; then the head of an immense *taktaZok* [lizard] rose above the surface. The old man killed it with a blow of his hatchet. Dragging it out he began again to dance. He brought out another, the female, not so large, but still heavy as an elk. They were small spring lizards, but the *Chenoo* had conjured them; by magic they were made into monsters.

He dressed the game; he cut it up. He took the heads and feet and tails and all that he did not want, and cast them back into the spring. "They will grow again into many lizards." he said. When the meat was trimmed it looked like that of the bear. He bound it together; he took it on his shoulders; he ran like the wind; his load was nothing.

The Indian was a great runner; in all the land was not his like; but now he lagged far behind. "Can you go no faster than that?" asked the *Chenoo*. "The

sun is setting; the red will be black soon. At this rate it will be dark before we get home. Get on my shoulders."

The Indian mounted on the load. The *Chenoo* bade him hold his head low, so that he would not be knocked off by the branches. "Brace your feet," he said, "so as to be steady." Then the old man flew like the wind–*nebe sokano 'vjaZ samastukteskuguZ cheZ wegwasumug weguz*–the bushes whistled as they flew past them. They got home before sunset.

Then the spring was at hand. One day the *Chenoo* told them that something terrible would soon come to pass. An enemy, a *Chenoo*, a woman, was coming like wind, yes–on the wind–from the north to kill him. There could be no escape from the battle. She would be far more furious, mad and cruel than any male, even one of his own cruel race, could be. He knew not how the battle would end; but the man and his wife must be put in a place of safety. To keep them from hearing the terrible war-whoops of the *Chenoo*, which is death to mortals, their ears must be closed. They must hide themselves in a cave.

Then he sent the woman for the bundle which he had brought with him, and which, had hung untouched on a branch of a tree since he had been with them. And he said if she thought it was offensive to her, to throw it away, but certainly to bring him a smaller bundle that was within the other. So she went and opened it, and that which she found therein was a pair of human legs and feet, the remains of some earlier horrid meal. She threw them far away. The small bundle she brought to him.

The *Chenoo* opened it and took from it a pair of horns–horns of the *chep-itchcalm* [dragon]. One of them has two branches; the other is straight and smooth. They were golden-bright. He gave the straight horn to the Indian; he kept the other. He said that these were magical weapons, and the only ones of any use in the coming fight. So they waited for the foe.

And the third day came. The *Chenoo* was fierce and bold; he listened; he had no fear. He heard the long and awful scream–like nothing of earth–of the enemy, as she sped through the air far away in the icy north, long ere the others could here it. And the manner of it was this: that if they without harm should live after hearing the first deadly yell of the enemy they could take no harm, and if they did but hear the answering shout of their friend all would be well with them. But he said, "Should you hear me call for help, then hasten with the horn, and you may save my life."

They did as he bade: they stopped their ears; they hid in a deep hold dug in the ground. All at once the cry of the foe burst on them like screaming thunder; their ears rang with pain; they were well-nigh killed, for all the care they had taken. But then they heard the answering cry of their friend, and were no longer in danger from more noise.

The battle begun, the fight was fearful. The monsters, by their magic with their range, rose to the size of mountains. The tall pines were torn up, the ground trembled as in an earthquake, rocks crashed upon rocks, the conflict deepened and darkened; no tempest was every so terrible. Then the male *Chenoo* was heard crying, "*N'loosook! Choogooye! Abog umumooe!*–My son-in-law, come and help me!"

He ran to the fight. What he saw was terrible! The *Chenoos*, who upright would have risen far above the clouds as giants of hideous form, were struggling on the ground. The female seemed to be the conqueror. She was holding her foe down, she knelt on him, she was doing all she could to thrust her dragon's horn into his ear. And he, to avoid death, was moving his head rapidly from side to side, while she, mocking his cries, said "You have no son-in-law to help you–*Neen nabujjeole*–I'll take your cursed life, and eat your liver."

The Indian was so small by these giants that the stranger did not notice him. "Now," said his friend, "thrust the horn into her ear!" He did this with a well-directed blow, he struck hard; the point entered her head. At the touch it sprouted quick as a flash of lightning, it darted through the head, it came out of the other ear, it had became like a long pole. It touched the ground, it struck downward, it took deep and firm root.

The male *Chenoo* bade him raise the other end of the horn and place it against a large tree. He did so. It coiled itself round the tree like a snake, it grew rapidly; the enemy was held hard and fast. Then the two began to dispatch her. It was long and weary work. Such a being, to be killed at all, must be hewed into small pieces; flesh and bones must all be utterly consumed by fire. Should the least fragment remain unburnt, from it would spring a grown *Chenoo*, with all the force and fire of the first.

The fury of battle past, the *Chenoos* had become of their usual size. The victor hewed the enemy into small pieces, to be revenged for the insult and threat of eating his liver. He, having roasted that part of his captive, ate it before her; while she was yet alive he did this. He told her she was served as she would have served him.

But the hardest task of all was to come. It was to burn or melt the heart. It was of ice, and more than ice; as much colder as ice is colder than fire, as much harder as ice is harder than water. When placed in the fire it put out the flame, yet by long burning it melted slowly, until they at least broke it to fragments with a hatchet, and then melted these. So they returned to the camp.

Spring came. The snows of winter, as water, ran down the rivers to the sea; the ice and snow which had encamped on the inland hills sought the shore. So did the Indian and his wife; the *Chenoo*, with softened soul, went with them. Now he was becoming a man like other men. Before going they built a canoe for the old man: they did not cover it with birch bark; they made it of moose skin. In it they placed a part of their venison and skins. The *Chenoo* took his place; they took the lead, and he followed.

And after winding on with the river, down rapids and under forest boughs, they came out into the sunshine, on a broad, beautiful lake. But suddenly, when midway in the water, the *Chenoo* lay flat in the canoe, as if to hide himself. And to explain this he said that he had just then been discovered by another *Chenoo*, who was standing on the top of a mountain, whose dim blue outline could just be seen stretching far away to the north.

"He has seen me," he said, "but he cannot see you. Nor can he, he is behind me now, but should he discover me again, his wrath will be roused. Then he will attack me; I know not who might conquer. I prefer peace."

So he lay hidden, and they took his canoe in tow. But when they had crossed the lake and come to the river again, the *Chenoo* said that he could not travel further by water. He would walk the woods, but sail on streams no more. So they told him where they meant to camp that night. He started over mountains and through woods and up rocks, a far, roundabout journey. And the man and his wife went down the river in a spring freshet, headlong with the rapids. But when they had paddled round the point where they meant to pass the night, they saw smoke rising among the trees, and on landing they found the *Chenoo* sleeping soundly by the fire which had been built for them.

This he repeated for several days. But as they went south a great change came over him. He was a being of the north. Ice and snow had no effect on him, but he could not endure the soft airs of summer. He grew weaker and weaker; when they had reached their village he had to be carried like a little child. He had grown gentle. His fierce and formidable face was now like that of a man. His wounds had healed; his teeth no longer grinned wildly all the time. The people gathered round him in wonder.

He was dying. This was after the white men had come. They sent for a priest.

He found the *Chenoo* as ignorant of all religion as a wild beast. At first he would repel the father in anger. Then he listened and learned the truth. So the old heathen's heart changed; he was deeply moved. He asked to be baptized, and as the first tear which he had ever shed in all his life came to his eyes he died.

# The Ojibwa

The Ojibwa, also called the Chippewa, are the third largest tribe in North America (behind the Cherokee and Navajo). Largely still occupying their traditional homelands, Ojibwa are located in Wisconsin, Minnesota, Quebec, and Ontario. Their language is a part of the Algonquian family. The traditional Ojibwa name for a wild man is *Puck Wudj Ininees*.

### *Puck Wudj Ininees*

Source: *North American Indian Legends,* by Allan A. Macfarlan, 1968. New York: Dover Publications, pp. 71-75.

There was a time when all the inhabitants of the earth had died, except two helpless children, a baby boy and a little girl. When their parents died, these children were asleep. The little girl, who was the elder, was the first to wake. She looked around her, but seeing nobody besides her little brother, who lay asleep, she quietly resumed her bed. At the end of ten days, her brother moved without opening his eyes. At the end of ten days more, he changed his position, lying on the other side.

The girl soon grew up to woman's estate, but the boy increased in stature very slowly. It was a long time before he would even creep. When he was able to walk, his sister made him a little bow and arrows, and suspended around his neck a small shell, saying, "You shall be called *Wa-Dais-Ais-Imid* [He of the Little Shell]."

Every day he would go out with his little bow, shooting at the small birds. The first bird he killed was a tomtit. His sister was highly pleased when he took it to her. She carefully skinned and stuffed it, and put it away for him. The next day he killed a red squirrel. His sister preserved this too. The third day he killed a partridge [*Peena*], which she stuffed and set up. After this, he acquired more courage, and would venture some distance from home. His skill and success as a hunter daily increased, and he killed the deer, bear, moose, and other large animals inhabiting the forest. In time, he became a great hunter.

He had now arrived to maturity in years, but remained an infant in stature. One day, walking about, he came to a small lake. It was in the winter season. He saw a man on the ice killing beavers. The man appeared to be a giant. Comparing himself to this great man he appeared no bigger than an insect. He seated himself on the shore, and watched the man's movements. When the large man had killed many beavers, he put them on a hand sled and went home.

When he saw him retire, *Wa-Dais-Ais-Imid* followed him, and wielding his magic shell, cut off the tail of one of the beavers, and ran home with his trophy. When the tall stranger reached his lodge, with his sled load of beavers, he was surprised to find the tail of one of them gone, for he had not observed the movements of the little hero of the shell.

The next day *Wa-Dais-Ais-Imid* went to the same lake. The man had already fixed his load of beavers on his *odawbon*, his sled, and commenced his return. But *Wa-Dais-Ais-Imid* nimbly ran forward, and overtaking him, succeeded by the same means in securing another of the beavers' tails. When the man saw that he had lost another of this most esteemed part of the animal, he was very angry. "I wonder," said he, "what dog it is that has thus cheated me. Could I meet him, I would make his flesh quiver at the point of my lance."

Next day he pursued his hunting at the beaver dam near the lake, and was followed again by the little man of the shell. On this occasion, the hunter had worked so fast that he had accomplished his object and nearly reached his home before our tiny hero could overtake him, but he nimbly drew his shell and cut off another beaver's tail. In all these pranks our hero availed himself of his power of invisibility, and thus escaped observation. When the man saw that the trick had been so often repeated, his anger was greater than ever. He gave vent to his feelings in words. He looked carefully around to see whether he could discover any tracks. But he could find none. His unknown visitor had stepped so lightly as to leave no track.

Next day the hunter resolved to disappoint him by going to his beaver pond very early. When *Wa-Dais-Ais-Imid* reached the place, he found the fresh traces of his work, but the hunter had already returned. Our hero followed his tracks, but failed to overtake him. When he came in sight of the lodge, the hunter was in front of it, employed in skinning his beavers. As he stood looking at him, he thought, "I will let him see me." Presently the man, who proved to be no less a personage than *Manabozho*, looked up and saw him. After regarding him with attention, "Who are you, little man?" said *Manabozho*. "I have a mind to kill you." The little hero of the shell replied, "If you were to try to kill me, you could not do it."

When he returned home he told his sister that they must separate. "I must go away." said he, "it is my fate. You too," he added, "must go away soon. Tell me where you would wish to dwell." She said, "I would like to go to the place of the breaking of daylight. I have always loved the east. The earliest glimpses of light are from that quarter and it is, to my mind, the most beautiful part of the heavens. After I get there, my brother, whenever you see the clouds in that direction of various colors, you may think that your sister is painting her face."

"And I," said he, "my sister, shall live on the mountains and rocks. There I can see you at the earliest hour, and there the streams of water are clear, and the air pure. And I shall ever be called *Puck Wudj Ininee*, or the little wild man of the mountains. But before we part forever, I must go and try to find some *Manitoes*." He left her, and traveled over the surface of the globe, and then went far down into the earth. He had been treated well wherever he went.

At last he found a giant *Manito,* who had a large kettle which was forever boiling. The giant regarded him with a stern look, and then took him up in his hand, and threw him unceremoniously into the kettle. But by the protection of his personal spirit, our hero was shielded from harm, and with much ado got out of the kettle and escaped.

He returned to his sister, and related his rovings and misadventures. He finished his story by addressing her thus, "My sister, there is a *Manito* at each of the four corners of the earth. There is also one above them, far in the sky; and last," continued he, "there is another, a wicked one, who lives deep down in the earth. We must now separate. When the winds blow from the four corners of the earth you must then go. They will carry you to the place you wish. I go to the rocks and mountains, where my kindred will ever delight to dwell."

He then took his ball stick, and commenced running up a high mountain, whooping as he went. Presently the winds blew, and as he predicted, his sister was borne by them to the eastern sky, where she has ever since been, and her name is the Morning Star.

> Blow, winds, blow! my sister lingers
> For her dwelling in the sky,
> Where the morn, with rosy fingers,
> Shall her cheeks with vermil dye.
>
> There, my earliest views directed,
> Shall from her their color take,
> And her smiles, through clouds reflected,
> Guide me on, by wood or lake.
>
> While I range the highest mountains,
> Sport in valleys green and low,
> Or beside our Indian fountains
> Raise my tiny *hip holla*.

# The Shawnee

The Shawnee were original residents of Ohio, Kentucky, and Pennsylvania. The current population resides in Oklahoma, Alabama, and Ohio. The Shawnee language is in the Algonquian stock.

## The Hairy Woman

Source: Interview of Joe Couch, Appalachia, Virginia, 1954. *Western Folklore,* Volume XVI, January 1957, No.1.

One time I's prowling in the wilderness, wandering about, kindly got lost and so weak and hungry I couldn't go. When it began to get cool, I found a big cave and crawled back in there to get warm. Crawled back in and come upon a leaf bed and I dozed off to sleep. I heard an awful racket coming into that cave, and something come in and crawled right over me and laid down like a big old bear. It was a hairy thing and when it laid down it went chomp, chomp, chawing on something. I thought to myself, "I'll see what it is and find out what it is eating."

I reached over and a hairy like woman was there eating chestnuts, had about a half a bushel there. I got me a big handful of them and went to chewing on them too. Well, in a few minutes she handed me over another big handful, and I eat chestnuts until I was kindly full and wasn't hungry any more. D'rectly she got up and took off and out of sight.

Well, I stayed on there till next morning and she come in with a young deer. Brought it in and with her big long fingernails she ripped its hide and skinned it, and then she sliced the good lean meat and handed me a bite to eat. I kindly slipped it behind me, afraid to eat it raw and afraid not to eat it being she give it to me. She'd cut off big pieces of deer meat and eat it raw. Well, I laid back and the other pieces she give over as she eat her'n. She was goin' to see I didn't starve.

When she got gone again I built me up a little fire and br'iled my meat. After being hungry for two or three days, it was good cooked–yes, buddy. She come in while I had my fire built br'illing my meat, and she run right into that fire. She couldn't understand because it kindly burnt her a little. She jumped back and looked at me like she was going to run through me. I said, "Uh-oh, I'm going to get in trouble now."

Well, it was cold and bad out, so I just stayed another night with her. She was a woman but was right hairy all over. After several days I learnt her how to br'ile meat and that fire would burn her. She got shy of the fire and got so she liked br'iled meat and wouldn't eat it raw any more. We went on through the winter that way. She would go out and carry in deer and bear. So I lived there about two year, and when we had a little kid, one side of it was hairy and the other side was slick.

I took a notion I would leave there and go back home. I begin to build me a boat to go away across the lake in. One time after I had left, I took a notion I would slip back and see what she was doing. I went out to the edge of the cliff and looked down into the mountain, and it looked like two or three dozen of hairy people coming up the hill. They were all pressing her and she would push them back. They wanted to come on up and come in. I was scared to death, afraid they's going to kill me. She made them go back and wouldn't let them come up and interfere.

Well, I took a notion to leave one day when my boat was ready. I told her one day I was going to leave. She follered me down to my boat and watched me get ready to go away. She was crying, wanting me to stay. I said, "No, I'm tired of the jungles. I'm going back to civilization again, going back."

When she knowed she wasn't going to keep me there, she just grabbed the little young'un and tore it right open with her nails. Throwed me the hairy part and she kept the slick side. That's the end of that story.

# The Northwest Coast Culture

# Northwest Coast Cultural Area

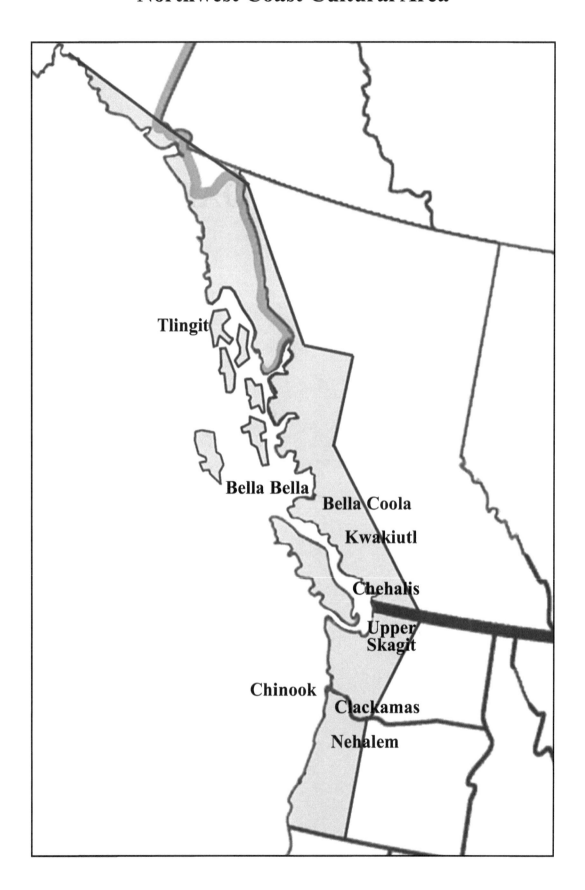

Tlingit

Bella Bella

Bella Coola

Kwakiutl

Chehalis

Upper
Skagit

Chinook

Clackamas

Nehalem

# The Bella Bella

The Bella Bella, also called Heiltsuk, still live in their traditional homeland along the central coast of British Columbia and west coast of Campbell Island. Their language is part of the Wakashan language group. Their traditional name for a female cannibal is *K!a;waq!a.*

### K!a;waq!a

Source: *Bella Bella Tales* by Franz Boas, 1932. New York: The American Folklore Society.

The *K!a;waq!a* carries a basket on her back in which she carries away children. Once upon a time she stole from the village *Xune!s* a boy whom she kept in her house for a whole year. One day, *Ask:a'naqs*, came to him and whispered into his ear, "the *K!a;waq!a* goes always down to the beach to get mussels and claims. When she comes up the steep mountainside, put the siphons of the clams on the tips of your fingers and move them towards her, opening and closing your fingers." The boy obeyed. When the *K!a;waq!a* came up he moved his fingers and shouted, "*ananai;dzedzeq!ei K!a;waq!a!*" She became frightened and asked him to stop. When he continued she fell down the cliff and was dead.

### K!a;waq!a (2)

Source: *Bella Bella Tales* by Franz Boas, 1932. New York: The American Folklore Society.

In *Hau'yat* where people lived in summer, children disappeared one after another at night time. The people did not know what happened to them. They asked four courageous men to watch all night. The watchers armed themselves with clubs, spears and lassoes. At midnight the *K!a;waq!a* appeared. They threw a lasso around her neck, speared her and cut off her head. The next morning the people deliberated what to do with her body. Some wanted to tied stones to it and throw it into the sea. Others wanted to burn it. Finally all agreed to burn it to ashes. Those who breathed in the smoke of the fire died of it. The others took to their canoes and left the place.

# The Bella Coola

The Bella Coola (also known as the Nux-alk) were original residents of British Columbia, along the Bella Coola River. Their language is part of the wide-spread Salishan of the Northwest Coast. There are two names known for a bigfoot-like animal, *Snanaik* (a female cannibal) and *boqs* (bush man).

### Boqs

Source: *Legends Beyond Psychology,* by Henry James Franzoni III and Kyle Mizokami.

[The *boqs*] somewhat resembles a man, its hands especially, and the region around the eyes being distinctly human. It walks on its hind legs, in a stooping posture, its long arms swinging below the knees; in height it is rather less than the average man. The entire body, except the face, is covered with long hair, the growth being most profuse on the chest which is large, corresponding to the great strength of the animal. The most peculiar feature of the animal is its penis, which is so long that it must be rolled up and carried in the arms when the creature is walking; it terrifies its enemies by striking tree-trunks and breaking branches with its uncoiled organ. It is said that a woman was once drawing water at the edge of a stream when a *boqs*, concealed on the other shore, extended its penis under the water to the further bank and had intercourse with her. The contact rendered her powerless, as if turned to stone; she could neither flee nor remove the organ. Her companions tried unsuccessfully to cut the organ until one of them brought a salalberry leaf, whereupon the monster, dreading its razor-like edge, withdrew.

### Boqs 2

Source: *Legends Beyond Psychology,* by Henry James Franzoni III and Kyle Mizokami.

Not many years ago a certain *Qaklis* was encamped with his wife and child in the Bay of the Thousand Islands, *Altukwlaksos*, about two miles above *Namu*, one of the haunts of the *boqs*. He heard a number of the creatures in the forest behind him and seized his gun, at the same time calling out to them to go away. Instead, the breaking of branches and beating upon tree-trunks came nearer. Becoming alarmed, he called out once more: "Go away, or you shall feel my power." They still approached and *Qaklis* fired in the direction of the sounds. There followed a wild commotion in the forest, roars, grunts, pounding, and the breaking of branches. The hunter, now thoroughly alarmed, told his wife and child to embark in the canoe while he covered their retreat with his gun. He followed them without molestation, and anchored his craft not far from shore. The *boqs* could be heard plainly as they rushed to and fro on the beach, but only the vague outlines of their forms were visible in the darkness. Presently, though there was no wind, the canoe began to roll as if in a heavy sea. *Qaklis* decided to flee to Restoration Bay, but before he had gone far his paddle struck bottom, although he was in mid-channel. Looking up, he saw that the mountains were higher than usual; the *boqs* had, by their supernatural power, raised the whole area so that the water had been almost entirely drained away. They are the only supernatural beings with this power. *Qaklis* jumped overboard into the water, which reached only to his knees, and towed his canoe to Restoration Bay, the *boqs* following him along the shore.

This is not the only occasion on which *boqs* have appeared near Restoration Bay. Within the life-time of the father of an informant, a chief set out with some friends from *Kwatna*, bound for *Namu*. They traveled overland to Restoration Bay, thence by canoe, making the journey without incident. When returning, they decided to gather clams on the rocky point of the bay. As the craft shot around the tip of the promontory, they saw a *boqs* gathering shellfish. The paddlers backed their canoe behind some rocks whence they could watch without being seen. The creature acted as if frightened, it kept looking backwards, then hurriedly scraped up some clams with its forepaws, dashed off with these into the forest, and came back for more. The chief decided to attack the animal. A frontal approach was impossible owing to the lack of cover, so he landed and crept stealthily through the forest, armed with his Hudson's Bay Company's musket. Presently he stumbled upon a heap of clams which the animal had collected. He waited until it returned with another load, then raised his musket and fired. Instead of killing the *boqs*, its supernatural power was so great that the hunter's musket burst in his hands, though he himself was not injured. The *boqs* shrieked and whistled as if in anger, and at once hordes of its mates came dashing out through the forest. The frightened chief rushed out on the beach and called to his comrades to save him. They brought the canoe close to the shore so that he could clamber aboard, and then paddled away unharmed.

### The Child and the Cannibal

Source: Unknown.

Once upon a time there was a youth whose name was *Anutkoats*, who was playing with a number of girls behind the village. While they were playing, a noise like the cracking of twigs was heard in the woods.

The noise came nearer and nearer. The youth hid behind a tree, and saw that a *Snanaik* was approaching. She was chewing gum, which caused the noise. He advised the children to run away, but they did not obey. When they saw the gum, they stepped up to the *Snanaik* and asked her to give them some. The *Snanaik* gave a piece of gum to all the children, and when she saw *Anutkoats*, who was advising the children to return home, she took him and threw him into the basket which she was carrying on her back.

Then she took all the other children and threw them on top of him into her basket. After she had done so, she turned homeward. Then *Anutkoats* whispered to the girls to take off their cedar-bark blankets, and to escape through

a hole that he was going to cut in the basket. He took his knife, cut a hole in the bottom of the basket, and fell down. The girls also fell down one by one until only one of them was left.

All the children returned home and told their parents what had happened. The mother of the girl who had not been able to escape began to cry, mourning for her daughter. She cried for four days and four nights. Then her nose began to swell, because she had been rubbing it all the time. She had thrown the mucus of her nose on the ground. Now when she looked down, she saw that something was moving at the place where it had fallen.

She watched it from the corners of her eyes, and soon she discovered that her mucus was assuming the shape of a little child. The next time she looked, the child had grown to the size of a new-born baby. Then the woman took it up, and the child began to cry. She carried it into the house, and washed the baby for four days.

Then the child, who was very pretty and had red hair, began to speak, and said, "My father, the Sun, sent me to ask you to stop crying. I shall go out into the woods, but pray don't cry, for I am sent to recover your daughter. I know where she is. Make a small salmon-spear for me, which I shall need." Thus spoke the boy.

Then the woman asked an old man to make a salmon-spear, which she gave to her son. His mother gave him earrings made of abalone shells, and the boy played about with his spear, and always wore his ear ornaments.

One day when his mother was crying again, the boy said, "Mother, I ask you once more, don't cry, for my father the Sun sent me down to bring back your daughter. He will show me where she is. I shall start today to recover my sister from the *Snanaik*, who stole her. Don't worry about me."

Then the boy went up the river. After he had gone some distance, he came to a tree which overhung the river. He climbed it, and looked down in order to see if there were any fish in the water. Soon he heard a noise some distance up the stream, and gradually it sounded nearer. Then he saw the *Snanaik* coming down the river. When she reached the tree, she stopped and looked down into the clear water. She saw the image of the boy, who was sitting on the tree, and thought it was her own reflection.

She said, "How pretty I am!" and she brushed her hair back out of her face. When she did so, the boy imitated her movements in order to make her believe that she was looking at her own reflection. When she laughed, he laughed also, in order to deceive her. But at last the *Snanaik* looked upward, and saw the boy sitting in the tree.

Then she addressed him with kindly words, and asked him to come down. She said, "What did your mother do in order to make you so pretty?"

The boy replied, "You cannot endure the treatment I had to undergo in order to become as pretty as I am."

The *Snanaik* begged, "Oh, come down and tell me. I am willing to stand even the greatest pain in order to become as pretty as you are. What are you doing up there?"

Then the boy said, "I was watching for salmon, which I desire to harpoon with my salmon-spear."

The *Snanaik* repeated, "Oh, come down, and do with me whatever you please in order to make me as pretty as you are."

The boy replied, "I don't believe you can endure the wounds that I have to inflict upon you."

She replied, "You may cut me as much as you please. I want to become as pretty as you are."

Then the boy climbed down the tree, and the *Snanaik* asked, "What must we do first?"

He said, "We must go up this river to find two stone knives with which my mother used to cut off my head."

They walked up the river, and found the stone knives. Then the boy said to the the *Snanaik*, "Now lie down on this stone. Put your neck on the knife."

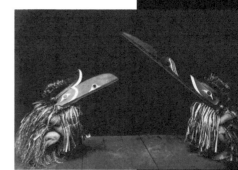

The *Snanaik* did as she was bidden. Then the boy took the other knife, told the *Snanaik* to shut her eyes, and cut off her head. The head jumped back to the body, and was about to unite with it, when the boy passed his hands over the wound, and thus prevented the severed head from joining the body again. Thus he had killed her.

Then he went to the *Snanaik*'s house. He found his sister whom the *Snanaik* had killed and smoked over her fire. He took the body down, and patted it all over with his hands. Thus he resuscitated the girl.

On looking around in the house, he found the dried bodies of other children, whom he also brought back to life. Then he took the girl and the other children home.

# The Chehalis

The Chehalis (also known as the Sts'Ailes) occupy an area near the Fraser River in their homeland of British Columbia. Their traditional word for a bigfoot-like creature is *Saskehavis*, meaning "wild man." John W. Burns, a teacher for the Chehalis reserve in Harrison Mills from 1925-1945, coined the word "sasquatch" based on the various names used by tribes within the Salishan language group. In 1980, the Chehalis band in British Columbia adopted a sasquatch image as their symbol.

## What happened to Serephine Long?

Source: "The Hairy Giants of British Columbia," by J.W. Burns, 1940. *The Wide World,* January 1940, Vol. 84, No. 502.

I was walking toward home one day many years ago carrying a big bundle of cedar roots and thinking of the young brave *Qualac* [Thunderbolt], I was soon to marry. Suddenly, at a place where the bush grew close and thick beside the trail, a long arm shot out and a big hairy hand was pressed over my mouth. Then I was suddenly lifted up into the arms of a young sasquatch. I was terrified, fought, and struggled with all my might. In those days, I was strong. But it was no good, the wild man was as powerful as a young bear. Holding me easily under one arm, with his other hand he smeared tree gum over my eyes, sticking them shut so that I could not see where he was taking me. He then lifted me to his shoulder and started to run.

He ran on and on for a long long time–up and down hills, through thick brush, across many streams never stopping to rest. Once he had to swim a river and then perhaps I could have gotten away, but I was so afraid of being drowned that I held on tightly with my arms about his neck. Although I was frightened I could not but admire his easy breathing, his great strength and speed of foot. After reaching the other side of the river, he began to climb and climb. Presently the air became very cold. I could not see but I guessed that we were close to the top of a mountain.

At last the sasquatch stopped hurrying, then he stooped over and moved slowly as if feeling his way along a tunnel. Presently he laid me down very gently and I heard people talking in a strange tongue I could not understand. The young giant next wiped the sticky tree gum from my eyelids and I was able to look around me. I sat up and saw that I was in a great big cave. The floor was covered with animal skins, soft to touch and better preserved that we preserve them. A small fire in the middle of the floor gave all the light there was. As my eyes became accustomed to the gloom I saw that beside the young giant who had brought me to the cave there were two other wild people–a man and a woman. To me, a young girl, they seemed very very old, but they were active and friendly and later I learned that they were the parents of the young

sasquatch who had stolen me. When they all came over to look at me I cried and asked them to let me go. They just smiled and shook their heads. From then on I was kept a close prisoner; not once would they let me go out of the cave. Always one of them stayed with me when the other two were away.

They fed me well on roots, fish and meat. After I had learned a few words of their tongue, which is not unlike the Douglas dialect, I asked the young giant how he caught and killed the deer, mountain goats and sheep that he often brought into the cave. He smiled, opening and closing his big hairy hands. I guessed that he just laid in wait and when an animal got close enough, he leaped, caught it and choked it to death. He was certainly big enough, quick enough and strong enough to do so.

When I had been in the cave for about a year I began to feel very sick and weak and could not eat much. I told this to the young sasquatch and pleaded with him to take me back to my own people. At first he got very angry, as did his father and mother, but I kept on pleading with them, telling them that I wished to see my own people again before I died. I really was ill, and I suppose they could see that for themselves because one day after I cried for a long time, the young sasquatch went outside and returned with a leaf full of tree gum. With this he stuck down my eyelids as he had done before. Then he again lifted me to his big shoulder.

The return journey was like a very bad dream for I was light headed and in much pain. When we re-crossed the wide river, I was almost swept away; I was too weak to cling to the young sasquatch, but he held me with one big hand and swam with the other. Close to my home, he put me down and gently removed the tree gum from my eyelids. When he saw that I could see again he shook his head sadly, pointed to my house and then turned back into the forest.

My people were all wildly excited when I stumbled back into the house for they had long ago given me up as dead. But I was too sick and weak to talk. I just managed to crawl into bed and that night I gave birth to a child. The little one lived only a few hours, for which I have always been thankful. I hope that never again shall I see a sasquatch.

# The Chinook

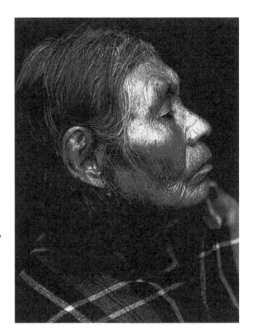

As part of the Penutian linguistic stock, the Chinook Tribe once occupied areas of the Columbia River, from British Columbia, Canada to Eastern Washington State, and all the way to the Pacific Ocean. The tribe is now split onto reservations in Washington and Oregon. The Chinook has several names for a bigfoot-type monster, depending on gender and location. The most famous, *Skookum*, is translated as "Evil God of the Woods" or mountain devil. Other terms include *At'at'ahila* (female monster), *Iekshthehlo* (female cannibal), and *Itohiul* (big feet).

## Coyote, the Transformer

Source: *The North American Indian, Vol. 8,* by Edward S. Curtis, 1930. Massachusetts: The Plimpton Press, p. 107 and 114.

The journeyings of Coyote began at the ocean, at the mouth of Columbia River, where lived an *At'at'ahila*, an evil creature who was constantly destroying people by tying them upon a baby-board and sending them adrift into the foggy distance, with the command, "Go forever!" After a time the board came floating back to her, and upon it there was nothing but bones, for on its voyage it had been to a place of such intense heat that the flesh was melted away. On the shore sat many people awaiting their turn to be set adrift. Their hearts would have run away, but the power of the *At'at'ahila* held them there. Then Coyote came among them, and after watching the evil one for a time, he told them, "I will try that, and soon I will return." So he was tied to the board, and, as he started to drift out into the fog, the old woman said, "Go forever!" But all the people cried out, "Come back again!" After a while the watchers could faintly see the board drifting closer, and they wondered if Coyote had been powerful enough to survive; and when it touched the shore they saw that he was alive, and all the people were glad. Then, to prove which was the stronger, the woman was placed on the board and went out into the fog, while Coyote and all the people shouted, "Go forever!" In time the board came drifting back with nothing but her bleached bones upon it. The people were happy that the evil was destroyed, and urged their deliverer to take from their number a wife. But he said: "No, I do not want a wife. I am to travel up the river." . . .

Coyote now proceeded to a village where he was told that an *At'at'ahila*, a female monster, and her husband, Owl, were carrying the people away and cooking them in a pit that they might eat them, and Coyote knew that he must change that. After thinking long he procured some green fir cones, cut them into bits, and dried them. He strung them, tied the strings around his legs, arms, and neck, in close rows, and threw his robe over them. Thus adorned, he went to the place where the monster usually was to be seen. She came to intercept him and kept in front of him, no matter in what direction he turned. Every time he stirred, the dry cones rattled. She said, "Where are you going?" He answered: "You see where the sun comes out in the morning? That is where I am going. My wife died a few days ago and I feel sad and do not wish to remain at home. She was a good wife. So I do not like to talk to women yet." He started to dance, and the cones rattled loudly. She ran up to him to take his arm, but he eluded her. Again she tried, and he pushed her with his staff and told her not to touch him. She asked, "How did you become so that you could make that sound when you dance?" "You need not ask that," he replied, "because I would not tell you, no matter how much you might pay me. If I told you that, you would never have to hunt for food, but only dance thus and the people would come to you. Then you would have only the work of cooking them." He started to leave her, but she came up with him again, and when she asked him once more how he made that sound, he at last, with apparent reluctance, consented to disclose the secret, provided she would promise to tell him the source of her own power. To this she agreed, and he said: "Then I will tell you how to dance and make your bones rattle as I do mine. I had my body completely covered with pitch, eyes and all. Then I was put on the fire. The pitch burned over my skin, and my bones were gradually roasted dry. That is why they rattle, because they are dry and charred. Hear my head!" and he shook it: "Hear my legs!" and he shook them. "Good!" said the *At'at'ahila*. "I am glad to know this, and I shall do it. Let us go up and you can work on me." She took him up to the pit where she was in the habit of cooking her victims. All around the edge of this great hole sat her captive people, old and young, awaiting their turn to be roasted. All were wailing, and everywhere about the pit were piles of the bones of those devoured by the *At'at'ahila* and Owl. Coyote told the waiting victims to go into the woods and collect fresh pitch, and they scattered among the trees, soon returning with quantities of it. Stones were heated, and Coyote proceeded to cover the *At'at'ahila* from head to foot with pitch, being careful not to leave a single bare spot, and all the while she was shifting her body to make sure that no spot should be missed. "You must agree that I am to be the judge of when you are done," said Coyote. "I will punch your arms and your head with this pole, and in that way I can tell when the work is done, because your bones will rattle." The *At'at'ahila* stood beside the roaring fire, and Coyote pushed her into it. Immediately she began to blaze. Coyote quickly gave each of five men a forked stick, one to hold her down by the neck, the others by the legs and arms. They pinned her down, and whenever Coyote ordered her to be turned, they rolled her over. When the pitch had burned out of her mouth, she cried, "I am burning! Take me out!" but Coyote only reminded her that he was the judge of when it was time for her to be taken out. "This will punish you for roasting people!" he said. In a short time the creature was dead, and Coyote told the people they were free to go home, and as they ran away they were happy, and sang. Soon after this Coyote saw Owl, the husband, coming home, leading a great number of captives. He picked up a handful of ashes, threw it at Owl, and said: "This is not the way. It is wrong to roast these people. There is going to be another kind of people here, and this must stop. I have killed your wife because she did it. From now on you will be nothing but a bird, and your name will be Owl, and you will live among these rocks. Once in a great while you will be heard, and when you are, some one will die." An owl's voice is always sad because he is mourning for his wife, and his feathers are mottled because of the ashes.

## The Transformers

Source: *The North American Indian,* Vol. 8, by Edward S. Curtis, 1930. Massachusetts: The Plimpton Press, p. 118-124.

One day the chief proposed to marry the girl, and it was so arranged. She never talked except privately with her husband, and she never laughed. Jaybird once remarked, "It is strange that our chief's wife never laughs." She said to him, "I am going to laugh." Then she went outside and laughed five times, "Ha-ha-heeee!" and the people fell dead. She devoured them all. Then she looked inside the house for her husband, but she could not find him, for, as soon as she began to laugh, Jaybird and the chief had run out of the house, and they had been the first ones to fall dead, although she had not intended to kill them. Not one person was left in the place.

When she realized that she had swallowed her husband, she thrust her finger down her throat and vomited all that she had swallowed, and he was the last one to come out, as he had been the first to go down. His legs had been bitten off. She washed him, legless as he was, put him in a basket, and sang, and after a while he came out laughing, but without legs. She replaced him in the basket, and hung it up in the house. Soon after this she bore two boys. They were *Mus'p* and *Skomoh'l*. She bathed them daily and nightly so that they would grow quickly. She warned them not to go in a certain direction, for she wished them not to find the place where she had vomited up the bodies of the people. One day they followed her to the prairie where she was digging camas, and as they were shooting, *Skomoh'l*, the younger, broke his bowstring. They returned to the house, and, searching for something which they could use for a string, they saw the basket hanging there. They took it down, thinking to find something suitable for a bowstring, but they found a person, who said, "Oh, my children; oh, my children!" He told them that they had a village of people in a certain place, to which he pointed, and that their mother was not human, but *iekshthehlo*. When their mother came home that evening, she noticed that they were morose, and she asked: "What is the matter, my children? We are alone here, but do not be downhearted." At dark they went to bed, and the younger said: "Tomorrow let us go where our mother told us not to go, and see what is there. There must be something." The next morning, while she dug camas, the boys visited the forbidden place, which they found covered with bones and old houses in ruins. *Skomoh'l* said: "Surely she is *iekshthehlo*. She has eaten our old people." He now began to think constantly what he should do.

The next morning they again took down the basket, and the younger tried to put legs on his father, but he could not. Then, leaving the basket and their father inside the house, they set fire to the structure, and smoke rose and fell over the fields like feathers. The woman caught some in her hand and, looking at it closely, said, "Ha! I will catch you!" She knew what her boys had been doing. When she went toward the house, the two boys were running to meet her, and she thought, "I will eat the elder first." But while she was waiting for him, the other ran round behind her, seized her hair, and shook her. All the bones fell rattling out of her skin, which he threw to the ground, and it turned into a female dog.

Then the two started to travel, the dog following them. The two brothers traveled on until after a long time they came to a man, of whom *Mus'p* inquired, "What are you doing?" The man answered: "I am making a knife. I have heard that two men are coming, and I am going to kill them." "Let me see that knife," said *Mus'p*. He took it and began to examine it, and said: "Are you going to kill those two men who are coming? You will never kill them. Your name is Beaver. Turn around!" He touched the knife to the man and it remained there like a tail, and *Mus'p* commanded him, "Now go and dive!" Beaver dived, and came up, and *Mus'p* said, "Now slap the water with your tail!" Beaver slapped the water as beavers have done ever since. "Now sing!" He began to sing in the way beavers do now in the mating season.

The two went on and found another man working on two knives. *Mus'p* got up on his back. "What are you doing?" he asked. "I am making knives with which to kill those two men who are coming," was the answer. "Let me

see your knives," said the boy. He took the two knives, and said, "Come here, closer." He put the two knives on the man's head, and said, "Now jump!" He jumped. "Turn around and look at me!" The man did so. "Now run!" The man ran. "You will never be a man again and kill people; you will be Deer," said *Mus'p*; "people forever will kill you and eat you!" The man became a deer, and the two knives his horns.

Again they went on, and came to a town, a large town. At one end of it *Mus'p* called out, "All you people, get your nets!" The people brought out their dip-nets. He directed them to get sticks to make a weir, and they began to build the trap in a creek where the tide came in. Then *Mus'p* showed them how to catch herring with a net held between two canoes and raised by ropes when full of fish. These people were *Yuhluyuhlu*.

The two came to another village, and *Mus'p* called out: "Come and see this whale in the river! Get your spear poles! Take five canoes and spear this whale!" So they did as he directed, and killed the whale. These were *Qunita'ih* [Makah] at Neah bay. They put some buoys on the whale and the five canoes towed it ashore, and the head-man distributed the flesh and blubber.

They arrived at another large town, and *Mus'p* called out, "Come and catch these blue-back salmon!" He then showed these *Tqinaiyuhlkhl* [Quinault] how to make the trap and take the salmon.

At Damons point they showed the *Tqiyanuhliks* how to use a stick in digging razor clams.

Next day they crossed the bay [Grays harbor] and found a large village at the mouth of a stream [Chehalis river]. When *Mus'p* told the people to get their nets, they ran into the houses and brought out their dip-nets, and he cried: "You are mistaken; I did not say dip-nets! But keep them, and you shall always be herring catchers."

At the mouth of Nemah River, where the people slept in hanging baskets because the beds were infested by fleas, the two brothers showed them how to sweep out their houses and thus rid themselves of vermin.

They crossed the river in a canoe and came to a small village, *Winiipu*, where they heard a man in a house, shouting. It was raining. They entered, and beheld a man shooting at the roof, and yelling. Wherever the water dripped through and fell on any one, that person died. So Jaybird was shooting at the rain. "What are you doing?" asked *Mus'p*. "I am killing those people who come to fight us," answered Jaybird. *Mus'p* looked up at the roof, and said: "That is not the way to make a roof. I will fix it." Then he showed them how to repair the leaky roof.

The two crossed the bay to *Tiapsuyi*, and there on the beach was Jaybird spearing cockle clams. As they left the canoe, Jaybird said to himself, "These must be great chiefs, for they wear sea-otter robes." He prepared to give them food, and roasted the cockles in the ashes. *Mus'p* opened one, ate the meat, and then drank the juice. Jaybird thought it odd that this great chief drank the "cockle oil." They remained there that night, and the next day at ebb-tide the people all went out with their spears for cockles. *Mus'p* and his brother walked out over the flats, and each time they felt a cockle under foot they picked it up and put it in a basket. They told the people that was the way to gather cockles, and Jaybird said, "I was thinking a long time ago of doing it that way." They went upon the sand, made a fire and heated stones, dug a pit, and showed the people how to pack the cockles in it. They taught them also how to hang cockles on a string to dry. "Have you any whale oil?" asked *Mus'p*. They brought some oil and he showed them how to eat fresh cockles with whale oil. Said Jaybird, "I thought of that a long time ago."

Again the two went on, this time to *Nakahuti* [Cape Disappointment], where they found a woman at play, a monster of the kind called *okohl*. She was killing children. On the beach was a great rock over which she threw them, crying, "Go forever!" and they fell on the sand beyond, dead.

The two brothers looked on from a distance, then went down close. "Where is your mother?" asked the woman. "She is coming," said *Mus'p*. The little dog was still following them, and it was her power that enabled them to do what they did. The woman then said, "I am glad you have come; we will have play." Said *Mus'p*: "You and I will play; my brother is always sick and never plays. You throw me over that rock first." So she took him by the hair, swung him, and threw him over the rock. He landed on his feet unhurt. The ground there was covered with children, some dead, some yet alive. He quickly made them well. Then he came around the rock, and the woman cried, "Oh, my nephew, I thought you were dead!" He said, "Now I will throw you over the rock." She was not pleased, but he assured her, "It did not hurt me." He had made the stones on the other side sharp flints, and had told the children that if the woman fell over there half dead they must cut her up. So he caught her by the hair and flung her over the rock, crying, "Go forever!" and the children fell upon her with the flints and cut her into pieces. Then *Mus'p* sent them back toward the east to the homes from which the woman had stolen them. The two brothers now walked across the point to *Walumluim* [Fort Canby]. Entering the first house of the village, they beheld two old women, who said, "Oh, young men, whence do you come?" "We have come a long distance," answered *Mus'p*, "and have been telling the people how to live." They said: "We have a great chief here. We catch all kinds of fish and hunt all kinds of game." But in fact they ate only the chief's excreta, for he devoured all the food. When the tide came in, the people went down to the beach. *Skomoh'l* said to *Mus'p*, "Do nothing until we see what that man is going to do." Just then the chief came to a canoe, and took out a sturgeon, which he raised, about to swallow it, but it slipped past his mouth and fell on his shoulder. This mishap was caused by *Mus'p* watching him. Lightning began to flash from the chief's eyes, and Jaybird cried, "Now we shall all die!" *Mus'p* and his brother went out from the house of the two old women toward the place where the chief was, and as he turned about and saw them, the lightning began again. *Mus'p* went toward him and stamped on the beach, and the chief sank to his ankles. Again he stamped, and the chief sank farther. Five times *Mus'p* stamped, and the chief was in the sand over his knees. Then *Mus'p* said: "In no other place do the people eat the excreta of their chief. They get fish and game, and give him some of it. You will remain here, and you will be a rock." The chief's name was *Iekauhsitk*, and this is what that rock is now called. The two old women were turned into mice, and Jaybird became as he is now. The others remained people.

The brothers next came to *Hlakhahl*, where they saw a person walking on his hands and carrying a stick between his legs. "Stand up!" commanded *Mus'p*; and he showed the man how to make a bundle of sticks and carry it on his shoulder. They went on to *Tsinuk*, where *Mus'p* told the people to get their nets, and he showed them how to use the seine for salmon. He told them: "When you catch the salmon, do not eat them at once, but lay them in the house. Then at the next flood-tide cook and eat them. Call in the people and have a feast, and if any fish remain, throw them into the fire and burn them. Do not attempt to keep them. Do this five days, and after that you may eat them at any time, and keep what you do not eat." In the last house of this place *Mus'p* found an old woman cooking. He asked her what she was preparing,

147

and she said she was cooking *iekshthehlo*. "If you eat this you will die," she said. "I am hungry," he answered; "give me that!" She filled a large wooden bowl with the soup and he ate five spoonfuls. Feeling a pain in the stomach, *Mus'p* went outside, and the two brothers, followed by the dog, went up a hill [Scarborough hill]. This soup had been made of human bones, and *Mus'p* began to vomit; and each time a hill was formed, until there were five. He said to his brother, "We will turn into rocks and remain here forever." So they became stone: *Mus'p*, his brother, and the dog.

## *Kihlktagwah*, the *Itohiul*

Source: *The North American Indian,* Vol. 8, by Edward S. Curtis, 1930. Massachusetts: The Plimpton Press, pp. 150-153.

In the old times many men were killed because of trouble over women. There was an *itohiul* who could walk across the river on the water. He had strong *yuhlmah*, and, being greatly feared, he took many girls and made them his wives. He once crossed to the southern side of the river at the Cascades, where lived a widow with a daughter of about fourteen years, and, although he had a very large house with two fires, and so many women that they occupied all the space around the walls, this girl, whose name was *Nadaiat*, he took also, and carried her back with him. In due time she had a child.

Now it was the custom of *Kihlktagwah* to kill his male children, but to permit the others to live. When this child was born, he came to its mother and asked roughly, "What kind of baby have you?" She said, "A girl," although it was a boy, and thus she retained her son. She immediately wound a fringed sash of the hair of the mountain-goat around the baby, the usual dress for women and girls. *Kihlktagwah* now started out again on a trip in search of women, and the Cascade girl crossed the river in a canoe, and returned to her people. In a few years the child began to talk, and his grandmother informed him what kind of father he had, and that he would have been killed had his sex been known. Soon the boy began his trips into the mountains in his search for *yuhlmah*, and at about ten years of age he found something, the same power his father had, which was given by a kind of water-skipper.

He was just coming into manhood when one day he crossed the river, walking on the water, and went to his father's house a little distance below the Cascades. Arriving there about dark, he entered and saw a tall man sleeping beside a woman in the corner near the door. Daylight came, the woman awoke, and the boy said, "Do you know me?" "No," she answered. "My name is *Wakisu* [Hair Girdle]," he said, and he told her how he had received the name. "Now you are my wife," he informed her. He was planning to kill his father. *Kihilktagwah* always had his women carry soft sand from the river and smooth it around the house, so that nobody could pass in or out without leaving proof of his movement. "Watch what I am going to do," said the boy. The woman stood in the door and looked while he walked boldly about in the sand; then she went back inside, and the boy returned to his home.

When *Kihlktagwah* awoke and stepped outside, he saw his own track, apparently, but he was sure he had not previously been out. He examined it carefully, and put one foot into the first print, but it did not quite fill the track.

After sleeping all day the boy returned to the northern side of the river, walked over the smooth sand, and found his father sleeping beside the next woman. This one also he called to the door and told to watch while he walked across the sand. In the morning the *itohiul* again saw what seemed to be his own footprints, but again he found that his foot did not fill them. He cut a stick, measured the footprints, gave the stick to two slaves, and told them to search for a man with a foot of that size. They went looking far down the river and back on the northern side, but never found one whose foot approached that size. They were gone six days. The next morning they started eastward on the northern side, measuring the foot of every man; then they crossed to the south and came back to the Cascades. One of the slaves proposed that they go to the house of that wife of their master who had run away with her baby, and see how large her daughter had grown to be. They entered and saw *Wakisu* lying on the bed asleep, with one foot on top of the other, so that the two nearly reached the roof, and they thought that their master must have come over to visit his former wife. The woman gave them food, and while they ate, *Wakisu* awoke, and, seeing that one of the slaves had a stick, he said, " Bring that stick, and measure my foot." From toe to heel his foot was found to be exactly as long as the stick. The slaves spent the night there, and in the morning *Wakisu* told them to say to their master, his father, that he would come over to see him. They went back and reported how they had found the man with the long foot. *Kihlktagwah* made no comment, but soon he told them to cross again, and to summon all the people to that place, as there was going to be a great battle with *Wakisu.*

The people came hurrying up the river in great numbers, so that the stream was full of canoes. Some were in favor of *Wakisu,* and those he sent into the woods with orders to strike every branch, in order to see if they could not thus kill his father's *yuhlmah.* At nightfall the crowd came home unsuccessful. Behind them walked two boys, one of whom stopped, while the other waited for him on the opposite side of an elderberry bush. The one who was resting began to shake, seized his hatchet, struck the bush, and cried: "*Yuhlmah* for which everybody is looking, this is it!" Immediately there was a roll of thunder above, and hail fell, as *Wakisu* had predicted would be the case when the *yuhlmali* was found. At the same time *Wakisu* knew that the *yuhlmah* had been discovered. People were sent to ascertain who had found it, and they came upon two young men prone on the ground, one on each side of an elderberry bush. *Wakisu* made medicine, and they recovered. Then a stalk about three feet long was cut from the bush, and formed into the shape of a baby, with features, and, painted red, it was brought to *Wakisu,* who said, "No, I do not want this red paint; wash it off." So the red paint was washed off, and it was painted just a little around the mouth and on its fingers and feet. Now *Wakisu* was ready to fight.

He wrapped the effigy in a piece of cattail matting and began to sing his songs. A dog was brought in and slit open, and a man scooped up a handful of blood and drank it, five times in all. Each man did this, and many dogs were killed. It was now nearly daylight, and *Kihlktagwah* was about to start across to make war on his son. *Wakisu* led to the river five girls, each about seven years of age, and made them stand on the edge of the bluff, while he himself went down to the water's edge. His father was already on his way, walking across, and his followers came on behind in canoes. *Wakisu* beheld his father coming, and when the latter was close he gave a signal to the girls and began to sing, while the girls threw the image of the baby, wrapped in matting, down the bluff. It rattled and tumbled down, and at once there was a sound of thunder, and hail fell, and a great storm rising destroyed the boats and the people. The *itohiul* turned back and made hastily for his own shore,

while *Wakisu* stood looking at his father; but still the storm raged. He went to his house and dispatched a slave to bring the image from the river bank, where it had been thrown, and he wrapped it up and stood it beside the fire. When this was done, he sang and placed his hands on the top of the stick, which sank down into the ground. The two young boys who had made the stick opened their hearts and sang. The next morning *Wakisu* crossed the river, intending to kill his father, but he found that *Kihlktagwah* had run away, although the women were still there. He released all except the two whom he had spoken to, and these he took for his own wives. *Wakisu* was recognized as a chief from Hood River down to Washougal, on both sides of the river, but he was not *itohiul*, only a great man.

## The Thunder's Son-in-Law

Source: *North American Indians Myths and Legends,* by Lewis Spence, 1914. New York: George G. Harrap and Co., pp. 332-335.

There were five brothers who lived together. Four of them were accustomed to spend their days in hunting elk, while the fifth, who was the youngest, was always compelled to remain at the camp. They lived amicably enough, save that the youngest grumbled at never being able to go to the hunting. One day as the youth sat brooding over his grievance the silence was suddenly broken by a hideous din, which appeared to come from the region of the doorway. He was at a loss to understand the cause of it, and anxiously wished for the return of his brothers. Suddenly there appeared before him a man of gigantic size, strangely appareled. He demanded food, and the frightened boy, remembering that they were well provided, hastily arose to satisfy the stranger's desires. He brought out an ample supply of meat and tallow, but was astonished to find that the strange being lustily called for more. The youth, thoroughly terrified, hastened to gratify the monster's craving, and the giant ate steadily on, hour after hour, until the brothers returned at the end of the day to discover the glutton devouring the fruits of their hunting. The monster appeared not to heed the brothers, but, anxious to satisfy his enormous appetite, he still ate. A fresh supply of meat had been secured, and this the brothers placed before him. He continued to gorge himself throughout the night and well into the next day. At last the meat was at an end, and the brothers became alarmed. What next would the insatiable creature demand? They approached him and told him that only skins remained, but he replied: "What shall I eat, grandchildren, now that there are only skins and you?"

They did not appear to understand him until they had questioned him several times. On realizing that the glutton meant to devour them, they determined to escape, so, boiling the skins, which they set before him, they fled through a hole in the hut. Outside they placed a dog, and told him to send the giant in the direction opposite to that which they had taken. Night fell, and the monster slept, while the dog kept a weary vigil over the exit by which his masters had escaped. Day dawned as the giant crept through the gap. He asked the dog: "Which way went your masters?" The animal replied by setting his head in the direction opposite to the true one. The giant observed the sign, and went on the road the dog indicated. After proceeding for some distance he found that the young men could not have gone that way, so he returned to the hut, to find the dog still there. Again he questioned the animal, who merely repeated his previous movement. The monster once more set out, but unable to discover the fugitives, he again returned. Three times he repeated these fruitless journeys. At last he succeeded in getting on to the right path, and shortly came within sight of the brothers.

Immediately they saw their pursuer they endeavored to outrun him, but without avail. The giant gained ground, and soon overtook the eldest, whom he slew. He then made for the others, and slew three more. The youngest only was left. The lad hurried on until he came to a river, on the bank of which was a man fishing, whose name was the Thunderer. This person he implored to convey him to the opposite side. After much hesitation the Thunderer agreed, and, rowing him over the stream, he commanded the fugitive to go to his hut, and returned to his nets. By this time the monster had gained the river, and on seeing the fisherman he asked to be ferried over also. The Thunderer at first refused, but was eventually persuaded by the offer of a piece of twine. Afraid that the boat might capsize, the Thunderer stretched himself across the river, and commanded the giant to walk over his body.

The monster, unaware of treachery, readily responded, but no sooner had he reached the Thunderer's legs than the latter set them apart, thus precipitating him into the water. His hat also fell in after him. The Thunderer now gained his feet, and watched the giant drifting helplessly down the stream. He did not wish to save the monster, for he believed him to be an evil spirit. *Okulam* [Noise of Surge] will be your name," he said. "Only when the storm is raging will you be heard. When the weather is very bad your hat will also be heard." As he concluded this prophecy the giant disappeared from sight. The Thunderer then gathered his nets together and went to his hut. The youth whom he had saved married his daughter, and continued to remain with him. One day the youth desired to watch his father-in-law fishing for whales. His wife warned him against doing so. He paid no heed to her warning, however, but went to the sea, where he saw the Thunderer struggling with a whale. His father-in-law flew into a great rage, and a furious storm arose. The Thunderer looked toward the land, and immediately the storm increased in fury, with thunder and lightning, so he threw down his dip-net and departed for home, followed by his son-in-law.

# The Clackamas

Closely related to the Chinook Tribe, the Clackamas lived in the northern part of Oregon and share the traditional word of "*Skookum*" or mountain devil with them. Their language is part of the Penutian family.

### Unseen Bigfoots

Source: *Attitudes Toward Bigfoot in Many North American Cultures,* by Gayle Highpine, 1992. In: *The Track Record* #18.

The Clackamas Indians maintain that in the lands of the headwaters of the Clackamas river, adolescent Bigfeet beings have to pass a test to become an adult members of the Bigfoot tribe. They must jump in front of a human on a trail, and wave their hands in front of the human's face, without being seen.

### The *Skookum's* Tongue

Source: Unknown.

After *Tallapus* [Coyote] fashioned a wondrous device to harvest salmon at the Willamette Falls, he made a foolish mistake and the fish-trap refused to work for all time. Only by their own labor could the Indians catch fish at the falls. "However, in the course of time, the Indians became very prosperous and a large village was built on the west side of the [Willamette] River.

But while they were thus prospering, a gigantic *skookum* that lived upon the Tualatin River began to commit fearful depredations. His abode was on a little flat about two miles from the Indian village but, so long was his tongue, that he was in the habit of reaching it forth and catching people as he chose. By this, of course, the village was almost depopulated and when, after a time, *Tallapus* returned, he was very angry to see that the benefits of his fishery had gone, not to the people, but to the wicked *skookum*.

*Tallapus* therefore went forth to the monster and cried out to it, "O, wicked *skookum*, long enough have you been eating these people." And with one blow of his tomahawk cut off the offending tongue and buried it under the rocks upon the west side of the falls; after which the people flourished.

When, a long time later, a canal was dug to go around the falls and connect the Tualatin River to Waluga [that is, Sucker or Oswego] Lake, "this was nothing more than laying bare the channel made for the tongue of the *skookum*."

# The Kwakiutl

The Kwakiutl were made up of several tribes that occupied the Northwest Coast and whose traditional languages were in the Wakashan language group. The tribes are better known today as the Kwakwaka'wakw and primarily occupy north Vancouver Island and British Columbia. The Kwakwaka'wakw has five different names for bigfoot, which depends on gender. These include *Be'a'-nu'mbe* ("Brother of the Woods"), *Bukwas* ("Wildman of the Woods"), *Dzunukwa* (*Dsonoqua*) ("Wild Woman of the Woods"), *Tsonaqua* ("Wild Woman of the Woods"), and *Tsunukwa* ("Female giant covered with hair with bigfeet"). It should be noted that Bukwas is the son of Dzunukwa and a human male, as told in the first story.

## *Dzunukwa*

Source: Unknown.

*Dzunukwa* [or *Dzoonokwa, Dzonoqua,* or *Tsonoqua*] is fearsome giantess of the dark forest that is not-quite-human female. She is also known as Wild Woman of the Woods or Property Woman. She has black hair, pendulous breasts, heavy eyebrows, deep-set eye sockets with half-closed eyes and has pursed lips…she cries "*Ooh-ooh, ooh-ooh.*" She is stupid, clumsy and sleepy. She captures children who are crying and who venture into the forest, carrying them away in a basket on her back to devour them. Her house is filled with wonderful treasures such as boxes of food, coppers, canoes, and more. Through special encounters with her, a person can acquire some of the wealth and supernatural powers.

One day she stole some dried fish from a Kwakiutl man. The man pursued her and caught her. They became lovers and produced a son, *Bukwas*. One day a young man found her baby in its cradle in the forest. He teased the baby by pinching it, causing it to cry loudly. *Dzunukwa* heard the cry and called out, "Whoever you are that may be teasing my baby, let him alone and I will give you a spear."

Pleased at such good fortune, the young man pinched the baby three more times and was offered the Water of Life, a magic wand, and a supernatural canoe if he would leave the baby alone. Satisfied, the man stopped teasing the child, returned home with his gifts and, because of his encounter with *Dzunukwa*, became rich and powerful.

### *Dzunukwa* and *Bukwas*

Source: *Bella Bella Tales* by Franz Boas, 1932. New York: The American Folklore Society.

When *Dzunukwa* steals a female child, she keeps it as her daughter and picks salmon berries for her. She also likes to steal salmon from the village. She throws aside the roof boards and reaches down to take the fish from the drying frames. Her son *Bukwas* is in the habit of striking trees with a piece of wood. His body is hairy and he is shy.

### Thunderbird and *Tsonoqua*

Source: Unknown.

Chief Splashing-Waters was having difficulties with the Wild Woman of the Woods. Thunderbird, *Kwun-kwane-kulegui*, came to his rescue and turned the savage *Tsonoqua* into stone. In remembrance of this help, the Chief decreed that Thunderbird would be respected as the Protector of Man and as the Spirit that made wishes come true. *Tsonoqua* was placed under him, to be ruled by him, and why he is often shown in totem poles with him sitting on the savage's head. Songs, dances, and masks were made to honor *Kwun-kwane-kulegui*. *Tsonoqua* would now forever be represented with pouting lips, symbolizing that she blows the wind in the forest.

### The Transformer, and Origin of the *Koskimo*

Source: *The North American Indian, Vol. 10,* by Edward S. Curtis, 1930. Massachusetts: The Plimpton Press, p. 248.

Now the brothers were alone. One day they went up the river and built a basket-trap. On their return journey *Kanikila* rolled up one corner of his blanket and rubbed it in the water. Soon a fish leaped into the canoe; the water was full of sockeye salmon, brought forth from this blanket of the *Oulachon* Woman.

Their trap caught many salmon, which they cut up, roasted, and hung above the fire to smoke. One day they found that something had stolen all the drying fish. This occurred many times, and then instead of going to their trap they concealed themselves in the house. Soon entered a very large woman with huge, hanging breasts, and as she reached up for the fish, *Kanikila* drew his bow and shot her in the breast. She ran out, and *Kanikila* said to his brother: "Take care of yourself! I am going to follow her. I must not lose my valuable arrow."

*Kanikila* followed the great tracks of the *tsunukwa* to a lake, where he sat down beside a spring and watched a house which stood near the forest. Soon appeared a weeping girl.

He asked, "Why do you weep?"

"My grandmother is ill. She was hurt while fishing for salmon."

"Let me go in and I will cure her," he said.

The girl went into the house and said to the *tsunukwa*, "There is a man beside the spring who says he can heal you."

"Great is your word!" exclaimed the *tsunukwa*. "Call him in to heal me."

When *Kanikila* entered he saw his arrow in the breast of the *tsunukwa*, who did not know what was hurting her. He sat beside her and pretended to suck her skin like a healer, but he really took the arrow between his teeth and drew it out. "He...!" said the *tsunukwa*. "It is as if you had pulled the sickness out of me!" Soon she was quite well, and she said: "Now, you see this house. The carving of it came from my body. You shall have it. You shall dance with the clothing I wear." She meant with her skin, for she wore no clothing. "You shall have the life-giving water. No matter how long your parents or your friends have been dead, this will bring them to life."

## The Adventures of *Gyamalagilaq*

Source: *The North American Indian,* Vol. 10, by Edward S. Curtis, 1930. Massachusetts: The Plimpton Press, p. 262-263.

In a cave at the top of a steep slope leading from the sea, and at the foot of a perpendicular wall of rock, lived *Gyamalagilaq* [born to be leader]. The place was *Awis* [in Belize inlet near the left entrance to Alison sound]. His daughter was *Kaiyfiuhlaka* [rich in property woman], and his sons were *Kiki-akalagilaq* [born to be frightener of all] and *Patlilagilaq* [born to be flier].

The canoe of *Gyamalagilaq* was called *Tahltahl* [to fold up]; for he could fold it up and thus turn it into a small canoe, and then unfold it and make a large one. Instead of keeping it in the water, he would drag it up the hill and into the cave. He had two paddles: a large one, which, dipped into the water twice in a day, caused the canoe to go flying over the sea; and an ordinary paddle used when the canoe was small. The large one was called *Hailpa* [go and return in one day], for no matter where he wished to go, he could go and return in the same day. Like the canoe it was *nawalaq*. Around the neck of *Gyamalagilaq* was the necklace *Yayinkyayuhaa* [necklace that strikes in return], from which hung a knife. When he became angry, he would shake the necklace, and it would give forth a hollow, metallic rattle.

In front of the cave was a fine beach, and the children, unable to swim, would play in the shallow water. One day their mother came to the entrance of the cave and called: "Do not play, my children. Your father is in the cave working on his canoe, and there must be no play nor noise while he is at it. Come up!" Just then the little girl was snatched into the water by some unseen thing. The woman cried: "*Kakyu* [slave], something is taking our child! Quick, jump down!" Again the woman shouted: "Slave, you say you are afraid of nothing! You say you are *nawalaq*! Get ready quickly and we will go to find her!"

Then *Gyamalagilaq* pushed *Tahltahl* down the hill and put on *Yaylnkyayuhdaa*. He shoved the canoe into the water and commanded: "Open! You will go fast today!" The canoe opened, and they embarked. He dipped *Hailpa* into the water, and the canoe flew out into the narrows and stopped at the foot of a cliff rising from the water.

*Gyamalagilaq* dived to the bottom, and there on the mud lay *Hwulqis* [mud-shark], a *yakyim* [evil thing]. With his knife he slashed it in twain across the belly, but his child was not there, and bringing the head of *Hwuilqis* to the surface, he reembarked. Another stroke of *Hailpa* brought the canoe to the tide-rips at the entrance of the inlet, and *Gyamalagilaq* dived to the bottom. There where the water was quiet he found *Nanis* [grizzly-bear of the sea]. He

lay down on the back of *Nanis*, grasped the hair of its head, drew the head back, and severed it. Then he cut into the belly, but the child was not there, and with the head he returned to the surface.

He went next to the very entrance of the inlet, where the water was very bad, and dived down to *Tsunukwis*, whose head he brought up after looking in vain into its belly. Another stroke brought them to *Tseqafti* [sea-gull home] a great precipice overhanging the water on the mainland at the entrance of Tribune channel, opposite Gilford Island]. Here he dived and found *Nuimhyalikyu* [one chief one], which was like an enormous halibut. Its back looked like a beach where the wavelets have left the sand in ripples. As he walked along its great back, he could see the edges moving slowly up and down. Coming to its head, which was sluggishly rising and falling, he drew it up and looked beneath it, but his daughter was not there. Then he cut it off and brought it to the canoe.

Now *Gyamalagilaq* turned back past his home to the head of the inlet, where there was an overhanging rock. He dived, and there found *Pgwis* [man of the sea], who had a huge, man-like body and very long hair. He was squatted on the bottom with his hands on his wife's shoulders and his head bent over touching hers, and she was in the same position with her hands on his shoulders. Beneath their arms and heads crouched the little girl. *Gyamalagilaq* approached and shook his necklace. Their power left them, and he seized them by the hair, one with each hand, and drew their heads apart. He slashed at their necks, and the heads fell off; for the mere motion of this knife would cause a head to fall. With the heads and his daughter he rose to the surface and returned home. Because of these deeds *Gyamalagilaq* changed his name to *Kikyilakifiu*, and his daughter's name to *Kikyilakifiimka* [striker under the water woman].

### Origin of the *Tsunukwa* Images

Source: *The North American Indian,* Vol. 10, by Edward S. Curtis, 1930. Massachusetts: The Plimpton Press, p. 293-294.

*Hlahwunala* [criticized disparagingly], a lazy youth of the *Gyigyilkuim* gens [clan], lived with his parents at *Oqiowas* on *Hanwati*. Salmon becoming scarce, the family followed them up the river to *Kawakyas* [true pool]. Now it began to be noticed that some of the drying fish on the scaffold over the fire were missing, and one day the boy's mother struck him with a stick and chided him: "You lazy boy! Why do you not go and *kekuila* [wash ceremonially in order to acquire supernatural power], so that you may find out what has been doing mischief to our salmon?"

The boy took the reproof hard and was so grieved at being struck by his mother that early in the morning he went to wash himself in the stream, and he continued to do so each day. One morning he remembered a small stream flowing into the river below them, and he went down to it. When he came to a place where the brook tumbled down a hillside, he saw a man standing in the water rubbing himself with hemlock twigs. This was *Hliluqekelis* [strong side of the stream], who stands at the edge of the river, bracing himself against the current and the tide, and holds the river in its place. The boy went toward the bather, and reached for one of two used bunches of twigs, the one

lying farther downstream. But the man exclaimed, "No, no, take the upstream one!" So the youth took it, and the man said, "Scrape your body with it four times."

*Hlihwuinala* sat in the water and rubbed his body, and the man said, "Go and pull down that yew sapling and twist it into a rope." The youth began to twist it, but soon his strength failed. Then the man made him go into the water and rub his body four times with another bunch of twigs; and though *Hlahwuinala* this time succeeded in twisting the sapling down to the middle, he was sent back to wash a third time. This gave him strength to twist the tree nearly to the bottom, and after the fourth washing he was able to twist it down to the very roots.

"Go now to the mouth of this stream," said the man, "and there you will find four large rocks. Throw them into the river. Then take four round stones just large enough to fit your hand, and you will be ready for what you wish to do. These stones you shall use on him." All this the youth did, and with the four round stones he walked up the river, went into the house, and lay down in his bed. At evening he sat in the back door and saw a broad trail which he had never before noticed. He followed it for a while, carrying his four stones, and just before darkness fell, as he sat beside the path a *tsunukwa* came walking along. He threw one of the stones, and it struck her in the forehead and passed through the head. She fell lifeless, but still *Hlahwuinala* sat there. Soon another came, and this one he killed in like manner. He waited all night, but no more came, and just before dawn he went home and lay down in his bed, waiting for the day. Then he called his father and led him back into the woods to the dead creatures, and explained, "There are the things that have been stealing our food."

Farther they went to the house of the *tsunukwa*, where they found a little *tsunukwa* sleeping and another sitting in the corner. There were quantities of stolen salmon, with much flesh of mountain-goats and bears, dried berries, and skins of goats, bears, and lynxes. These things, together with the children of the *tsunukwa*, they carried out to their house, and transported in a canoe down the river and around to the village *E'awigyilis*. There *Hiahwuinala* built a great house and invited the different tribes to a dance. He took the dancing name of *Tsunukwa*.

Four days the people were assembling, and he fed them with the food taken from the house of the *tsunukwa*. On the fifth day they danced. The two young *tsunukwa* were kept concealed in the house, and when in the dance *Hlihwuinala* exhibited them, everybody became as if intoxicated. While they were helpless, the young man murdered many of them, and among the others he distributed the skins before they departed. Having killed the *tsunukwa* and captured their children, *Hlahwuinala* celebrated his deed by placing four carved images of *tsunukwa* before his house.

### The Children Who Killed a *Tsunukwa*

Source: *The North American Indian,* Vol. 10, by Edward S. Curtis, 1930. Massachusetts: The Plimpton Press, p. 295-296.

Twelve children were playing on the beach and eating mussels, and *Tsumkyihsta*, a harelipped girl whom all the others despised and hated, came to join them. They exclaimed: "Do not come with us! We do not want you!"

Then she began to sing: "*Tsaistntoquhl, fsaisintoquhl, fsehfsekyalakyil-slah antlotanalasaskyatus* [oh, I see something, I see something showing its head behind that rock lying on the ground]!"

"Ye...!" cried the children. "You try only to frighten us so that you may come with us. We do not want you!"

"*Alamiuntoquhl, alamuntoquhl; awulihaantequulfie Itekyalakylslah ant-lotanalasaskyatus* [true is what I saw, true is what I saw; mischief-making I saw, showing its head behind that rock lying on the ground]!"

"Ye...!" they shouted in derision. "You wish only to join us. We do not want you!"

But while they sat eating their mussels came Awuli [a child's name for the ogress-like *tsunukwa*] with a great basket on her back and muttering in a low voice, "*U...! U...!*" Perceiving that she would be the first one taken, *Tsumky-ihsta* stooped and picked up a mussel-shell. Then the *tsunukwa* seized her and dropped her into the basket, and took the others one by one. Without delay the hare lipped girl began with her mussel-shell to cut a hole in the basket, and soon she dropped to the ground. Five others of the smallest followed her. Hearing something fall, *Awuli* muttered to herself: "Hemlock leaves are falling, hemlock leaves are falling, hemlock leaves are falling."

She carried her captives into her house, kindled a fire, and built a crib of huge logs for heating stones. While she was outside getting a mat with which to cover the children in steaming them, they heard a voice calling to them, and now they saw a very pretty woman in one corner of the room. She was *Tlopakyastulihl* [roots from the buttocks in all directions], for she was rooted to the ground. "When those stones are red-hot," she said, "then you will sit down and begin to sing this song." And she gave them a song which mentioned the name of *Awuli*. "This will make her sleepy, and you can push her into the fire." Just then the *tsunukwa* returned, and the children gathered in one place and began to sing. She seemed to like the song, for she danced round the fire. Then she sat down, her head drooped, and she slept. Softly the children crept to her, and pushed her into the fire! Then quickly they threw the pail of water on the stones and covered them with the mat, and the woman in the corner said: "Go to yonder corner and hide behind the boxes, and when the children of *Awuli* come home, I will tell them to remove the mat and eat what their mother has cooked for them."

So the children concealed themselves, and soon the four children of the *tsunukwa* came home and saw the steaming mat. The woman said, "Your mother told me to tell you to uncover what she has cooked for you, and eat it." As they ate, one of the boys behind the boxes called: 'U...! You are eating what was your mother!" Another one added: "U...! You are eating the nipple of your mother's breast!" One after another they repeated such things, and the four children of *Awuli* left the house and disappeared. The boys then dug out the roots that held *Tlopakyastilihl* to the ground and took her to their home.

## The First *Tsunukwa* Dance

Source: *The North American Indian,* Vol. 10, by Edward S. Curtis, 1930. Massachusetts: The Plimpton Press, p. 296-297.

A hunter and his wife one evening went down *Hanwati* to fish, and landed at the mouth of the stream, where they had a small hut. The next morning the man caught some salmon, and his wife cleaned them and laid them on a scaffold under the smoke-hole. Late in the night she heard something on the roof. Her husband was snoring. She watched the smoke-hole, and seeing a dim shape moving on the roof, she nudged her husband and whispered, "There is a man over the smoke-hole!" He looked up and caught sight of a person moving the boards aside to get at the drying salmon. The hunter's bow lay at his side. He cautiously strung it, put an arrow on the string, and shot with the full strength of the bow. The person fell back and rolled down the roof; there was a crash in the brush, and the noise of something creeping away.

Early in the morning the hunter went to see what he had shot, and after following the trail a short distance he found the body of a strange creature with great, hanging breasts and a round, protruding mouth. It was a male *tsunukwa*. He covered the body and returned to the hut, and said, "I killed that thing. It was a *tsunukwa*. We will go home." They paddled up the river to the village, from which they could see their camping place.

On the morning after their return a party of men going down the river saw on the top of a rock in the stream a huge female *tsunukwa*, crying. They at once turned and hurried homeward to report what they had seen, and the hunter whispered to his wife, "This *tsunukwa* is crying for the one I killed!" Some reckless young men said they would go to see it, but they were warned: "Do not do it! Its eyes are enormous, and there seems to be fire inside them. Its head is as big as a storage box."

"Oh," said the young men, "we will go. We are not afraid of it." So they brought their canoe close to the rock and asked the *tsunukwa* why she was crying. She said, "I have lost my son!" Then they hurried back to the village, for they thought she had come to kill some one out of sorrow for her son.

An ugly young man, a very quiet youth who seldom spoke, got up without a word. In some way he knew that the hunter had killed the *tsunukwa*, and where the body was lying. He took his paddle and poles, and in a small canoe paddled downstream. He let his canoe drift quite close to the rock before he spoke: "What are you crying about, good one?"

"I have lost my son, and whoever will show me which way he has gone, I will make him a rich man."

He had now backed the canoe right up to the rock, and she took hold of it. "Whoever will show me where my son is, I will take that man to my house," she said.

"Go ashore," answered the young man. She made one step to the shore, and he landed and conducted her to the house of the hunter. He entered and looked at the smoke-hole, then came out and followed the trail to the body. The *tsunukwa* took it up and said, "Come, we will go to my house." She no longer wept. Before long she led him into a great house. "Now," said she, "all these things are yours." She pointed to dressed skins and dried mountain-goat flesh, and a mask which was just like her face. "With this," she said, "you will be *tsunukwa* dancer. Come, see what I will do with my son."

In the corner of the room was a circular hole containing water, some of which she now sprinkled on her son, and he became alive. This was the living water, and she told the young man he should have it. She threw some of it on him, and he became very handsome.

Then he said: "My father and my mother have long been dead. That is why I am unhappy."

"You can bring them to life if you know where they are," she answered. "I am going to leave this house. I will go now to a safe place where no one can harm my son." So the two *tsunukwa* departed. The young man loaded his canoe with skins and meat, and then went home to get his people to help him with larger canoes.

Then he gave the first winter dance. While they were singing to bring back the disappeared ones, chief of whom was his cousin, he himself brought in the bodies of his father and mother, sprinkled on them the living water, and saw them sit upright, rub their eyes, and say, "We have slept long!" The next day the disappeared ones were brought in and the *tsunukwa* dance was performed. The skins and the meat found in the house of the *tsunukwa* were sufficient for the feasting and the presents.

Now the hunter disputed with the young man: "I killed the *tsunukwa*, and this dance should be mine. I got it by blood, but you did not."

But the young man retorted: "*Tsunukwa* gave me this dance. She did not say, 'Take this dance and give it to the one who killed my son.' She gave it to me." And to this day jealousy and enmity exist between the descendants of those two men.

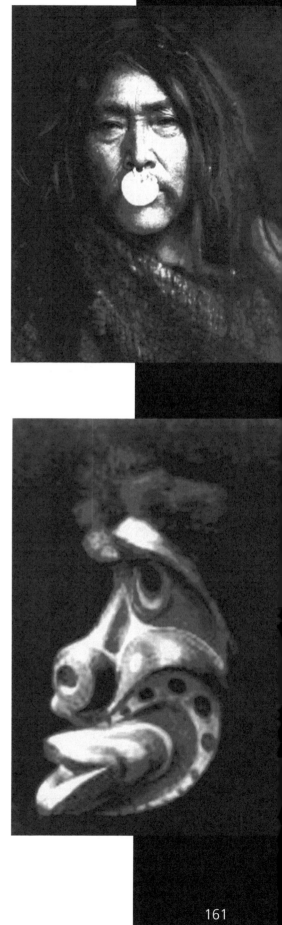

## Big Figure

Source: *Kwakiutl Legends,* by James Wallas and Pamela Whitaker, 1989. Blaine: Hancock, pp. 154-157.

There were no schools in the days of which I speak, but there was a spot near the forest, a playground, where children used to play. One little boy that played there had a knife–what kind I don't know; it happened a long, long time ago.

The other children wanted to borrow that knife but the boy told them, "My mother and father won't allow me to lend it. My mother said you might cut yourself with it, then blame me. My father said you might lose it and never return it. That is what my parents told me."

Well, you know what kids are like. The children decided they would not play with the little boy with the knife. "Let him go by himself," they said to one another. They taunted the boy and teased him. Their backs were to the forest.

Suddenly the boy with the knife cried, "Hey I see a big figure in the trees!"

The children did not turn around and look but kept their backs to the forest. "You're just saying that because we won't play with you," they shouted.

"No, I'm not," argued the boy. "There it is again! A big figure. It's watching us."

But the children would not listen. "You're just trying to fool us but it won't work," they chided. "We're not going to have anything to do with you."

"It's coming!" screamed the boy. "It's coming!"

The children saw it then. It was a big, big man, bigger than any other. He had hair all over his body and his eyes were set deep in his face. He carried a large basket on his back. The children's strength drained out of them in fear. They were helpless.

The woods giant grabbed the boy that had the knife first and threw him in his basket. Then he threw all the rest of the children on top of him. He set off through the forest while the children peeked through the cracks of the basket, trying to se where he was taking them.

The boy with the knife was right at the bottom of the basket and could hardly move with all the children on top of him. Finally he was able to cut a slit in the basket big enough to squeeze through and he dropped to the ground. The man did not notice, and the boy ran back to his village crying, "Big Figure has taken all the children!"

The men of the village gathered together. They asked the boy to lead the way that Big Figure had gone. They traveled over roots and under logs. At the place the boy had fallen through the basket the trail became harder to follow. They could see where something big had gone through the bush and followed that till eventually the trail ended at a large cave.

The men of the village could dimly see some of their children hanging by the feet in the dark cave. A huge figure of a man was tying up the other children's feet and putting pitch in their eyes. Hs wife and children were helping him.

"What are you doing with our children?" the villagers cried.

"We're going to smoke them," answered the giant.

"Those are our children! We want to take them home with us," said the villagers.

"We're going to smoke them and eat them," replied the big man. He and his wife finished tying the children's feet and started hanging them up, one by one, with the other children.

"Don't do that," the fathers of the children pleaded. "Let us take them home with us."

The big man started building a fire under the children. Then he said to the men, "Why are your faces so nice and smooth and not rough like mine? You have nice eyes. They don't sink way in your head like mine do."

The villagers thought fast. One of them said, "You can have a face just like ours. We can fix you up. Go outside and get a big flat rock and another small rock with a sharp end."

So the big man did what they asked. It was easy for him to carry the big

flat rock because he was so strong. Then the men of the village said to the giant, "Lie down and use this flat rock for a pillow. We're going to fix you up just like us."

"How long will it take?" he asked as he lay down and put his head on the flat stone.

"Just four days," they answered. "Close your eyes. Close your eyes tight." Then they took the rock with the sharp end and sunk it between the big man's eyes. He was dead.

"How long is he going to lie there?" asked the giant's wife.

"Oh, about four days," answered the men. They took their children, untied their legs and removed the pitch from their eyes. Then they went home to their village where the people were very happy.

## Big Figure and the Smoked Salmon

Source: *Kwakiutl Legends,* by James Wallas and Pamela Whitaker, 1989. Blaine: Hancock, pp. 158-161.

A family was camped by a river so that they could put up salmon for the winter. The salmon they had caught were hanging in a split cedar smokehouse.

One day before he went to bed with his family in the shelter they had made, the eldest boy went into the smokehouse and noticed some gaps between the fish that were hanging there. "Some of our smoked salmon seems to be missing," he told his father.

"We're the only ones here," his father replied. "Our family is camped all alone. Just forget about it–we'll get some more."

The next morning when the boy built the fire in the smokehouse, he noticed even more of the smoked salmon was missing. "Tonight I am going to hide in the smokehouse and find out who it is that is taking the salmon," he announced. "I will have my bow and arrow with me, but if it is a man that comes I will not use it."

That night they did not bank the fire very high and it soon went out. The boy hid in the corner of the dark smokehouse and waited. Except for the rush of the wind in the cedar trees and the voice of the river, the camp was quiet.

It was not long before the boy heard a new sound–footsteps. Heavy footsteps were approaching the camp. They came closer and closer and stopped just outside the smokehouse. The boy was frightened but he had his bow and arrow ready.

Slowly the roof of the smokehouse lifted up. The boy pulled his bowstring taut. He dimly saw a huge hairy arm reach in toward the salmon and sent his arrow where the arm was coming from.

There was a terrible cry that woke up the others. "I think I got it! I think it's the woods giant!" shouted the boy to his parents. "Let's go after him."

"We will wait 'till morning," said his father. "He will be a lot easier to trail in the daylight and if you wounded him he might be dead by then."

The family rose early the next morning. The boy, his father and younger brother headed out on the trail of the giant. The trail they found had a few drops of blood on it. It led deep into the forest and ended at a cedar bark house. A pool of fresh water was nearby with a tree leaning over it.

"You wait here," the father said to his elder son, "and your brother and I will skirt around the back of the house."

While he was waiting, the elder boy climbed up the tree, as it was a good place to see from. Soon a large hairy girl came out of the cedar bark house with a bucket in her hand and walked over to the pool of water that the tree leaned over.

When she stooped to scoop up some drinking water, she saw the boy's reflection in the pool. "My, I didn't know how pretty I was," she exclaimed. "I'm different from the rest of my family. Their eyes all sink in their heads and mine don't. They are hairy and I have smooth skin."

The boy above her moved in the tree, and a branch broke and fell into the water. The girl jerked her head up and saw him. "Oh, it is you that I see in the water," she cried. Then she paused and added, "My father has been terribly sick since he came home last night. Can you come and help him?"

"I'll get my father," the boy answered. "This must be where the person lives who was stealing fish from us," he said when he reached his father and brother. "I think he is very sick from my arrow. His daughter wants us to help him."

"Okay," said the father, "let us go in."

They went in the cedar bark house and a big hairy man more than six feet tall lay almost dead with an arrow deep in his chest. His wife and children were standing around him.

The boy who shot the arrow walked up to the big man and tried to pull the arrow out. It would not come out straight, and he had to twist it this way and that way. Finally it pulled free.

"I feel better already," said the giant weakly. "You have helped me, so I will give my daughter to one of you to marry."

"No!" cried the elder boy. "I do not wish to marry your daughter."

"I do not wish to marry your daughter either," exclaimed the younger son.

"Have you another offer, then?" asked the father of the two boys.

"Yes, my offer is this. You may use us on your totem pole and face mask. No one else can make our likeness, only you. You can make the mask just like our face."

The father and his sons accepted the giant's offer and went home. They took their arrow with them. No one else had a mask like theirs. It was a frightening mask with the eyes sunk deep in the head.

### Big Figure's Wife

Source: *Kwakiutl Legends,* by James Wallas and Pamela Whitaker, 1989. Blaine: Hancock, pp. 162-164.

One day, Hunter was deep in the wilderness hunting for deer or elk when he heard a noise that sounded like someone working with an axe.

"That sounds like a canoe maker," he thought, "But who would be working this far back in the woods?" He knew that it was no one from his village. Hunter moved noiselessly toward the sound of the worker, and it led him to a clearing where a big figure was hollowing out a large cedar tree with an axe. Her back was to him, but he could see that it was a huge figure of a woman. Her baby was seated behind her in the hollowed-out tree.

Hunter did not wish to startle the giantess, so he crept up to the back of the canoe and pinched the baby's little toe. The infant cried out. Without turn-

ing around the mother said, "That could be Hunter, who pinches you–the one who hunts on water and on land."

The hunter pinched the baby's toe again and it started to cry. "It's just that hunter teasing you, don't cry," said the giantess again without turning.

Finally the hunter came around to the front of the woods giant's woman. "Yes, it is I," he said. "What are you making that canoe for?"

"We live beside a long lake," said the giantess. "'We will use it there. Why have you come to me?" she asked him.

"I followed the sound of your axe," he replied, "and now I have found you I want something from you."

"What is it that you want?"

"I am a provider of food for my people and I have not had much luck lately in hunting. Can you help me?"

"I will help you," responded the lady. "I will use my power to bring elk, deer and bear to you. When you are hunting in the water, seal will come to you."

The hunter was pleased at the big woman's generosity, yet he asked her for one more favor. "I want to use your features in a dance mask," he said.

"If you use me, you must use all of me and my four children too," she replied. "This baby is the youngest of the four. You may use us all in a dance."

After that the hunter became a very successful provider of food, and a dance was created showing the huge woman with her four babies being born one by one.

## Big Figure and the Limpets

Source: *Kwakiutl Legends*, by James Wallas and Pamela Whitaker, 1989. Blaine: Hancock, pp. 165-166.

There were four or five children laughing and having fun on a beach. Their parents had taken a canoe and gone to a good place for digging clams.

The children were playing on the sand near a pit in which they had built a fire. They put rocks in the fire and, when the rocks were red hot, they baked limpets on them and ate them. The little limpet shells fitted perfectly on the children's fingers, and they were having fun playing with them.

At first they did not notice a big figure creep slowly out of the woods and advance on one of the children. It looked like a big, big man with sunken eyes and covered with hair.

Finally one child spotted him but made no outward indication that he had noticed. He whispered to the others, "It's Big Figure. Don't scream, don't run away. Pretend you are not afraid." All the children put limpet shells on their fingertips and circled around to the other side of the huge figure so they were between him and the forest.

The giant turned toward them, his back to the fire. The children were trembling but the eldest bravely said, "We are ones that can scare people too." They opened and closed their fingers as if they were blinking. Slowly they advanced on the giant, continuing to blink their fingers with the limpet shells on the tips.

Big Figure started backing up as the children advanced. He took several steps and suddenly tumbled backward into the pit with the red hot stones in it. The big creature was badly burned, and the jack-knife position he found himself in made it hard for him to get up.

"Cover him up! Cover him up!" screamed the children, and they quickly buried him with sand and gravel.

When the parents returned to the beach where they had left their children, the giant was dead. "We might not have been here when you came back," the eldest child cried, as all the children ran down to meet their parents' canoe. They all spoke at once. "Big Figure was here!" they said. "We buried him in the cooking pit."

# The Nehalem

Strongly associated with the Clatsop Tribe, the Nehalem occupied the Oregon Coast from Tillamook Head to well south of Tillamook Bay. The tribe still lives in Oregon today. Their language is part of the Penutian group. The Nehalem had two names for a bigfoot-like creature which depended on the gender of the animal. A *Qe'ku* was a wild woman while a *Yi' dyi'tai* was a wild man.

### Wild Man

Source: *Nehalem Tillamook Tales,* by Elizabeth Derr Jacobs, 2003. Corvallis: University of Oregon Books.

People were drying fish up the Nehalem River. They heard a noise, the brush was crackling loudly, they knew that no wind nor common animal could be making that kind of noise. They hurried into their canoes and crossed over to the other side of the river. They forgot their little dog. They crawled into a place and lay down to listen. Their little dog barked and barked, then suddenly quit. Then they heard a terrific noise as Wild Man knocked down one side of the house. Then he must have gone back into the woods. They could not sleep they were so frightened, although they knew it was such a deep river he would be unable to wade it.

The next day one fellow went over in a canoe to have a look. One side of that large house where they had dried fish was smashed to pieces. The dog was lying there dead, and Wild Man's huge tracks were all around. That fellow came back and told the people, "Yes, I saw his tracks." They put all of their belongings and their fish in canoes and left that place for good. They would not live there any more for fear he might come again. After that no one would camp on that side of the river.

That really happened.

### Wild Men

Source: *Nehalem Tillamook Tales,* by Elizabeth Derr Jacobs, 2003. Corvallis: University of Oregon Books.

There must have been a whole tribe of Wild Men because there were always some around.

A Nehalem man was not married. He would go hunting and permit the married people to have the meat he got. One summer he killed an elk, and he saved the blood. He took the elk's bladder and filled it with the blood. He made a camp near there. He placed that bladder of blood near his feet, lay down, and went to sleep. Wild Man came and helped himself to the elk meat.

The man awoke. He was too warm, he was sweating. "Goodness! What is the matter?" he asked himself, looking about. It was like daylight, there was such a great fire burning there. Wild Man had placed large pieces of bark between the man and the fire so the man would not get too hot while he slept. You see, he treated that fellow well. When he spoke to him, Wild Man called the man "my nephew."

The man awoke to see Wild Man, that extremely large man, sitting by the fire. He had the fat ribs and front of that elk on a stick, roasting them by the fire. He said, "This is how I am getting to be. I am getting to be always on the bum, these days. I travel all over, I cannot find any elk. I took your elk, dear nephew, I took your elk meat."

That man stretched himself, he had forgotten about that bladder of blood. He kicked it with his feet, causing it to make a noise. Wild Man looked around; he said, "It sounds as if a storm were coming." (A Wild Man does not like to travel when it is storming.) Wild Man was afraid of that noise, he kept kicking that bladder of blood. He said, "Yes, a storm is coming." Wild Man asked, "My dear nephew, would you tell me the best place to run to?" That man showed Wild Man a high bluff. "Over in that direction is a good place to run," he told him. Wild Man started out running. Soon the man heard him fall over that bluff.

The man did not go back to sleep any more that night. In the morning he went to look. There Wild Man lay, far down at the foot of the bluff. He went around by a better route and climbed down to see the body. He took Wild Man's quiver, he left Wild Man lying there. Then he became afraid, so he made ready and returned from the woods taking as much meat as he could carry. He said, "Wild Man found me. He jumped over the bluff." He too found all kinds of bones in that quiver.

They must have been lucky pieces because elk would come down from the mountain for him, and only he could get sea lions on the rocks.

# The Tlingit

The Tlingit still live in their traditional homelands along the coast and islands of British Columbia. Their language is part of the Athabaskan linguistic family.

### How Mosquitoes Came to Be

Source: Unknown English source, 1883

Long ago there was a giant who loved to kill humans, eat their flesh, and drink their blood. He was especially fond of human hearts. "Unless we can get rid of this giant," people said, "none of us will be left," and they called a council to discuss ways and means.

One man said, "I think I know how to kill the monster," and he went to the place where the giant had last been seen. There he lay down and pretended to be dead.

Soon the giant came along. Seeing the man lying there, he said: "These humans are making it easy for me. Now I don't even have to catch and kill them; they die right on my trail, probably from fear of me!"

The giant touched the body. "Ah, good," he said, "this one is still warm and fresh. What a tasty meal he'll make; I can't wait to roast his heart."

The giant flung the man over his shoulder, and the man let his head hang down as if he were dead. Carrying the man home, the giant dropped him in the middle of the floor right near the fireplace. Then he saw that there was no firewood and went to get some.

As soon as the monster had left, the man got up and grabbed the giant's huge skinning knife. Just then the giant's son came in, bending low to enter. He was still small as giants go, and the man held the big knife to his throat. "Quick, tell me, where's your father's heart? Tell me or I'll slit your throat."

The giant's son was scared. He said: "My father's heart is in his left heel."

Just then the giant's left foot appeared in the entrance, and the man swiftly plunged the knife into the heel. The monster screamed and fell down dead.

Yet the giant still spoke. "Though I'm dead, though you killed me, I'm going to keep on eating you and all the other humans in the world forever!"

"That's what you think!" said the man. "I'm about to make sure that you never eat anyone again." He cut the giant's body into pieces and burned each one in the fire. Then he took the ashes and threw them into 'the air for the winds to scatter.

Instantly each of the particles turned into a mosquito. The cloud of ashes became a cloud of mosquitoes, and from their midst the man I heard the giant's voice laughing, saying: "Yes, I'll eat you people until 'the end of time."

And as the monster spoke, the man felt a sting, and a mosquito, started sucking his blood, and then many mosquitoes stung him, and he began to scratch himself. The giant got his revenge.

## The Giant of *Tâ'sna*

Source: *Tlingit Myths and Texts,* by John R. Swanton, 1909. Bureau of American Ethnology Bulletin 39, pp. 187-188.

At *Tâ'sna,* near the mouth of the Yukon, was a large village in which everybody had died except one small boy. His mother was the last to perish. This boy was very independent, however, remaining in his mother's house all the time instead of going around to the other houses in the place. Every day he went out with his bow and arrows and shot small birds and squirrels for his sustenance.

On one of these hunting trips, however, he met a very large man with bushes growing on one side of his face. The big man chased him, and, being very quick, the boy tried to climb up a tree, but the big man reached right up after him and pulled him down. Then the big man said, "I am not going to hurt you. Stand right here." So he put the boy on a high place, went some distance away and said, "Take your bow and arrows and shoot me right here," pointing at the same time to a spot between his eyebrows. At first the boy was afraid to do so, and the big man begged him all that day. Finally, when it was getting dark, he thought, "Well! I will shoot him. He may kill me if I don't, and he will kill me if I do." The moment he shot the man, however, he saw his mother and all the village people that had been lost. All had been going to this big man. That was why the man wanted the boy to shoot him. It brought all the people back.

## The Boy and the Giant

Source: *Tlingit Myths and Texts,* by John R. Swanton, 1909. Bureau of American Ethnology Bulletin 39, pp. 212-214.

At a certain place in the interior lived a manly little boy who was very fond of hunting. He would take his lunch and go off hunting very early in the morning and stay all day, bringing home two or three porcupines in the evening. One morning he started earlier than usual and came upon a giant as tall as the trees. He was very much frightened and ran away with the big man in pursuit. As the giant was not a very fast runner, the boy kept ahead of him until he came to a sort of cave like a house at the foot of a hill and entered it. When the big man saw this, he said, "Come here, my grandson." The boy refused, and the giant continued his entreaties for a long time. At last the boy

consented to go with him, so the giant said, "Get inside of my shirt. I will carry you that way." Then the boy vaulted in there, and they started off.

After they had gone, along in this manner for some time, the boy, who had his head out, saw a very small bird called old-person [*Lagu-qâ'k!u*] and said, "Grandpa, there is a bird I would like to have." Then the big man stopped and let him down, and he shot the bird with an arrow and put it into his bosom, after which he crawled back into the big man's shirt. But now this bird had increased the boy's weight so much that the giant could scarcely move along. At every step he took he sank deep into the moss. When the boy noticed this, he said to himself, "How is it that, since I picked up this small bird, I have gotten very heavy, and it is hard for him to walk?" Then he threw the bird away and the giant walked on again as lightly as before. The boy enjoyed so much being with this giant that he had forgotten all about his father and mother. After that they traveled on together until they came to a very large lake. In it the boy saw beaver houses, and the beaver dam ran right across it. He thought, "This is a beaver lake. This is the kind of place my father has told me about." Then the big man tore a hole through the top of a beaver house, took all of the beavers out, and made a fire right back of the lake at which to cook them. They camped there for several days, living on beaver meat and drying the skins. But the first evening the giant said, "Keep a look out. If you hear any noise during the night, wake me up. There is a bigger man than I of whom I am much afraid." He also said to the boy, "Sleep some distance away from me, or I might move against you or throw my leg on you so as to kill you."

The second night they encamped there the boy heard the bushes breaking, and sure enough the second giant came along. He was so tall that his head was far up above the trees, and they could not see it. This second giant had been looking for the other for a long time unsuccessfully, so he rushed upon him, threw him down, and lay on top of him. Then the boy's friend cried, "Grandson, take that club of mine out and throw it at him." The boy ran to the big man's bed, took his club, which was made from the entire skeleton of a beaver, out from under it, and threw it at the intruder. As soon as he let it go out of his hands it began chewing at the second giant's leg, and, as he was unable to feel it, the club chewed off both his legs. Then the other, who had been almost smothered, killed him and threw his body into the lake.

After this the boy's companion had nothing to fear, and wandered from lake to lake, and the boy was so fond of hunting that he forgot all about his father and mother. It was now winter time, and that winter was very severe. From the time the second giant had been killed he had been doing nothing but killing beaver.

One evening, however, the boy began thinking of his father and his mother, and was very quiet. Then the big man said, "Why is it that you are so quiet this evening?" The boy answered, "I have just thought of my father and mother. I feel lonely [i.e., homesick] for them." Then his companion said, "Would you like to go to them?" "I can't go to them because I don't know where they are. I don't know which way to go to get to them." Then the big man said, "All right, you can go," but the boy did not know what he meant. Now the big man went to a small tree, broke it off, trimmed it well for the boy, and said to him, "Take this along and as soon as you feel that you are lost, let it stand straight up and fall over. Go in the direction in which it falls. Keep on doing this until you get to your father's place."

At first the boy was afraid to start off alone, but finally he did so. Whenever he was in doubt about the direction he let the tree fall, and it led him at last right down to his father's village, where all were exceedingly glad to see him.

# The Upper Skagit

The Upper Skagit traditionally occupied the Upper Skagit and Sauk rivers in Washington State. Today, their reservation is located in the Skagit River Valley. Their language is in the Salishan family.

## Cannibal Basket Woman, Defeated by Clever Children

Source: *Haboo–Native American Stories from Puget Sound,* by Vi Hilbert, 1985.
Seattle: University of Washington Press, pp. 42-44.

A group of children knew a woman who lived all alone near the river. The children knew that she was lonely, and they wanted to go visit with her. When they asked their parents for permission to go, their parents said, "No. You can't go, because it is too far away: the Giant Woman might get you when you are away from home. The Giant Woman is powerful. She would put you in her huge clam basket."

The children ignored their parents. They got into a canoe and went on their way to visit the lonely woman. When night came, they made themselves a camp on the other side of the river. They built a fire and cooked their supper. One of the children was a hunchback. When the children divided their supper, Hunchback was given the tail part.

They traveled for several days. Each evening they would stop to camp overnight and eat their supper. Every time, they would give Hunchback the tail part for his share.

Hunchback finally said, "If you folks are always going to be giving me the tail part when I would really rather have the tips, I will call the Giant Woman!"

When night came again and they stopped to camp and eat their supper, it was still the tail part, which he was given. Now Hunchback hollered! He hollered:

"Come downhill, Giant Woman, Come downhill, Giant Woman. It is just the tail part that I am given by my playmates!"

The Giant woman heard right away. "Oh, there is someone hollering at me!" She put her basket on her back and she walked. She was a huge person, this Giant Woman. She chewed on everything as she traveled.

She arrived where the children were. Right away she began to pick up the children one by one and put them into her basket. She grabbed Hunchback first and put him there. When all of the children were in the basket, the Giant Woman walked. She carried these children upland. Suddenly she could feel something catch at her basket. She thought, "Oh, it must be Hunchback who has caught onto something."

Hunchback had squirmed and squirmed until he managed to get himself up on top of the other children. Each time he came to a leaning tree he tried to grab a hold of it. No. He couldn't do it. On the fourth try, he did it.

Giant Woman went on walking. When she arrived at her home with the children she immediately gathered rocks and placed them on her fire to heat. When they were good and hot she began to take the children out of her basket. Then she found that Hunchback was missing. "Oh, Hunchback isn't here! Where is he? Maybe he managed to run away."

Giant Woman ran!

Hunchback was in the canoe, shoving off from shore. He had a paddle with holes in it. This paddle had holes. When Giant Woman threw rocks at him, he held up his paddle and the rocks just went through. Hunchback paddled hard. Each time she threw a rock at him, he raised his paddle and the rock just went through a hole.

Giant Woman gave up. She went home and put more rocks on her fire. She wanted the rocks to be very hot to cook her supper fast.

The children huddled together and began talking to each other. They watched the Giant Woman heating all of those rocks on the fire.

Giant Woman noticed and said to them, "What are you children saying?"

The children carefully answered, "Oh, it is just that we are so happy for you that you are heating rocks. We would like for you to sing and dance before you cook us there."

Giant Woman was so flattered at the request that she said, "All right!"

The children said, "You will dance!"

She proudly said, "Yes, I will." Now Giant Woman danced. She sang this as she danced:

> The children will be roasted on the rocks.
> The children will be roasted on the rocks.
> The children will be roasted on the rocks.
> The children will be roasted on the rocks.

The children said, "Oh my, but your song is so nice. Sing more." And again Giant Woman sang and danced.

The oldest and strongest of the children were making plans: "We had better push her onto the hot rocks."

Giant Woman asked, "What are you children saying?"

They cautiously answered, "Oh, we are just so happy for you."

They whispered to each other, "When she comes near us, let's all push her."

Old Giant Woman was coming closer, singing:

> The children will be roasted on the rocks
> The children will be roasted on the rocks
> The children will be roasted on the rocks
> The children will be roasted on the rocks

As she came close to them, all of the oldest, strongest children pushed her. Right onto the hot rocks she fell. She screamed, "Remove me, children. Remove me from the fire and I will return you to your home."

One of the children said, "Get a forked stick, and we shall remove your grandmother from the fire. We shall remove her. Get a forked stick."

However, the children took the forked stick, and everyone pressed her down onto the hot rocks until she was just stuck there, roasting.

That is the end of the story.

## Basket Woman's Sister Eats Her Last Meal

Source: An unknown source, but a variant of the first story.

Basket Ogress spoke to her little daughter, Tree Roots. "Little Roots, I want you to build a fire and heat those rocks. We are going to have tender roasted children for our supper."

Basket Ogress put her huge clam basket on her back and hurried down to the water where the little children were playing. She grabbed them all up and stuffed them into her basket. Little Hunchback kept wriggling himself up over the children. He managed to be at the top of the basket as ogress lumbered upland thinking about her supper.

Little Hunchback saw a tree branch that was hanging sideways.

He grabbed a hold of it and swung himself out of the basket as ogress crawled under with her pack. Then he ran. He went home. When he got there he told how the bad Basket Ogress had stolen the children. The people immediately prepared themselves to go and rescue them. They should kill that ogress.

When Basket Ogress arrived at home with her basket full of children, she took them out and seated them around the fire. As she thought about her dinner, she began to sing and dance:

> The children will now be roasted,
> The children will now be roasted,
> The children will now be roasted,

Around the fire she went. It was a great big fire, and her daughter, little Tree Roots, had lots of rocks heating there. Ogress was very happy. She was glad because now she had lots of tender little children to eat. She became lightly dizzy as she danced around the fire, and she staggered just a little. Oh,

but she was so happy as she thought about the dinner she would have in just a little while. It was such a big, hot fire!

The older boys and girls noticed how she had staggered as she danced. They whispered to each other, "She could burn! We could push the dirty thing, because she gets dizzy when she dances and staggers toward the fire. We could push her down and push her neck onto the fire with a forked stick."

"We could all poke her and hold her down on the fire. We could manage to kill her. It would be a good thing if she died, anyway!"

The children discussed their plan; then one of them ran and brought back a forked stick. They said to little Tree Roots, "Little Tree Roots, go and get a forked stick so that we can get your mother out of the fire if she should get dizzy and fall there." Little Tree Roots went and returned with the good forked stick that they used when they were out hunting.

Now they watched carefully as Basket Ogress happily danced around her big hot fire. As soon as she staggered just a little, they pushed her toward the fire and poked her neck onto the hot rocks with the forked sticks. She thrashed around for a little while.

Then she died in the fire! They kept her pressed onto the fire. Basket Ogress, the monster who liked to eat children, died. She would have eaten them if she had not been killed herself.

It was little Hunchback who ran and told. Then the people came. They made certain that she was truly dead. There was still a little life left in her when the relatives of the children arrived, so they completely killed her. She died!

After Basket Ogress was dead they covered her over with ashes and left her there. Her little daughter, Tree Roots, left. She walked at first, but then she went running away from the place where her mother had died.

The younger sister of Basket Ogress, had been hunting far away from home. Now she quietly returned. As she glanced around the area, she noticed that a big fire had died down, but there appeared to be something there covered with ashes.

Then she chuckled to herself and said, "Well, well as usual, the great, powerful one has her game cleverly hidden. This is probably her game that she has roasted and hidden here." She went closer to investigate what was covered at the fire. She knew it had been roasted. She uncovered part of it. True! It was cooked and falling apart, it was so well done! This younger sister had been out hunting and hadn't had time to stop and cook herself a good meal. She was so hungry.

Now she ate. She thought that this was some game that her sister had cooked and left covered at the fire.

After she had eaten her fill she began to feel a little sick, and she said,

"Oh, my goodness, this tastes like it might have been the dear one I…" She realized now that it was her own sister whom she had eaten. She got scared and went away from there.

She walked a long way until she came to some people in a village. She asked them, "Where is your door?

They answered, "It is through the roof that people enter who come here." They already knew, however, that Basket Ogress's, sister would be traveling, and they had built a huge fire beneath the roof. When she came through the hole in the roof, they threw her into the fire, where she died.

Now both monsters were dead, and that is why there are no monsters here on top, the way the world is now. They would still be here if they hadn't been killed in the fire, the bad Basket Ogress and her younger sister.

The younger sister was also bad. This story is about the way it was in the beginning. Those monsters liked to eat children. They killed them. They didn't eat old people, just the children. The daughter of Basket Ogress, little Tree Roots, lived. Coming generations will now be all right, because the monsters were killed.

That is the end.

HEY-hey-hey-hey! What about that daughter, when she grows up? You kids better WATCH OUT, you see some big ugly old lady with a basket on her back.

# THE
# PLATEAU
# CULTURE

# Plateau Cultural Area

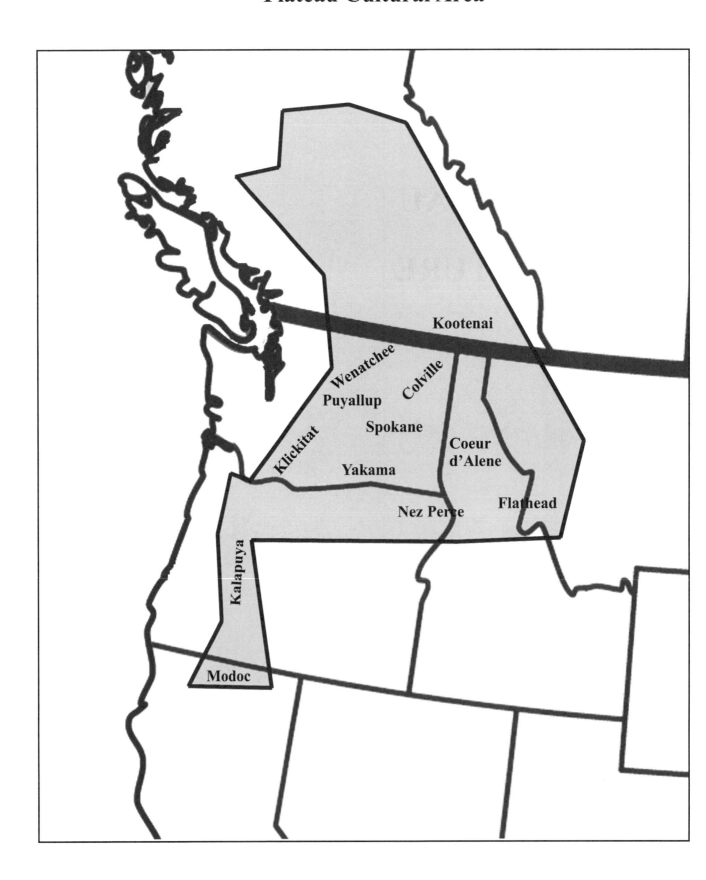

Kootenai

Wenatchee

Colville

Puyallup

Klickitat

Spokane

Coeur
d'Alene

Yakama

Nez Perce

Flathead

Kalapuya

Modoc

# The Coeur d'Alene

The Coeur d'Alene (also known as the Schitsu'umsh) homelands once consisted of northern Idaho, eastern Washington, and western Montana. Their reservation is now located solely in Idaho. Their traditional Salishan word for bigfoot is not known.

## Giants

Source: *Indian Legends from the Northern Rockies,* by Ella Clark. Norman: University of Oklahoma Press, pp. 113-114.

Giants were formerly common in Coeur d'Alene country. They had a very strong odor, like the odor of burning horn. Their faces were black–some say they were painted black, and the giants were taller than the highest tipis. When they saw a single tipi or lodge in a place, they would crawl up to it, rise, and look down the smoke hole. If several lodges were together, the giants were not so bold.

Most of them dressed in bearskins, but some wore other kinds of skins with the hair left on. They lived in caves in the rocks. They had a great liking for fish, and often stole fish out of people's traps. Otherwise, they did not bother people much. They are said to have stolen women occasionally in other tribes, but there is no tradition of their having stolen women in the Coeur d'Alene country.

## Origin of Indian Tribes (From Parts of Monster)

Source: *Myths of Idaho Indians* by Deward E. Walker Jr., 1980. Moscow: University of Idaho, pp. 70-74.

Rabbit had a house near Grizzly Bear's. Grizzly was always starving and Rabbit always had to feed him. Besides eating everything he wished, Grizzly always wanted to take some food along home with him. Then he became so greedy that he thought he would kill Rabbit and get all the food. "Let's play," he proposed. Rabbit said, "We are no children to be playing." "Oh, come on, let's play. Let's go swimming."

When they were in the water Grizzly said, "Let's splash. Let me be first." He took water and threw it at Rabbit, then laughed. Rabbit took a big spoon made of elk antler. While Grizzly was laughing he filled it with water and threw it down Grizzly's throat. Grizzly almost choked, but Rabbit ran away into his house before Grizzly recovered. He threw Grizzly's food out at him and saw him eat it greedily. Then Grizzly laughed again, "We are only playing," but to himself he said, "I'm going to shoot him in the eye."

Rabbit took a bladder, blew it up and put it in his eye.

Grizzly shot at him and the bladder burst. Grizzly laughed, "My, isn't that fun!" Then came Rabbit's turn. He shot and put out Grizzly's eye. Grizzly

growled in fury and pain, but Rabbit ran home. Then Rabbit ran into the timber and soon came to the house where a wicked old woman lived with her daughter and son-in-law. The husband of the girl was gone, so Rabbit killed the girl. He took a knife and began to skin her. As he did so he asked the old woman, "Are my ears getting longer?" "Yes," she said. Then as he cut the daughter down the back he asked, "Is my fat showing?" "Yes," the old woman was compelled to answer.

The girl had an understanding with her husband when they first got married. She had told him, "If one of your arrows breaks when you are hunting then you will know I am dead." He had told her, "If ever your digging stick breaks when you are digging camas you will know I am dead."

Now when the husband was out hunting he was warned of his wife's disaster by the breaking of his arrow. He hurried home. "Mother-in-law, what does this mean?" he asked. "Rabbit came in, killed our daughter, cut her open and went away again."

Rabbit had escaped into the timber but the man went after him. Rabbit made all kinds of tracks in the timber so the man could not track him easily, but nevertheless he followed. Then Rabbit put cooked camas down at intervals. This was so the man would be delayed by picking it up to eat. Finally Rabbit came to the open prairie. Just as he got a good start forward, he ran into Coyote. Rabbit said, "You shouldn't delay me this way, a monster is chasing me."

Coyote took up some jointgrass, pulled the joints apart and hid Rabbit in it. Rabbit was shaking with fear, so Coyote blew the jointgrass so it looked as if it was shaking in the wind. Then he consulted his powers. The first one said, "The monster who is after you has a dog, the Grizzly Bear, so I'll be your dog and my name will be the same. I'll be very small." The second power said, "I'll be a knife at the back of your dog's head." The third said, "I'll give you the power to gobble everything up."

Then they saw the monster coming with his dog. "Did you see what I am chasing?" he asked roughly. Coyote asked, "What are you chasing?" "A rabbit," replied the monster. "I didn't see him," Coyote said. The monster said, "Maybe he passed before I came." The monster's dog began to growl. "Be quiet, Grizzly!" said Coyote to his own dog. "Why, we call our pets by the same name!" said the monster.

Coyote answered, "Aha! My father and his father had the same name for their dogs." Then the monster became angry and walked toward Coyote's pet. He said, "Make your dog stop growling or we might kill you." Coyote said, "You stop yours." "You better listen to me, he will kill you," the monster warned. Coyote laughed, "We might kill you." "Oh, no," said the monster. Then Coyote proposed, "Let's let our dogs fight."

So they turned the dogs loose and they fought: Coyote's dog was bitten and stepped on, but Coyote just laughed. He called, "What is the matter with you, Grizzly? Why don't you put your head under him?" and he laughed again. Again he egged him on. The Coyote's dog crawled under Grizzly dog and ripped his stomach open with the knife behind his head. The Grizzly dog fell dead.

The monster mourned for his dog, but Coyote said, "It's too bad. I told you to call off your dog when they started to fight. I saw they were mad." The monster retorted, "Shut up! I'll gobble you up! Coyote answered, "Do you mean that you will gobble *me* up? I'll gobble *you* up. Let's see if we can gobble up that tree. You try first."

The monster tried, but left about three feet of the stump standing. Coyote laughed, "I thought you were smart. Now look at me!" He gobbled and when he was through not a splinter of the tree was left. "Now look," said Coyote. "That is the way real gobblers gobble. Let's go and gobble that cliff. You go first." The monster gobbled at it but when he had done his best some rocks were left. Coyote laughed. He gobbled and not a pebble was left. "You are not like me," he bragged, "I am the smart one!" "I might gobble you up," said the monster. "All right," said Coyote, try it!"

Before Coyote could look he found himself inside the monster's stomach. There were lots of people there playing games. Some were playing the stickgame, others cards, still others were dancing a war dance. Coyote said to them, "What's the matter with you all? You are pitiful. Don't you know you are in the belly of a monster? I am going out of here. Get yourselves ready. Soon I'll be back, then I'll fix it so you can come out."

He tickled the monster's heart until he was spat out and landed far away. Coyote picked up a stick to make a hoop and continued making hoops as he talked to the monster. "Your insides show you are a good gambler. You are a card player." Coyote had made a hoop the size of the monster's mouth and was now fashioning two smaller ones the size of his nostrils. "You are a good war dancer."

The monster answered, "I vomited you up because you are no good. I eat only good things." Coyote said, "You only think so. You eat mice. I am the one who eats really good things." The monster said, "Just a minute ago I got through eating two nice, neat, good-looking people." Coyote said, "I was the one who ate those two." "If that's true vomit them out," the monster replied angrily. "Come," said Coyote, "sit down there and close your eyes. I'll close mine and we will see what we can vomit. You do it first!"

The monster vomited two people and Coyote four mice.

Coyote threw the mice in front of the monster and put the people on his side. Then he said, "Let's open our eyes." Coyote laughed, "Those nice-looking ones are the ones I ate." The monster could not believe his eyes. "They are the ones I ate. I never did eat mice." "Look where they are," said Coyote. "They're on your side." "I'll gobble you up!" shouted the monster. "You're a mouse-eater!" replied Coyote. Coyote had the hoops in his hand and held them flat. "All right, go on, gobble me up," teased Coyote.

Again in a twinkling he was in the monster's stomach.

"Hello!" he said to the people. "Wait till I run out, then you can get out too." He ripped open the stomach and it was light again. The people ran out while Coyote cut off the monster's heart. Then he set the large hoop so it would hold the mouth open and the smaller ones in the nostrils. Everyone came out. The monster died and Coyote ran off.

Coyote went back to the joint grass where Rabbit was hiding and took him out. Rabbit was glad to be free. Then Coyote told Rabbit to cut the monster up. Rabbit cut him all up and Coyote took the pieces and threw them about. He threw a leg and said, "You will become the Blackfoot Indians, you will be tall." He threw a rib saying, "You will be the Nez Perce, you will have good heads." The paunch became the Gros Ventre, "You will have big bellies." Then he threw the heart. "You'll be the Coeur d'Alene, you'll be courageous." He threw all the pieces away. Then he wiped his hands on some grass and threw the grass away. "You will be the Spokane, you will be poor," he decreed.

That is the end of my road. Now you know how the Indian tribes came about.

# The Colville

Once occupying areas throughout Washington State, today the Colville's maintain a reservation outside Spokane. Although their language is part of the Salishan group, their traditional word for a bigfoot-like creature is *Skanicum*, meaning Stick-Indian, which is similar to other tribes in the area despite different language groups.

*Skanicum*

Source: *They Walked Among Us–Scweneyti and the Stick Indians of the Colvilles,* by Ed Fusch, 2002, p. 30.

Note: *Skanicum* is a stick Indian, a human being to the Colville. *Skanicum's* cry sounds like "*iiieee!*"

*Skanicum* could turn into a tree. One time he was followed in to a ravine along the bottom of which flowed a creek with a heavy growth of trees. The Colville sat down on the hillside where they could see the entire area including the hillsides. After a while when *Skanicum* did not leave the ravine, some of the Indians went down into the ravine while others maintained a lookout. They searched for *Skanicum*, but he wasn't there, only trees. No Indian would dare to start chopping into the trees with an ax. All the Indians know that *Skanicum's* color and natural camouflage enables him to stand motionless against a tree and not be seen.

## *Skanicum* Kidnaps a Girl

Source: *They Walked Among Us–Scweneyti and the Stick Indians of the Colvilles,* by Ed Fusch, 2002, p. 33.

Back a long time ago, the Indians set up a fishing camp near Keller on the San Poil River. In the evening the men would return to camp with the days catch. The women would work all evening processing the fish and putting it on drying racks to dry. While cooking dinner one of the women, a recent bride took a kettle and went off for water. Minutes later they heard her screaming. The men rushed to the river but could only watch as a *Skanicum* carried the bride off. They knew that *Skanicum* was very vengeful and if harmed, the captive would be injured and the mountains would not be safe for any Indian. As she was carried away she tore off and dropped pieces of her slip, leaving a trail for the men to follow. She was with *Skanicum* all summer, when the men, still searching for her on horseback, saw her gathering wild potato roots. *Skanicum* was asleep nearby. When she saw the men, she emptied her lap of the potatoes, crept quietly to them, leaped up on one of the horses, and escaped. When they returned to camp, all the Indians immediately broke camp and left the area. During her stay with the *Skanicum*, the woman had to gather roots which they shared. The *Skanicum* eats anything that other people eat but loves tule or cattail plants.

185

# The Flathead

Also known as the Salish, the Flathead lived between the Cascade Mountains and Rocky Mountains. As part of the Confederated Salish and Kootenai Tribes of the Flathead Nation, the Flathead reservation is located in Montana. They speak a language in the Salishan group.

### Coyote Kills a Giant

Source: *American Indian Myths and Legends,* by Richard Erdoes and Alfonso Ortiz, 1984. New York: Pantheon Books, pp. 223-225.

Coyote was walking one day when he met Old Woman. She greeted him and asked where he was headed.

"Just roaming around," said Coyote.

"You better stop going that way, or you'll meet a giant who kills everybody."

"Oh, giants don't frighten me," said Coyote (who had never met one). "I always kill them. I'll fight this one too, and make an end of him."

"He's bigger and closer than you think," said Old Woman.

"I don't care," said Coyote, deciding that a giant would be about as big as a bull moose and calculating that he could kill one easily.

So Coyote said good-bye to Old Woman and went ahead, whistling a tune. On his way he saw a large fallen branch that looked like a club. Picking it up, he said to himself, "I'll hit the giant over the head with this. It's big enough and heavy enough to kill him." He walked on and came to a huge cave right in the middle of the path. Whistling merrily, he went in.

Suddenly Coyote met a woman who was crawling along on the ground.

"What's the matter?" he asked.

"I'm starving," she said, "and too weak to walk. What are you doing with that stick?"

"I'm going to kill the giant with it," said Coyote, and he asked if she knew where he was hiding.

Feeble as she was, the woman laughed. "You're already in the giant's belly."

"How can I be in his belly?" asked Coyote. "I haven't even met him."

"You probably thought it was a cave when you walked into his mouth," the woman said, and sighed.

"It's easy to walk in, but nobody ever walks out. This giant is so big you can't take him in with your eyes. His belly fills a whole valley."

Coyote threw his stick away and kept on walking. What else could he do?

Soon he came across some more people lying around half dead. "Are you sick?" he asked.

"No," they said, "just starving to death. We're trapped inside the giant."

"You're foolish," said Coyote. "If we're really inside this giant, then the cave walls must be the inside of his stomach. We can just cut some meat and fat from him."

"We never thought of that," they said.

"You're not as smart as I am," said Coyote.

Coyote took his hunting knife and started cutting chunks out of the cave walls. As he had guessed, they were indeed the giant's fat and meat, and he used it to feed the starving people. He even went back and gave some meat to the woman he had met first. Then all the people imprisoned in the giant's belly started to feel stronger and happier, but not completely happy. "You've fed us," they said, "and thanks. But how are we going to get out of here?"

"Don't worry," said Coyote. "I'll kill the giant by stabbing him in the heart. Where is his heart? It must be around here someplace."

"Look at the volcano puffing and beating over there," someone said. "Maybe it's the heart."

"So it is, friend," said Coyote, and began to cut at this mountain.

Then the giant spoke up. "Is that you, Coyote? I've heard of you. Stop this stabbing and cutting and let me alone. You can leave through my mouth; I'll open it for you."

"I'll leave, but not quite yet," said Coyote, hacking at the heart. He told the others to get ready. "As soon as I have him in his death throes, there will be an earthquake. He'll open his jaw to take a last breath, and then his mouth will close forever. So be ready to run out fast!"

Coyote cut a deep hole in the giant's heart, and lava started to flow out. It was the giant's blood. The giant groaned, and the ground under the people's feet trembled.

"Quick, now!" shouted Coyote. The giant's mouth opened and they all ran out. The last one was the wood tick. The giant's teeth were closing on him, but Coyote managed to pull him through at the last moment.

"Look at me," cried the wood tick, "I'm all flat!"

"It happened when I pulled you through," said Coyote. "You'll always be flat from now on. Be glad you're alive."

"I guess I'll get used to it," said the wood tick, and he did.

# The Kalapuya

The Kalapuya historically occupied western Oregon. However, the tribe was devastated by smallpox in the 1800s and survivors were integrated into the Siletz and Grande Ronde reservations. Although their traditional language was part of the Penutian family, the language is nearly extinct.

### The Cave Monster of the Willamette Valley

Source: *Indian Legends of the Pacific Northwest,* by Ella Clark, 1953. Berkeley: University of California Press, pp. 101-102.

A monster was frightening all the people in the valley of the Willamette River. At night he would come out from his cave, seize as many people as he could carry, and return to his cave to eat them.

When Coyote came to the valley, the people left in the villages begged him to save them from the cave monster.

"I will," promised Coyote. "I will get rid of this monster before the new moon comes again."

Coyote did not know what to do, so he talked with his good friend Fox. "The monster always lives in the dark," said his good friend Fox. "He cannot stand the daylight."

Then Fox and Coyote put their thoughts together and made a plan. Next day the sun was very bright. When it was high in the sky, Coyote took his bow and arrows and went to the top of a big mountain. There he shot an arrow into the sun. He shot a second arrow into the end of the first arrow, a third arrow into the end of the second. He kept on shooting until he had a rope of arrows from the sun to the earth.

Then he pulled on the rope of arrows. He pulled very hard. He pulled the sun down and hid it in the Willamette River.

The monster thought that night had come again, so he left his cave to get someone to eat. As soon as he grabbed the first man, Coyote broke the rope of arrows with held the sun down in the river. At once the sun sprang back up into the sky. It made so much light that the monster was blinded. Then Coyote killed him. The people were freed from their terror.

After many, many summers and many, many, many snows, white people found the bones of the monster and carried them away. The Indians living in the Willamette Valley told them that evil would come from moving the bones of a monster of a long-ago time. But the white people would not listen.

# The Klickitat

In prehistoric times, the Klickitat (also known as the Klikitat) were residents of the headwaters of the Cowlitz, Lewis, White Salmon, and Klickitat rivers. They now occupy a reservation with the Yakama in south central Washington. In their traditional Penutian language, the Klickitat word for a bigfoot-like creature is *Nashlah*, meaning "cannibal monster." Because they were also closely related to other tribes, the Klickitat shared additional bigfoot names with the Yakama (*Qah lin me* and *Qui yihahs* ["The Hairy brothers"]) and the Puyallup (*Seatco* [Stick Indian]).

## Coyote and the Monster of the Columbia

Source: *Indian Legends of the Pacific Northwest,* by Ella Clark, 1953. Berkeley: University of California Press, pp. 89-91.

One time on his travels, Coyote learned that a monster was killing the animal people as they traveled up and down Big River in their canoes. So many had been killed that some of the animal people were afraid to go down to the water, even to catch salmon.

"I will help you," promised Coyote. "I will stop this monster from killing people."

But what could he do? He had no idea. So he asked his three sisters who lived in his stomach in the form of huckleberries. They were very wise. They knew everything. They would tell him what to do.

At first his sisters refused to tell Coyote what to do.

"If we tell you," they said, "you will say that it was your plan all the time."

"If you do not tell me," said Coyote sternly, "I will send rain and hail down upon you."

Of course the berries did not like rain and hail.

"Do not send rain," they begged. "Do not send rain or hail. We will tell you what to do. Take with you plenty of dry wood and plenty of pitch, so that you can make a fire. And take also five sharp knives. It is *Nashlah* at Wishram that is killing all the people. He is swallowing all the people. You must let him swallow you."

"Yes, my sisters, that is what I thought," replied Coyote. "That was my plan all the time."

Coyote followed his sisters' advice. He gathered together some dry wood and pitch, sharpened his five knives, and went to where the monster lived. The monster saw Coyote but did not swallow him, for he knew that Coyote was a great chief.

Coyote knew that he could make *Nashlah* angry by teasing him. So he called out all kinds of mean names. At last the monster was so angry that he took a big breath and sucked Coyote in with his breath. Just before entering his mouth, Coyote grabbed a big armful of sagebrush and took it in also.

Inside the monster, Coyote found many animal people. All were cold and hungry. Some were almost dead from hunger, and some were almost dead from cold.

"I will build a fire in here for you," said Coyote. "And I will cook some food for you. While you get warm and while you eat, I will kill *Nashlah*. I have come to help you, my people. You will join your friends soon."

With the sagebrush and the pitch, Coyote made a big fire under the heart of the monster. The shivering people gathered around it to get warm. Then with one of his sharp knives Coyote cut pieces from the monster's heart and roasted them.

While the people ate, Coyote began to cut the cord that fastened the monster's heart to his body. He broke the first knife, but he kept cutting. He broke the second knife, but he kept cutting. He broke his third and his fourth knives. With his fifth knife he cut the last thread, and the monster's heart fell into the fire.

Just as the monster died, he gave one big cough and coughed all the animal people out on the land.

"I told you I would save you," said Coyote, as the animal people gathered around him on the shore of the river. "You will live a long time, and I will give you names."

Coyote went among them and gave each creature a name.

"You will be Eagle, the best and the bravest bird. You will be Bear, the strongest animal. You will be Owl, the big medicine man, with special powers. You will be Sturgeon, the largest fish in the rivers. You will be Salmon, the best of all fish for eating."

In the same way Coyote named Beaver, Cougar, Deer, Woodpecker, Blue Jay, and all the other animals and birds. Then he named himself. "I am Coyote," he told them. "I am the wisest and smartest of all the animals."

Then he turned to the monster and gave him a new law. "You can no longer kill people as you have been doing. A new race of people are coming, and they will pass up and down the river. You must not kill all of them. You may kill one now and then. You may shake the canoes if they pass over you. For this reason most of the canoes will go round your pool and not pass over where you live. You will kill very few of the new people. This is to be the law always. You are no longer the big man you used to be."

The law that Coyote made still stands. The monster does not swallow people as he did before Coyote took away his big power. Sometimes he draws a canoe under and swallows the people in it. But not often. Usually the Indians take their canoes out of the water and carry them round the place where the monster lives. They do not pass over his house. He still lives deep under the water, but he is no longer powerful.

# The Kootenai

The Kootenai (also known as the Kutenai) Tribe is indigenous to the area now known as Montana, Idaho, and British Columbia. Their language, often referred to as Kutenai, is isolated into the Kitunahan language group due to no known relation with any other language. Some anthropologists suggest a connection to the Salishan languages, but the relationship is unclear. The tribe is located in Montana as part of the Confederated Salish and Kootenai Tribes of the Flathead Nation.

## The Giant

Source: Unknown.

There was a town. One day two brothers went out hunting. As they were going along, the older one saw a bighorn sheep and shot it. He carried it down, but toward sunset he became hungry. He thought, "I'll make a fire and roast a piece of meat. When I have finished eating, I will cut up the meat and dry it." Then he threw a piece of the bighorn sheep meat into the fire. When it was cooked he ate it, but it was without taste. He thought, "I'll cut a piece of my own body and I'll roast it in the fire." Then he cut a piece off of himself and threw it into the fire. When it was done he ate it. It tasted good. He cut off another piece and threw it into the fire and ate it. After two days he had devoured himself entirely. Only his bones were left. The younger brother had gone on home, and the following morning he thought, "I'll go and look for my older brother." He went along to the place where they had been hunting. When he arrived, he heard a strange sound. He stood still and listened. He heard the sound from a hill in front of him and walked there. A little way off there was a fire. He went there and heard his older brother making that noise. The older brother was saying, "Oh, I love my brother and it will take me two days to eat him!" When the younger brother arrived there, the older brother saw him and ran after him and killed him.

Meanwhile, those at home said they ought to look for the brothers. The older one's wife took her son and started looking for them. As they went along, the woman heard a sound. She went in that direction and saw her husband sitting down. He was saying, "Oh, I love my son! It will take me two days to eat him." The woman was behind a hill and something told her, "Take sharp stones and stick them on your clothing. He will strike you and the stones will cut him. Then he will not be able to catch you." Then she stuck stones on her clothing and went nearer. He struck her, and he was cut. She carried her child, but her husband could not catch her. She started to run and he pursued her. Because he was only bones, he could not run fast.

When she got back, she said, "My husband ate his younger brother, and he intended to eat my son. He is coming." Then they said, "We will move camp." Someone said, "Who has enough courage to stay and kill him when he comes?" Coyote said, "I will stay," but everyone said, "Don't." Crane, said, "I will stay," and he was told, "That is good." Crane and the wife and the son of the older brother stayed. Everyone else moved from camp, but the three stayed there. Not long after Crane left too.

Then the brother arrived, but there was nobody left except his wife and his son. When he saw his wife, he said to her, "Give me the child." She gave it to him. When he took it, he killed it. He thought he would eat it, but his wife said to him, "Hand it to me, I shall go and wash it." He gave it to his wife and she carried it down to the water. Then she went behind and threw it away. She began to run after the other people. When she reached them, she said, "He arrived at the place where we moved camp. He has killed his boy." Then Crane was told, "Go back and kill him." Crane went back. He made a hole as long as his legs in a steep bank. Then he stayed there.

The brother remained at the camp. When his wife did not come back, he thought, "I'll go and kill her," so he went in the direction in which she had gone. There was nothing there. Only his son was lying there, and he ate him. Then he started in the direction in which his wife had gone. He went along the steep bank. The trail passed close to the bank, and Crane stayed there waiting. The brother did not know that Crane was there. He walked past that hole and when Crane saw him, he stretched out his foot quickly and kicked him over the bank. The brother fell into the water and was killed. Then Crane went off. He had been the first of the cannibal giants.

# The Modoc

The Modoc were historic residents of northeastern California and central southern Oregon. Today, as a result of the Modoc War of 1872-1873, they are split into two major tribes, one living on a reservation in Oregon and the other in Oklahoma. Their language is part of the Penutian family. The traditional Modoc word for bigfoot is *Matah Kagmi*. The Modoc/Klamath traditional word is *Yah'yahaas*.

### *Matah Kagmi*

Source: "Encounters with the Matah Kagmi," *Many Smokes,* (National American Indian Magazine), Fourth Quarter, 1968. Modoc County, California.

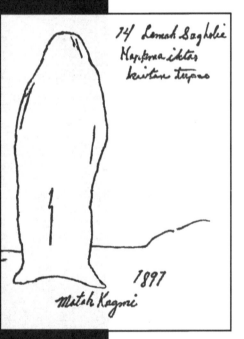

[Grandfather] was walking along a deer trail near a lake just about dusk, when he saw up ahead something that looked like a tall bush. Upon coming a little closer he became aware of a strong odor, sort of musky. He then gave a close look at the bush, and suddenly realized that it was not a bush at all, for it was covered from head to foot with thick coarse hair, much like horsehair. He took a step closer, but the creature made a sound that sounded like "*Nyyaaaah!*" Grandfather now knew this was the one the old ones spoke about, a Sasquatch!

Although it was growing darker, Grandfather was able to see quite clearly two soft brown eyes through the hairy head part, then the creature moved slightly, and Grandfather made a motion of friendship and laid down the string of fish that he had been carrying. The creature evidently understood this, as it quickly snatched up the fish and struck out through the timber nearby. It stopped only for a moment and made a sound that my grandfather never forgot–a long, low "*Aaagoooooooouummmmt.*" Grandfather called them people. He referred to them as people called '*mahtah kagmi.*'

It was only a few weeks after his encounter with the *matah kagmi* that he was awakened one morning by some strange noises outside his cabin. Upon investigating, he found a stack of deerskins fresh and ready for tanning. Off in the distance he heard that strange sound once again, "*Aaagoooooooouummmm!*" After this there were other items left from time to time, such as wood for fuel, and wild berries and fruits.

It was a few years later that Grandfather had his second, but far more amazing contact with the Sasquatch. [A timber rattler had struck him in the leg while guiding men searching for gold. He had gone ahead of the group and was therefore alone with this occurred.] Grandfather killed the snake and started to come back down to a more comfortable spot, but soon found it difficult to go on, and as best as he can remember he became sick at his stom-

ach and fainted. When he came around again, he thought he was dreaming, for three large Sasquatch about eight to ten feet tall surrounded him. He noted that they had made a small cut on the snakebite and had somehow removed some of the venom, and placed cool moss on the bite. Then one of the *matah kagmi* made a kind of grunting sound and the two lifted him up and took him down a trail that he did not know. Finally after some little descent down the mountainside, they placed him under a low brushy tree and left. Again Grandfather heard that mournful cry of the Sasquatch, "*Aagooooooouummmmm.*"

After a while he began to feel better, and then took his old .44 caliber cap and ball pistol and began to fire some shots in the air. Finally the gold party found him. Grandfather said nothing about what happened concerning the Sasquatch. He was taken back to where the pack mules were tied, and then on to the nearest little town where he rested for a few days, and then returned to Tulelake. Grandfather told only his immediate family about this encounter, and after this would never take anyone for any amount of money to the Mount Shasta region. He would only say: "*matah kagmi* live! That Holy Place, I have friends there."

For many years after, in the still of the evening or sometimes late at night, he would still hear the sound he now knew, "*Aagoooooouumm,*" the call of the Sasquatch. Grandfather went on to relate that the *matah kagmi* were not vicious, but were very shy, especially of the white man, and they generally only came out in the evenings and at night. They lived chiefly on roots they dug and berries, and only ate meat in the bitterest of cold weather. Their homes are in deep mountain side burroughs, unknown to man.

*Note: The drawing shown on the opposite page was made by the grandfather. It depicts the creature when it was first seen. The inscription states, "Fourteen hand above," meaning that the creature was fourteen hands high.*

# The Nez Perce

A large nomadic tribe, the Nez Perce historically inhabited north central Idaho, where their reservation is today. However, they were also known to have extended into southeastern Washington, northeastern Oregon, and western Montana and Wyoming. The Nez Perce have been known by multiple names. The tribe calls themselves the Nimi'ipuu, while ethnographers often used the name Te-taw-ken. Their language is in the Penutian family.

**How the *Te-taw-ken* Came to Be**

Source: *A Book of Tales–Being Some Myths of the North American Indians,* by Charles Erskine Wood, 1929. New York: Vanguard Press, pp. 81-83.

The name of the Nez Perce is *Te-taw-ken* or *We the people*. Once upon a time there were four giants and their giant sister who lived in the Salmon River and Palouse country. The sister wanted some otter liver to make big medicine. The great otter lived in the Palouse, which was a smooth river at that time, from the Snake to its head. So the four brothers took their spears and bows and went to hunt him.

They stationed themselves along the river; and the lowest, seeing the great beast asleep, shot an arrow into him. At this the otter fell into the water and shivered. This made the first rapids of the Palouse. As the otter swam upstream, the next brother also shot an arrow into him; again he shivered, and this made the second rapids. Still he swam upstream, lashing the water into foam with his tail; and the third brother shot him. At this he made some tremendous struggles, and thus came the rapids just below the falls. At this time the last giant ran down and thrust his spear through the otter; and the dying animal tore up the earth and rocks, and threw them about like sand. This made the falls of the Palouse.

Then the sister cut the beast into pieces, and threw some here, some there; where a piece fell there was made a band of the *Chu-te-pa-lus* or *Ne-me-pus* nation, Cayuses, Spokanes, Okanokanes, Umatillas, Walla Wallas. But the Nez Perces themselves–the *Te-taw-ken*, who are truly the people–they came from the strong heart of the otter. Then, when the giants saw the earth was filled with brave men (*homonick*), they took stations to watch over them; and, standing so long on guard, they were turned into mountains. There they still stand, white snow mountains above the earth.

## Coyote and the Monster of Kamiah

Source: *Nu-Mee-Poom Tit-Wah-Tit: Nez Perce Legends* by Allen Slickpoo, 1972. Idaho: Nez Perce Tribe of Idaho.

This story tells how Coyote made the different people, including the Nez Perce, and how certain animals came to look as they do today. Without Coyote's cleverness in outwitting the Monster, the people and animals today would still be imprisoned in the Monster's belly.

Once upon a time, Coyote was tearing down the waterfall at Celilo and building a fish ladder, so that salmon could go upstream for the people to catch. He was very busy at this, when someone shouted to him, "Why are you doing that? All the people are gone now because the Monster has eaten them."

"Well," said Coyote to himself, "then I'll stop doing this because I was doing it for the people, and they are gone. Now I'll go along, too."

From there he went upstream, by way of the Salmon River country. As he was walking along, he stepped on the leg of Meadowlark and broke it. Meadowlark got mad and shouted, "*Lima, lima, lima*! What chance do you have of finding people, walking along like this?"

Coyote said, "My Aunt! Please tell me what is happening, and I will make for you a new leg from the wood of a chokecherry tree."

So the Meadowlark told him, "Already all the people have been swallowed by the Monster."

Coyote replied, "Well, that is where I, too, am going." Then he fixed Meadowlark's leg with a chokecherry branch.

From there, he traveled on. Along the way he took a good bath, saying to himself, "I will make myself tasty to the Monster."

Then he dressed himself all up, saying, "This is so he won't vomit me up."

Coyote tied himself with rawhide rope to three great mountains, *Tuhm-lo-yeets-mekhs* [Pilot Knob], *Se-sak-khey-mekhs* [Seven Devil's Mountain], and *Ta-ya-mekhs* [Cottonwood Butte]. After the people came, these same mountains were used by young men and women as special places to seek the wey-a-kin, or spirit who helped guide them through life.

From there, Coyote went along the mountains and over the ridges. Suddenly, he saw a great head. He quickly hid himself in the grass and gazed at it. Never before in his life had he seen anything like it. The head was huge, and somewhere off in the distance was its big body.

Then Coyote shouted to him, "Oh Monster, let us inhale each other!"

The big eyes of the Monster looked all around for Coyote, but did not find him, because Coyote's body was painted with clay and was the same color as the grass.

Coyote shouted again, "Oh Monster, let us inhale each other!" Coyote shook the grass back and forth where he sat.

Then suddenly the Monster saw the swaying grass and said, "Oh you Coyote, you inhale first. You swallow me first."

So Coyote tried. Powerfully and noisily he drew in his breath, but the great Monster only swayed and shook.

Then Coyote said, "Now you inhale me. You have already swallowed all the people, so you should swallow me too, so I won't be lonely."

The Monster did not know that Coyote had a pack strapped to his back with five flintstone knives, a flint fire-making set, and some pure pitch in it.

Now the Monster inhaled like a mighty wind.

He carried Coyote right towards him, but as Coyote went, he left along

the way great *keh-mes* [Camas bulbs] and great serviceberry fields, saying, "Here the people will find them and will be glad, for only a short time away is the coming of the *La-te-tel-wit* [Human Beings]."

Coyote almost got caught on one of the ropes, but he cut it with his knife. Thus he dashed right into the monster's mouth.

Coyote looked around and walked down the throat of the Monster. Along the way he saw bones scattered about, and he thought to himself, "I can see that many people have been dying."

As he went along he saw some boys and he said to them, "Where is the Monster's heart? Come, show me." As they were heading that way, Grizzly Bear rushed out at them, roaring.

Coyote said, "So! You make yourself scary only to me," and he kicked Bear on the nose. Thus, the bear today has only a short nose.

As they went on, Rattlesnake rattled at them in fury. "So, only towards me you are vicious. We are nothing but dung to you." Then he stomped on Rattlesnake's head, and flattened it out. It is still that way.

Coyote then met Brown Bear who said, "I see the Monster has kept you for last. Hah! I'd like to see you try to save your people!"

But then, all along the way, people began to greet Coyote and talk to him. His close friend, Fox, greeted him from the side and said, "The Monster is so dangerous. What are you going to do to him?"

Coyote told him, "You and the boys go find some wood or anything that will burn."

About this time, Coyote had arrived at the heart of the Monster. He cut off slabs of fat from the great heart and threw them to the people. "It's too bad you are hungry. Here, eat this." Coyote now started a fire with his flint, and smoke drifted up through the Monster's eyes, nose, ears, and anus.

The Monster said, "Oh you Coyote! That's why I didn't trust you. Let me cast you out."

Coyote said, "If you do, people will later say, 'He who was cast out is giving salmon to the people'."

"Well, then, go out through the nose," the Monster said.

"But then they will say the same thing."

"Well, then, go out through the ears," the Monster said.

"If I do," answered Coyote, "they will say, 'There is old ear-wax, giving food to the people'."

"*Hn, hn, hn*, Oh you Coyote! This is why I didn't trust you. Then, go out through the anus."

And Coyote replied, "Then people will say, 'Old feces is giving food to the people'."

The fire was now burning near the Monster's heart, and he began to feel the pain. Coyote began cutting away on the heart, but then broke one of his stone knives. Right away he took another knife and kept cutting, but soon that one broke, too.

Coyote then said to the people, "Now gather up all the bones around here and carry them to the eyes, ears, month, and anus of the Monster. Pile them up, and when he falls dead, kick them out the openings." With the third knife he began cutting away at the heart. The third knife broke, and then the fourth, leaving only one more.

He told the people, "All right, get yourselves ready because as soon as he falls dead, each one of you must go out through the opening that is closest to you. Take the old women and old men close to the openings so that they may get out easily."

Now the heart hung by only a small piece of muscle and Coyote was cutting away on it, using his last stone knife. The Monster's heart was still barely hanging when Coyote's last knife broke. Coyote then threw himself on the heart, just barely tearing it loose with his hands. Then the Monster died and opened up all the openings of his body. The people kicked the bones out and then went out themselves. Coyote went out, too.

The Monster fell dead and the anus began closing, but Muskrat was still inside. Just as the anus closed he squeezed out, barely getting his body out, but his tail was caught. He pulled and pulled and all the hair got pulled right off it.

Coyote scolded him, "Now what were you doing? You probably thought of something to do at the last minute. You're always behind in everything."

Then Coyote told the people, "Gather up all the bones and arrange them well."

They did this. Then Coyote said, "Now we are going to cut up the Monster."

Coyote smeared blood on his hands and sprinkled this blood on the bones. Suddenly there came to life again all those who had died while inside the Monster. Everyone carved up the great Monster and Coyote began dealing out parts of the body to different areas of the country all over the land, towards the sunrise, towards the sunset, towards the north, and towards the south. Where each part landed, he named a tribe and described what their appearance would be. The Cayuse were formed and became small and hot-tempered. The Flatheads got a flat-headed appearance. The Blackfeet became tall, slender, and war-like. The Coeur d'Alene and their neighbors to the north became skillful gamblers. The Yakima became short and stocky and were good fishermen.

He used up the entire body of the Monster in this way. Then Fox came up to Coyote and said, "What is the meaning of this, Coyote? You have used up

the body of the Monster and given it to far away lands, but have given yourself nothing for this area."

"Well," snorted Coyote, "Why didn't you tell me this before? I was so busy that I didn't think of it."

Then he turned to the people and said, "Bring me some water with which to wash my hands."

He washed his hands and made the water bloody. Then with this bloody water, he threw drops over the land around him and said, "You may be little people, but you will be powerful. You will be little because I did not give you enough of the Monster's body, but you will be very brave and intelligent and will work hard. In only a short time, the *La-te-tel-wit* [Human Beings] are coming. And you will be known as the *Nu-me-poo* [later referred to as Nez Perce], or *Tsoop-nit-pa-lu* [People Crossing over into the Divide]. Thus, the *Nu-me-poo* Nation was born.

## The Seven Devils Mountains

Source: *Indian Legends of the Pacific Northwest,* by Ella Clark, 1953. Berkeley: University of California Press, pp. 63-64.

Long, long ago, when the world was very young, seven giant brothers lived in the Blue Mountains. These giant monsters were taller than the tallest pines and stronger than the strongest oaks.

The ancient people feared these brothers greatly because they ate children. Each year the brothers traveled eastward and devoured all the little ones they could find. Mothers fled with their children and hid them, but still many were seized by the giants. The headmen in the villages feared that the tribe would soon be wiped out. But no one was big enough and strong enough to fight with seven giants at a time.

At last the headmen of the tribe decided to ask Coyote to help them.

"Coyote is our friend," they said. "He has defeated other monsters. He will free us from the seven giants."

So they sent a messenger to Coyote. "Yes, I will help you," he promised. "I will free you from the seven giants."

But Coyote really did not know what to do. He had never fought with giants.

He had fought with monsters of the lakes and the rivers. But he knew he could not defeat seven giants at one time. So he asked his good friend Fox for advice.

"We will first dig seven holes," said his good friend Fox. "We will dig them very deep, in a place the giants always pass over when they travel to the east. Then we will fill the holes with boiling liquid."

So Coyote called together all the animals with claws—the beavers, the whistling marmots, the cougars, the bears, and even the rats and mice and moles—to dig seven deep holes. Then Coyote filled each hole with a reddish-yellow liquid. His good friend Fox helped him keep the liquid boiling by dropping hot rocks into it.

Soon the time came for the giants' journey eastward. They marched along, all seven of them, their heads held high in the air. They were sure that no one dared to attack them. Coyote and Fox watched from behind some rocks and shrubs. Down, down, down the seven giants went into the seven deep holes of boiling liquid. They struggled and struggled to get out, but the holes were very deep. They fumed and roared and splashed. As they struggled, they scattered the reddish liquid around them as far as a man can travel in a day.

Then Coyote came out from his hiding place. The seven giants stood still. They knew Coyote.

"You are being punished for your wickedness," Coyote said to the seven giants. "I will punish you even more by changing you into seven mountains. I will make you very high, so that everyone can see you. You will stand here forever, to remind people that punishment comes from wrongdoing.

"And I will make a deep gash in the earth here, so that no more of your family can get across to trouble my people."

Coyote caused the seven giants to grow taller, and then he changed them into seven mountain peaks. He struck the earth a hard blow and so opened up a deep canyon at the feet of the giant peaks.

Today the mountain peaks are called the Seven Devils. The deep gorge at their feet is known as Hell's Canyon of the Snake River. And the copper scattered by the splashing of the seven giants is still being mined.

# The Puyallup

The Puyallup historically occupied western Washington. Today, their reservation is located near Tacoma. Their language is in the Salishan linguistic stock. The Puyallup have a close relationship with other tribes in the area and share traditional names for bigfoot. These includes *Steta'l* ("Spirit Spear") and *Tsiatko* (Wild Indians), shared with the Nisqually, and *Seatco* (Stick Indian), shared with the Yakama and Klickitat.

### The Demons in Spirit Lake

Source: *Indian Legends of the Pacific Northwest,* by Ella Clark, 1953. Berkeley: University of California Press, pp. 63-64.

The lake at the foot of the beautiful mountain *Loo-wit* was the home of many evil spirits. They were the spirits of people from different tribes, who had been cast out because of their wickedness. Banding themselves together, these demons called themselves *Seatco*, and gave themselves up to wrongdoing.

The *Seatco* were neither men nor animals. They could imitate the call of any bird, the sound of the wind in the trees, the cries of wild beasts. They could make these sounds seem to be near or seem to be far away. So they were often able to trick the Indians. A few times, Indians fought them. But whenever one of the *Seatco* was killed, the others took twelve lives from whatever band dared to fight against them.

In Spirit Lake, other Indians said, lived a demon so huge that its hand could stretch across the entire lake. If a fisherman dared to go out from shore, the demon's hand would reach out, seize his canoe, and drag fisherman and canoe to the bottom of the lake.

In the lake also was a strange fish with a head like a bear. One Indian had seen it, in the long-ago time. He had gone to the mountain with a friend. The demons who lived in the lake ate the friend, but he himself escaped, running in terror from the demons and from the fish with the head of a bear. After that, no Indian of his tribe would go near Spirit Lake.

In the snow on the mountaintop above the lake, other Indians used to say, a race of man-stealing giants lived. At night the giants would come to the lodges when people were asleep, put the people under their skins, and take them to the mountaintop without waking them. When the people awoke in the morning, they would be entirely lost, not knowing in what direction their home was.

Frequently the giants came in the night and stole all the salmon. If people were awake they knew the giants were near when they smelled their strong, unpleasant odor. Sometimes people would hear three whistles, and soon stones would begin to hit their lodges. Then they knew that the giants were coming again.

# The Demons in Spirit Lake

Source: *Indian Legends of the Pacific Northwest,* by Ella Clark, 1953. Berkeley: University of California Press.

A *Seatco* is in the form of an Indian but larger, quick and stealthy. He inhabits the dark recesses of the woods, where his campfires are often seen; he sleeps by day but sallies forth at dusk for 'a night of it.' He robs traps, breaks canoes, steals food and other portable property; he waylays the belated traveler, and it is said to kill all those whose bodies are found dead. To his wicked and malicious cunning is credited all the unfortunate and malicious acts which cannot otherwise be explained. He steals children and brings them up as slaves in his dark retreats; he is a constant menace to the disobedient child, and is an object of fear and terror to all.

# The *Tsiatko*

Source: *Indian Legends of the Pacific Northwest,* by Ella Clark, 1953. Berkeley: University of California Press.

In my grandfather's time, his people captured a *tsiatko* boy and raised it. The child slept all day, then went out nights when everyone else was asleep. In the morning they would see where he had piled up wood or caught fish or brought in a deer. Finally, they told him he could go back to his people. He was gone many years and then came back once. He brought his *tsiatko* band with him and the Indians could hear them whistle all around. He said he came just for a visit to see them. Then he went away for good.

# The *Tsiatko* and *Seatco*

Source: *Legends Beyond Psychology,* by Henry James Franzoni III and Kyle Mizokami.

A race of tall Indians, called "wild" or "stick" Indians, was said to wander through the forests. In general conversation they were referred to as *tsiatko* although another term, *steta'l*, from *ta'l*, spear, could also be applied to them.

The *tsiatko* lived by hunting and fishing. Their homes were hollowed out like the sleeping places of animals and could not be distinguished as human habitations. It was largely because of this lack of any houses or villages that they were characterized as "wild." They wandered freely through the wooded country, their activities being mainly confined to the hours of darkness. As has been said, they were abnormally tall, always well over six feet. Their language was a sort of a whistle and even when people could not see them they often heard this whistle in the distance. They had no canoes nor did they ever travel by water.

The giants played pranks on the village Indians, stealing the fish from their nets at night, going off with their half-cured supplies under cover of darkness, etc. Sometimes pranks on the persons of individual men, such as removing their clothes and tying their legs apart, were made possible by a sort of hypnotic helplessness engendered by the sound of the giants' whistle.

The giant were dangerous to men if the latter interfered with them or caused hurt to one of their members. Under these conditions their hatred was implacable and they always tracked the culprit down until they finally killed him with a shot from their bows. Occasionally also, they stole children or adolescents and carried them off to act as wives or as slaves. For this reason children were mortally afraid of going about alone at night and the *tsiatko* threat was used in child discipline. During the summer camping trips when mat houses with loose sides were used for shelter, children always slept in the center surrounded by their elders for fear that the *tsiatko* would lift the mats and spirit them away. Men avoided conflicts with the giants and women retained the fear of them throughout their lives. Thus, one informant, a woman approaching seventy, broke her habit of rising before dawn and going to an outhouse at some distance from her home because she heard the whistle of a giant one morning.

# The Spokane

The Spokane remain residents of their traditional homelands in Washington State. Their language is part of the Salishan. The Spokane word for bigfoot is *Sc'wen'ey'ti*, meaning "Tall Burnt Hair."

*Scweneyti*

Source: *They Walked Among Us–Scweneyti and the Stick Indians of the Colvilles,* by Ed Fusch, 2002, pp. 11-13.

*Scweneyti* [*Chwah-knee-tee*] is a "tall, hairy, smells like burnt hair." He is about nine feet tall and possesses a very strong stench. He never hurts humans, but does like to play tricks on people, like throwing rocks at them. He loves to tease horses and dogs. One day a family heard strange indistinguishable sounds coming from a draw far up in the mountains. The sounds, as of a man crying, drew nearer and echoed and resounded throughout the mountains until they were very close. The dogs were barking hard and suddenly were thrown against the flap of the te-pee. The daughter, the bravest and smartest, went outside and said, "Why are you terrifying us this way? We're already afraid! We know who you are. We know you are Cen. That this is your punishment for the sin you committed, and here on this earth there will be no end to your wanderings, roaming about. Then here you are, here terrifying us, scaring us. It is God's will that you be this way. Go! Turn yourself around and walk away! Get away! Back away from us!"

Suddenly all was quiet. After a little while they heard *Scweneyti's* voice again, but further away. He had left them, no longer bothering them and terrifying them.

## Fish and the *Scweneyti*

Source: *They Walked Among Us–Scweneyti and the Stick Indians of the Colvilles,* by Ed Fusch, 2002, p. 15.

Fish was known to be a favorite food in *Scweneyti's* diet, especially when cooked. With their racks full, the Indians would cook the heads and parts they did not want and leave them out for *Scweneyti*, who would not disturb their fish or camp nor torment their horses or dogs.

## *Scweneyti* is Captured and Bound

Source: *They Walked Among Us–Scweneyti and the Stick Indians of the Colvilles,* by Ed Fusch, 2002, p. 20.

While camped at Keller, Washington during the salmon harvesting season, Grandmother, two of her sisters, and her brothers wives found *Scweneyti* sleeping along a creek. These three sisters and two other women, knowing that when *Scweneyti* sleeps, he sleeps very soundly (he sleeps during the day), drove stakes into the ground all around him, then laced their braided Indian ropes crossed all over him, tying him very securely to the stakes. As he began to awaken they all sat on him, hoping to keep him down. He appeared to pay no attention to them and rose effortlessly, breaking the ropes. The women fell off as he arose and walked away. They had to destroy their clothes because of the stench from their contact with *Scweneyti.*

# The Wenatchee

The Wenatchee lived along the Wenatchee River in Washington. Their traditional language is in the Salishan family. The Wenatchee word for a bigfoot-like creature is *Choanito*, meaning "night people."

### *Choanito*

Source: *They Walked Among Us–Scweneyti and the Stick Indians of the Colvilles,* by Ed Fusch, 2002, p. 37.

In the fall of the year, October, a group of male members of the tribe were on a hunting trip near Wenatchee Lake. One of the men became separated from the rest of the party and was captured by *Choanito*. He was taken to a cave far up in the Rocky Mountains and held captive by a family of *Choanitos* throughout the winter until spring. The odor in the cave was terrible. They would not take him out hunting with them but made him remain in camp near the cave with the women. They were like a different tribe of Indians. In the spring they returned him to the place where they had captured him. Upon returning to his camp he was immediately recognized by the children who couldn't believe that he was back as he had been gone for so long. They thought that he bad been killed. He said that he bad been well treated by *Choanito*.

### *Choanito* and Camas Root

Source: *They Walked Among Us–Scweneyti and the Stick Indians of the Colvilles,* by Ed Fusch, 2002, p. 38.

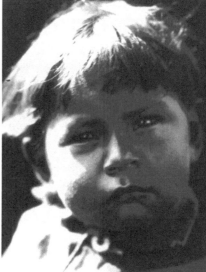

A woman had dug camas roots which they [native women] placed on the roof of their home, located near Nespelem Creek, where animals could not get at them. During the night she heard *Choanito* on the roof. In the morning the camas roots were gone and *Choanito* had put her puppy up on the roof. *Choanito* is still very active in the area. At night lights can be seen moving along the base of a nearby mountain as a pack of them travel along, and many have been reported on Keller Butte. People are always warned to be out of the mountains before dark.

# The Yakama

In prehistoric times, the Yakama inhabited parts of the Columbia Plateau (Idaho, Oregon, and Washington). They now occupy a reservation in south central Washington. In their traditional Penutian language, the Yakama words for a bigfoot-like creature are *Seat ka* and *Ste ye mah* ("Spirit Hidden by Woods"). Because they were also closely related to other tribes, they shared additional names with the Klickitat (*Qah lin me* and *Qui yihahs* ["The Hairy brothers"]); the Puyallup (*Seatco* [Stick Indian]), and the Shasta (*Tah tah kle' ah* ["Owl Woman Monster"]).

**Stick-shower**

Source: *Ghost Voices–Yakima Indian Myths, Legends, Humor, and Hunting Stories,* by Donald M. Hines, 1992. Issaquah: Great Eagle Publishing, Inc., pp. 52-53.

The *Ste-ye-hah' mah* or Stick-shower are a mysterious and dangerous people whose general habitat is the lofty forest regions of the Cascade Mountains. They haunt the tangled timber-falls, which serve them as domiciles, or lodges. They are as large as the ordinary Indian; their language is to mimic notes of birds and animals. Nocturnal in habit, they sleep or remain in seclusion during the day and consequently are seen only on very rare occasions. Under the cover of darkness, they perform the acts which have fastened upon them the odious appellation 'stick-shower.' It is then that they thrust sticks through any opening of the tepee or hunter's lodge, or shower sticks upon the belated traveler. The Indian who is delayed or lost from the trail is very apt to receive their attention. He may hear a signal, perhaps a whistle, ahead of him. Should he follow the sound, it will be repeated for a time. Then he will hear it in the opposite direction, along the path he has just passed. If he turns back, it will only be to detect the mysterious noises elsewhere, leading to utter confusion and bewilderment. When the traveler is crazed with dread, or overcome by exhaustion and sleep; it is then that the Stick-shower scores a victory. Regaining his head, or awakening from slumber, the wanderer is more than likely to find himself stripped of all clothing, perhaps bound and trussed with thongs. He is fortunate to escape with his life.

# Wild Stick-showers

Source: *Ghost Voices–Yakima Indian Myths, Legends, Humor, and Hunting Stories,* by Donald M. Hines, 1992. Issaquah: Great Eagle Publishing, Inc., p. 54.

The wild Stick-showers live in the mountains, in lodges underground. Doors to lodges are heavy, snow and earth. You cannot find them. They have no fire in these lodges. But they dry meat, dry salmon by fire somewhere in the woods where they hide. They dress in bearskins tied up the front with strings. Head of bearskin covers head of Stick-shower, keeps off rain and snow. That bearskin dress is warm, is dry and warm for coldest winter.

The Stick-shower is tall, is slender. He is good runner. He has medicine which gives him swiftness and strength. [Some Indians claim he has medicine that renders him invisible.] They go long distance in one night. Maybe they hunt over on the *n-Che'-wana* [Columbia River] near Dalles early in the night. Next morning, they are over here in Yakama country, all up Yakama River. Stick-showers are good hunters. Nothing can get away from them; nothing can escape them.

When you hunt on Goat Rocks, you have to watch. You have to watch close all the time. You are on a rock; maybe you cannot see around that rock, cannot see on either side. The Stick-shower pushes you off that rock. You fall down, fall far down to death. Some [Indians] get killed that way. To hunt where Stick-shower is, four or five of us go together. Three hunt, walking not far apart. One is here, one down below. One is higher up the mountain. We watch ahead, watch on each side. Fourth is behind. He watches back over the trail. Stick-shower might be following us. Must always watch for the bad Stick-shower.

## Whistling *Ste-ye-hah' mah*

Source: *Ghost Voices–Yakima Indian Myths, Legends, Humor, and Hunting Stories*, by Donald M. Hines, 1992. Issaquah: Great Eagle Publishing, Inc., p. 55.

An Indian, whose house stood by the side of a lagoon beyond which stretched a deep forest, lay on his bed at an open window one evening. He heard a whistling out in the timber. He answered it, supposing that it was someone lost. In turn, he was answered from the trees and at closer range. This was kept up for some time, the voice in the woods often taking the cadence of a bird song or other forest sounds. The Indian began to feel "queer" and "out of his head." Surmising that he was being "fooled with" by the Stick Indians, he closed the window and remained in the house.

## The *Ste-ye-hah'*

Source: *Ghost Voices–Yakima Indian Myths, Legends, Humor, and Hunting Stories*, by Donald M. Hines, 1992. Issaquah: Great Eagle Publishing, Inc., pp. 57-59.

It is the delight of the *Ste-ye-hah'* to carry away captive children who may become lost or separated from their people. Many snows ago two little ones, a brother and a sister, were missing from a hunter-village in the mountains. The parents and friends instituted a wide search and found their trail. Small footprints showed between the imprints of adult tracks, and at various places the children had left bits of their skin clothing along the path. It was readily seen that they had been carried off captive. But by whom? No hostile tribesmen were in that region. The alarmed and fearful people continued their quest and soon came upon undisputable proof that the dreaded *Ste-ye-hah'* had possession of the little ones. Recovery was hopeless, and at a point where the trail disappeared entirely, the pursuit was abandoned.

Long afterwards, perhaps twenty snows, the parents of the lost children were camped in the mountains gathering huckleberries. One night while sitting in their lodge, a stick was thrust through a small crevice in the wall. The old man immediately called out, "You need not come around here bothering me, *Ste-ye-hah'*! I know you! You took my two children, *Hom-chin-nah* and *Whol-te-noo*. We are all alone since you took our children. Go away!"

The *Ste-ye-hah'* withdrew from the side of the tepee. He was the lost boy. When he could not remember his native tongue, he recognized his own name spoken by the old Indian, his father. He lingered about the lodge, all night, fearing to enter. As daylight appeared, he went back to his people and told his sister what he had seen and heard, that their own parents were in the lone lodge at the berry patch. The next night he returned to the lodge, but did not enter nor let his presence be known. The third night he came again with his sister and entered the lodge. He made the old people to understand that they were their lost children, *Hom-chin-nah* and *Whol-te-noo*. It was the bow and arrows of the old man hanging on the lodge pole that had deterred him from entering the previous evenings. The children came often to see their parents, bringing them salmon in abundance. There has never been any salmon in that part of the Cascades, but the *Ste-ye-hah' mah* had this fish in quantity.

The old people went away with their children, who had married and had families of their own. Later, when Indians visited this place, only the empty lodge was to be seen. The parents stayed with the *Ste-ye-hah' mah* for one snow, then returned to the berry patch and rejoined their tribe. Ever since that time, when any of the Indians are in the mountains and hear the Chief of the *Ste-ye-hah' mah* hooting like an owl, calling to his people, they know the mysterious beings are abroad, bent on mischief. They listen. Presently they hear a cry like some bird, or the chattering of a chipmunk near their lodge. It is then that the startled inmates call out, "You need not come bothering around here! I am a relative of *Hoom-chin-nah* and *Whol-te-noo*! This invariably secures that particular lodge from further molestation by the mysterious *Ste-ye-hah*. They will not knowingly annoy the relatives of the two children whom they once captured and who resided with them so many years as members of their tribe.

## The Capture

Source: *Ghost Voices–Yakima Indian Myths, Legends, Humor, and Hunting Stories,* by Donald M. Hines, 1992. Issaquah: Great Eagle Publishing, Inc., p. 60.

Two *Ste-ye-hah'* captured a Yakama man and carried him on their shoulders to their home. One of the captors wanted to take him to his sister, but the other wanted to kill him. At last the friendly *Ste-ye-hah'* slipped the man away and told him to escape to his own land. He said to him, "Hurry away! There is a tall tree on the ridge where you will be overtaken by the darkness. Sleep on the top branches of this tree. The *Ste-ye-hah'* cannot climb the tree after you! The Indian did as instructed, and the pursuing *Ste-ye-hah'* came to the tree early after sundown and were under it all night. The Indian could hear his enemies constantly, but when the dawn came they left, and the man came from his perch and made the rest of his way home before another nightfall.

## The Other Tribe

Source: *Ghost Voices–Yakima Indian Myths, Legends, Humor, and Hunting Stories,* by Donald M. Hines, 1992. Issaquah: Great Eagle Publishing, Inc., p. 60.

There is another tribe of *Ste-ye-hah' mah*; a tall slender race having but one leg. They live far to the North and are seldom seen. They are the deadly enemy of the Cascade *Ste-ye-hah'*, who are mortally afraid of them. They too, are nocturnal and can cover vast stretches of country in a single night. Their mode of locomotion is supposedly long leaps, since the foot impressions appear at a considerable distance apart. Some Indians contend that these beings are possessed of two legs, the same as any other people, and the difference is in the foot alone. Both tracks (impressions) are identical, conforming to the right or the left foot exclusively.

# Spirit costume of the *Ste-ye-hah' mah*

Source: *Ghost Voices–Yakima Indian Myths, Legends, Humor, and Hunting Stories,* by Donald M. Hines, 1992. Issaquah: Great Eagle Publishing, Inc., pp. 146-151.

There was among the Yakamas a young man poverty-stricken and useless to his tribe. His parents and all his relations were dead; he had no home. He traveled from place to place, subsisting on the generosity of friends. If he ate out at one lodge, there were others where he might go. It is the Indian custom to turn away none without first supplying their physical wants. The young man was "The Wanderer" among the tribes.

The Wanderer came up the Yakama River to *Pah'-gy-ti-koot*. There he saw five Indians disputing and contending amongst themselves. They were *Ste-ye-hah' mah*, the Stick-Shower Indians. The Wanderer inquired the cause of their trouble, and one of them said, "You see these clothes, these buckskins? We found them here. We cannot agree how to divide them. This man wants the coat, the shirt. The other man wants the leggings. This man here wants the moccasins, while I want the headdress. That man over there wants the entire suit, we cannot agree."

The Wanderer thought for a moment. He knew that the *Ste-ye-hah' mah* were great runners. They were swifter than any other Indians. He said, "Let me decide this for you! I will help you out."

The *Ste-ye-hah' mah* replied "All right! We will let you manage it for us. You settle it for us."

The Wanderer rejoined, "Yes! I will do this for you, all of you go to *Ow-yah'*. Go to the big greasewood. Line up there for the race. The one who reaches here and puts his hand on the buckskins first gets them. He will have the entire suit."

The *Ste-ye-hah' mah* agreed, "That is good! We will do as you say. You are wiser than we."

The five *Ste-ye-hah' mah* then ran down to the big bush and were instantly coming like the wind. All touched the buckskins at the same time. The young man said, "You will have to go farther in this race. Go down to the trail crossing. Run from there."

The *Ste-ye-hah' mah* hurried to the starting place. It was out of sight, down the plain. They reached there; then they were coming back. The young man watched the dust. The racers burst into view; they came like the deer. Five hands touched the buckskins at the same time. The young man laughed. He had never seen such running among all the tribes. He said, "You must go farther away. Go to *Luts-an-nee'*. Run from there." The *Ste-ye-hah' mah* are tireless. You cannot tire them. They raced to *Luts-an-nee'*. There was the returning dust cloud. They were coming fast, fast as hawks can fly. All five touched the buckskins at the same time. The Wanderer laughed. He was surprised, but he laughed. He said, "Go this time to *Cee-cee*! Run from there. This business must be decided."

It was not long till the *Ste-ye-hah' mah* were at *Cee-cee* where the sand is not firm under foot. Soon the swirling dust cloud was seen. The *Ste-ye-hah' mah* were coming in a bunch. Five reaching hands touched the buckskins at the same time. The Wanderer was serious this time. He spoke, "You have raced four times. None of you have won the buckskins. The fifth time must decide who is to have them. Go to *Pal-lah h-lee'*! Run from there."

The *Ste-ye-hah' mah* were not tired. They hurried across the desert to *Pal-lah h-lee'*. The Wanderer thought, "I will look at these buckskins. They appear good."

The young man examined the buckskins. He found them fine and showy. He thought, "The *Ste-ye-hah' mah* will not be back soon. My own garb is poor. It is about worn out. I will see if these fit me." He tried on the buckskins, leaving his own on the spot where they had been lying. They fit him nicely. He thought, "I think that I would like to have these buckskins. I wish I could get away with them. But no! The *Ste-ye-hah' mah* can run faster than any Indians of all the tribes. They are good trailers. Nothing can hide from them. They would catch me sure. I had better let them alone. I had better replace the buckskins, better not have anything to do with them. The *Ste-ye-hah' mah* want these buckskins badly. Otherwise, they would not race for them as they do."

While thus debating, the Wanderer saw the approaching dust-cloud. It was far down the desert, but coming fast. The five runners were as eagles flying. The young man had decided too late. He could not change the buckskins. Instantly in view, the *Ste-ye-hah' mah* would be upon him, would catch him. Scared, he stood aside from his discarded garb. There was no use trying to run away, no use hiding. The five *Ste-ye-hah' mah* all touched the old buckskins at the same time. Then they saw what had been done. They began to accuse each other for the loss. They said, "You did this. You wanted all the buckskins, all the dress. Now this Indian has stolen all of them. We will get nothing!"

"No! You caused it. You wanted the shirt."

"No! It was you! You wanted the leggings."

"Had you not contended for the headdress, we would now have the entire suit. It was your fault that all are lost."

"Why do you say that? It was you that wanted the moccasins. You would have the moccasins, and now everything is gone."

During this trouble, the Wanderer stood only few steps away. None of the *Ste-ye-hah' mah* seemed to notice him. He wondered why this was, why they did not attack him and take the buckskins. But no! They began to fight among themselves. The young man knew that they would fight until all were dead, killed at the same time. He decided quickly what he would do. He would get away with the suit. It was fine! He began to think what an impression he would make at the village with such buckskins.

So while the *Ste-ye-hah' mah* were fighting to the death, fighting so equally matched that all would die at the same time, the Wanderer left. He went through *Pah'-gy-ti-koot*, traveling north. He reached the village at the mouth of the Naches. A great tribal festival was in progress. He was soon surprised and disappointed that none of his friends paid any attention to him. His fine costume counted for nothing. He was hungry. He went from group to group where they were eating. He stood close to his best friends, stood in front of them. None noticed him. None would look at him; none would speak to him. A woman carrying food would have walked over him had he not stepped aside. He began to think, wondering what was wrong. Maybe his friends did not want him? He went to different lodges. It was the same everywhere. Nobody noticed him. Then he remembered the *Ste-ye-hah' mah* had done the same thing, had not noticed him. Might it be the buckskins he was wearing? He would test it out.

Procuring some old buckskins, he went to the river. There under the bank, he changed his costume. He hid his new buckskins and went back to the village. Immediately some of his friends called to him, "Come and eat! You have been gone. For a long time we do not see you. Tell us what you know, what you have seen, what you have heard."

Yes! It must be the buckskins. Some great power was in them. He sat down to the feast. He talked of his travels among different tribes. He went to another group of feasters. As he approached, they called, "You here? When did you come? We are glad! Come eat."

It was so everywhere he went. He now understood that it was his *Ste-ye-hah'* costume. That was the mystery. The buckskins must be a spirit suit, invisible. But he held the secret from his friends, from all the people.

# THE
# SOUTHEAST
# CULTURE

# Southeast Cultural Area

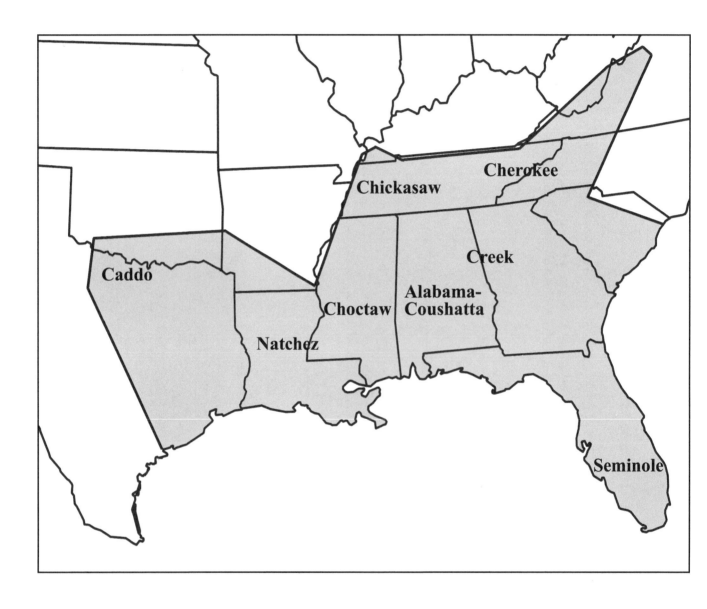

# The Alabama-Coushatta

Although originally located in Alabama, Mississippi and Georgia, due to forced relocation in the 1800s, most Alabama-Coushatta live in Texas today. In their traditional language, which is part of the Muskogean language stock, bigfoot is known as *Eeyachuba* or wild man.

## Outwitting the Cannibals

Source: *Myths and Folktales of the Alabama-Coushatta Indians of Texas,* by Howard Martin, 1977. Austin: The Encino Press, pp. 44-45.

Once there were six brothers living near the edge of a village. Each day five of the brothers would go hunting, while the sixth stayed home to do the cooking. None of them liked to miss a chance to go hunting, so they took turns cooking.

One day the youngest brother was serving as cook. While he was washing some potatoes in a creek, he lost his balance and fell into the water. As he struggled beneath the surface of the creek, his hand touched a piece of wood. He carried the piece of wood to the bank of the creek, where he found that the wood was really a baby-board. And fastened to the board was a tiny little girl, still alive!

When the other brothers returned from their hunting trip, they all looked at the baby girl and felt sorry for her. Since no one came around asking about her, the brothers decided to keep the little girl with them. As she grew older, she learned to do all the cooking and housework, so all six of the brothers could go hunting at the same time.

While the brothers were out hunting one day, a strange person slipped into the house, killed the girl housekeeper, and paddled away in a canoe. The girl returned to life, however, and later told the brothers what had happened.

On the following day the men pretended to go hunting again. This time they doubled back on their trail and hid near their house.

As the brothers had expected, the stranger came back to the house. On a certain signal, the six brothers started shooting arrows into the stranger, who died instantly.

One of the brothers pushed the visitor's canoe into the creek, and it went down the stream until presently it began circling in one spot. This seemed unusual to the brothers, so one of them left to make an investigation–but he did not come back. Another soon followed–and he, too did not return. A third went and did not return. Likewise, the fourth and fifth started out and failed to return.

Finally, the sixth departed to look for his brothers. At dinner time on the first day, he climbed into a persimmon tree and ate some of the fruit. While he was eating the persimmons, a female cannibal came under the tree carrying a basket and a club. When she looked up and saw the man, she said, "The other men who climbed that tree wrestled with me. Get down and let's wrestle."

After the cannibal had laid the basket and the club on the ground, the hunter climbed down and began wrestling with her. Quickly she threw him down, but he got up immediately. This happened several times. Presently, she threw him down near her club, whereupon he seized the club and killed her.

He cut off her head with a hatchet, but the cannibal's head reunited with her body. He cut the head off again, and again the head went back onto the body. But the third time he cut off the head it remained severed.

When the cannibal was dead, the young hunter cut her to pieces and threw the parts away. He took her heart and hit a tree with it. "Stick there and become tree fungus," he said. He hung the intestines on a tree, and from that day they have been clinging to trees in the shape of long blue vines. After he put the woman's nose and her club in the basket, he set out along the path from which the cannibal had come.

Presently he approached some girls who were pounding corn with a pestle. When they saw the nose in the basket, they said, "That's looks like our grandmother's nose.

"No," he explained, "it is a pipe which *Aba Mikko* sent me." And they said of the club. "This is like our grandmother's club." But he said, "No, *Aba Mikko* sent it to me. It is to tickle people. If you will lie down in a straight line, I will show you how it works." Accordingly, they all lay down, and he cut their throats.

A little later he asked a small boy where the cannibals threw the bones of people they had eaten. "In that direction," the boy answered, pointing to a large tree. Beneath this tree the young man found many bones. Among them were his brothers.

As he shot an arrow over one pile of bones, he said, "Look out! The arrow will stick into you." When he spoke these words, the dead brother awoke and sat up. Then the youngest brother shot an arrow over each of his other brothers until all had come to life.

"Don't look behind," he said to them. But, as they went along, one of them looked back, turned into a wildcat, and ran away growling. Another looked back, turned into a panther, and went off howling. The third looked back and turned into an alligator. In the same manner the fourth changed into an owl. Likewise, the fifth became a chicken hawk and flew away. The sixth brother returned home alone.

# The Caddo

In prehistoric times, the Caddo occupied areas of Arkansas, Louisiana, Texas, and Oklahoma. In the 1800s, the tribe was forcibly removed to a reservation in Oklahoma where the majority of Caddo live today. In their native language, Caddoan, giants are called *Ha'yacatsi*.

### Ten Brothers and the Cannibals

Source: *Texas Indian Myths and Legends,* by Jane Archer, 2000. Maryland: Republic of Texas Press, pp. 21-23.

Grandmother kept a safe and warm home for her ten grandsons. She told them stories around the fire at night, and they played during the day. They also farmed and hunted, providing plenty of food for the family.

One day the oldest brother went out to hunt, but he did not return. Grandmother worried about him, so the next day another brother went in search of him. He did not return either. Grandmother worried even more, so another brother went to find the first two boys. And so it went until the ninth brother failed to return.

Grandmother and the youngest boy waited and waited. With deep sadness in their hearts, they continued to work but they no longer played. They hoped to hear something about the other nine, but no word came to them. They grew sadder every day.

"I can wait no longer," the youngest boy said. "I must find my lost brothers."

"Oh no," Grandmother said. "You are all I have left. What if you never return? I will die of heartbreak."

"But they may await rescue."

"I fear whatever evil happened to them will happen to you."

"I must take a chance."

"You are too young to go alone into the woods."

"They are too old to be lost. I will find them."

He hugged Grandmother close, then prepared to go.

She packed food for him. He prayed for guidance. As he left home, he stuck an eagle feather in his hair, hoping it held hidden power to help him.

After walking a long time and far away, he saw a tepee in the distance. He crept near it and heard people talking inside.

"Another comes," a man said. "Cook some corn for we will soon have meat."

The boy understood what the man meant, but he was so sad, tired, and hungry that he no longer cared if he lived or died. He walked right up to the tepee.

219

A man wearing a facemask with a sharp iron nose came outside. "You look thin. Did you travel far?"

"Yes"

"Are you looking for your nine brothers?"

"Yes."

"I know where your brothers are now. I will even set you on the right trail to find them. First you must work for me. Will you do that?"

"Yes."

"See that big log over there?"

"Yes."

"Pick it up and put it on the fire."

The boy did not want to do anything the man suggested, but he thought maybe some power would help him.

"I will give you four chances. If you cannot lift the log, you must lay down on it and let me lift it."

The boy trusted nothing he heard, but he prayed for help to rescue his brothers. He tried to lift the log four times, straining and groaning and heaving, but he was not strong enough to move it.

"Now you must lay down and let me move it," the man said.

Reluctantly the boy kept his word.

As the man lowered his face to spear the boy with the iron nose of the mask, an unseen power jerked the boy off the log. The iron nose caught in the log and held the man so he could not get free.

"Boy, run into the tepee and take the corn powder away from the woman in there," a voice on the wind said. "Kill her, then bring it here and beat this man to death."

The boy jumped to his feet and followed the instructions exactly. When the man lay dead at his feet, he listened for the voice again.

"Go back inside the tepee. There you will find the bones of your brothers." A young man appeared beside the boy. "I will help you gather them."

Soon they carried the bones outside, and the young man sorted them into nine piles.

"Now put your buffalo robe over them," the young man said. "After that, shoot an arrow up into the sky and cry, 'Look out, brothers, the arrow will hit you!'"

Again the boy followed the instructions exactly, and his brothers jumped out from under the robe.

"Now burn the tepee with the man and woman inside it, then scatter the ashes," the young man said.

The ten brothers quickly finished the task.

"I am the Sun. I helped you destroy the cannibals. Now return to your grandmother." The young man disappeared in a flash of golden light.

The brothers hurried home. Grandmother greeted them with tears of joy. That night beside the fire they told her their story. "The Sun took pity and helped me," the youngest boy finished.

Thereafter the people knew the Sun was their friend and would always help them in times of trouble.

*Note: "Iron nose" is likely a mistranslation of shape features.*

# Death of a Cannibal

Source: *Texas Indian Myths and Legends,* by Jane Archer, 2000. Maryland: Republic of Texas Press, pp. 24-26.

One day at Tall-timber-on-top-of-the-Hill the people agreed to move to another village. As they packed, a woman whose husband had died gave birth to their child. She could not travel on such a long journey with her new baby. The people could not wait for her. They left her to follow when she regained her strength.

For many days she stayed alone with her baby in the village. She longed to be with her people. She shivered in fear at animal cries in the night. She grew more anxious to be gone with each setting of the sun.

One night she sat in her grass lodge rocking her baby in her arms. Flames from a warm fire cast menacing shadows on the walls. She listened for danger.

"Let me come inside," a man called from outside the lodge. She shivered in fright. "Did my people send you?"

"No. You may trust me because I often stay near their village at night."

She felt so lonely that she overcame her fear. "Come inside."

A tall stranger entered the lodge and sat down across the fire from her. "I am Spotted Wolf. I feel concerned for the safety of you and your child.

"Do not worry for us."

"You must not start your journey too soon. Many dangerous animal lurk in the woods."

"I hear them at night, but I must go to my people soon."

"Your life is in danger if you go now."

"I dare not wait much longer."

He handed her a leather pouch. "If trouble finds you, toss a pinch of this tobacco to the four directions, then call me. I will help you."

"Thank you." She watched him leave, clutching the tobacco pouch to her baby.

Several days later she placed her baby in a cradle board on her back, then started on her journey. At dusk on the third day, a strange being blocked her path. As she walked closer, she could not decide if it were man or beast.

The stranger fell to the ground, rolled over twice, and arose as an animal. She closed her eyes and shook her head to make sure she saw correctly. When she looked again, the animal was a person.

Now she knew great fear, for the creature must surely be a cannibal. They appeared as humans, then they turned into wild beasts and ate people. She could not move for her fear, sure that she and her baby would be eaten. The cannibal growled and then stalked toward her.

She remembered Spotted-Wolf. She pulled out the pouch he gave her, then she tossed a pinch of tobacco to the south, the west, the north, and the east. "Spotted Wolf, please help me and my baby." She repeated her request four times. A wolf howled in the south, another in the west, one in the north, and finally in the east. She sighed in relief. The cannibal looked around in fright, growls tapering to a whine.

The wolf from the south escorted the woman and her baby safely to her new village, then disappeared back into the woods.

# How the Cannibal Was Destroyed

Source: Unknown.

In the beginning of this world there lived many kinds of fierce animals. Among these animals was one especially that was called by the people living in those times, the cannibal.

One time there were three men who went out hunting. They went a long way from home and kept on going farther and farther in search of game. One day they came to a country timbered with many large trees. They came to one of these trees and saw that something had been climbing on the tree, and near the base there was a large hole. The men thought that a bear must have made the hole, and that the bear was in the hole. They gathered dry leaves and grass and made it up into a small bundle, and they set the bundle on fire and tied it to the end of a long pole and thrust the burning bundle into the hole. They kept on dropping bundles into the hole until they thought it about time the bear should come out. One of the bundles which was put into the hole dropped out from the hole, and then they knew that the bear was coming out. Finally some strange animal came and peeped out from the hole, and it was not a bear, but a hairy cannibal.

As soon as they saw and knew what kind of animal it was, they ran. The smoke cleared away and the cannibal came down from the tree and smelled around until he scented the tracks of the men, and then he began to follow them. These men were on foot and the cannibal was very swift, and so it was not long until he overtook one of the men and killed him. Then the animal took the man back to the woods, to the large tree, and went back after the other two men. After running a long way he overtook the second man. He killed him and carried him back and placed him by the side of the first man. Then he returned for the third man. When the third man was almost overtaken, and was running with all his might, he saw something flat on the ground in front of him, but he did not stop. He saw that it was a mountain-lion, lying there watching and waiting for the approaching cannibal. The man ran on a way, then turned around and looked back to see what the mountain-lion would do. The cannibal did not see the mountain-lion lying there, and before he knew anything the mountain-lion jumped upon him and seized him by the throat. Finally the cannibal was overpowered and killed, and then the man started on for his home. When he got home he told his people what had happened to the other two men. When they all heard this they started down where he last saw the cannibal, and when they got to the place they found nothing but many white and black wolves, which had already eaten the body, and there was nothing left but the bones of the cannibal. The men went on to the tree where the cannibal had lived. The tree was not burning, and so the men began to cut the tree down, and when it fell they found two bodies. They took the bodies out from the tree and buried them a short distance away.

## The Death of the Cannibals

Source: Unknown.

There is another kind of cannibal, though not so dangerous as the one who first appears as a human being, then turns to an animal. These cannibals live as human beings and eat people only after they are dead. Whenever they hear of any one who is sick and about to die they pretend to be sick, too, and when they hear that the sick person is dead, they pretend to die, too, and are buried; but in the night they jump out of their graves and steal the dead person before the spirits can take him away.

## Slaying the Monsters by Fire

Source: Unknown.

In the beginning of the world there were animals that lived with human beings and were kind and friendly, but there were other animals that were very strong and dangerous. At that time, when the earth was new, the grass was taller than the highest trees are now, and many wild animals prowled through the high grass, and that was the reason why the world was so very dangerous. One time the people met in council to make plans to kill all the dangerous animals in the world, and Morning Star, who was one of the head men in the council, arose and said: "There is only one way to kill these animals and that is to burn the grass all over the world. I know how large the world is and what a big task we have, but we must do it."

As every one was willing to try Morning Star's plan, he told a man who was present at the council that most of the work would fall to him, but that he would appoint two men to help him carry out the work. The man's name was Fire, and the first man appointed to help Fire was the fastest runner in the world, and his name was Black Snake; the second man was the slowest in the world, and his name was Skunk. Fire took hold of Black Snake's tail and put fire on the end of it, and then took hold of Skunk's hind foot and placed fire between his toes. They both started out at the same time, the one going to the north, the other around to the south, so as to meet somewhere in the west, since they started in the east. While these two were on their way the people decided to make a long rope out of soapweeds that would reach up to the sky. Everybody helped make the rope, and as they worked Pigeon would go up into the blue sky to see how near the fire had approached. After a time the people could see that the sky was getting very dark on account of the smoke from the fire, and so they worked hard and fast to get their rope long enough. Finally they had the rope finished, and they appointed Crow to take it up to the sky. Crow took the rope and flew and flew until he was out of sight, and it was a long time before he returned, but when he came he assured the people that he had the rope firmly fastened to the sky. The fire was approaching rapidly, and so the people began climbing up the rope. After the people had climbed up, all kinds of animals came and began to get hold of the rope, and all the bad animals came, and then the rope began to move upward. After the people were high up they sent a man down the rope as far as the first bad animal. This man's name was Bat, and because he had very sharp teeth he was sent to cut the rope. The animals saw him chewing something and asked him

what he was eating. Bat said that his grandmother had parched some corn for him and that he was eating it. He kept on cutting the rope, and finally it broke and let the bad animals fall down. When the animals dropped down to the ground Bat followed them down to see what would become of them. He saw a large hairy monster and heard it call all the other animals to enter his body through his nose, ears, and mouth. These animals went in, and so large was he, that he had room inside for all the bad animals. After all the others were in, Bat slipped in and began to pull out some hair from the hairy monster's nose. That made him sneeze, and he sneezed so hard that he threw all the other animals out through his nose. The animals were scattered every place and burned, for the fire was upon them.

Bat flew up where the people were, but he was scorched a little before he could get there, and that is the reason bats are yellowish in color. After the bad animals had all been burned the people returned to the world again, and ever since the world has been a good place to live upon.

# The Cherokee

When first contacted by Europeans, the Cherokee were a large tribe spread throughout most of the eastern and southeastern United States. Forced removal of over 20,000 people, known as the Trail of Tears, relocated the Cherokee to Oklahoma. The two federal recognized tribes are in Oklahoma and North Carolina, but there are smaller communities in Georgia, Kentucky, Missouri, Alabama, Arkansas, and Tennessee. As part of the Iroquoian language stock, the traditional Cherokee names for a big-foot-like creature are *Kecleh-Kudleh* (hairy savage) and *Nun' Yunu' Wi* (stone man).

## The Snake with the Big Feet

Source: Unknown.

Long ago, in that far-off happy time when the world was new, and there were no white people at all, only Indians and animals, there was a snake that was different from other snakes. He had feet–*big feet*. And the other snakes, because he was different, hated him, and made life wretched for him. Finally, they drove him away from the country where the snakes lived, saying, "A good long way from here live other ugly creatures with feet like yours. Go and live with them!" And the poor, unhappy Snake had to go away.

For days and days, he traveled. The weather grew cold and food became hard to find. At last, exhausted, his feet cut and frostbitten, he lay down on the bank of the river to die.

The Deer, *E-se-ko-to-ye*, looked out of a willow thicket, and saw the Snake lying on the riverbank. Pitying him, the deer took the Snake into his into his own lodge and gave him food and medicine for his bleeding feet.

The Deer told the Snake that there were indeed creatures with feet like his who would befriend him, but that some among these would be enemies whom it would be necessary to kill before he could reach safety.

He showed the Snake how to make a shelter for protection from the cold and taught him how to make moccasins of deerskin to protect his feet. And at dawn the Snake continued his journey.

The sun was far down the western sky, and it was bitter cold when the Snake made camp the next night. As he gathered boughs for a shelter, *Kais-kap*, the porcupine appeared. Shivering, the Porcupine asked him, "Will you give me shelter in your lodge for the night?"

The Snake said, "It's very little that I have, but you are welcome to share it."

"I am grateful," said *Kais-kap*, "and perhaps I can do something for you.

Those are beautiful moccasins, brother, but they do not match your skin. Take some of my quills, and make a pattern on them, for good luck." So they worked a pattern on the moccasins with the porcupine quills, and the Snake went on his way again.

As the Deer had told him, he met enemies. Three times he was challenged by hostile Indians, and three times he killed his adversary.

At last he met an Indian who greeted him in a friendly manner. The Snake had no gifts for this kindly chief, so he gave him the moccasins. And that, so the old Ones say, was how our people first learned to make moccasins of deerskin, and to ornament them with porcupine quills in patterns, like those on the back of a snake. And from that day on the Snake lived in the lodge of the chief, counting his coup of scalps with the warriors by the Council fire and, for a long time, was happy.

But the chief had a daughter who was beautiful and kind, and the Snake came to love her very much indeed. He wished that he were human, so that he might marry the maiden, and have his own lodge. He knew there was no hope of this unless the High Gods, the Above Spirits took pity on him, and would perform a miracle on his behalf.

So he fasted and prayed for many, many days. But all his fasting and praying had no result, and at last the Snake came very ill.

Now, in the tribe, there was a very highly skilled Medicine Man. *Mo'ki-ya* was an old man, so old that he had seen and known, and understood, everything that came within the compass of his people's lives, and many things that concerned the Spirits. Many times, his lodge was seen to sway with the Ghost Wind, and the voices of those long gone on to the Sand Hills spoke to him.

*Mo'ki-ya* came to where the Snake lay in the chief's lodge, and sending all the others away, asked the Snake what his trouble was.

"It is beyond even your magic," said the Snake, but he told *Mo'ki-ya* about his love for the maiden, and his desire to become a man so that he could marry her.

*Mo'ki-ya* sat quietly thinking for a while. Then he said, "I shall go on a journey, brother. Perhaps my magic can help, perhaps not. We shall see when I return." And he gathered his medicine bundles and disappeared.

It was a long and fearsome journey that *Mo'ki-ya* made. He went to the shores of a great lake. He climbed a high mountain, and he took the matter to *Nato'se*, the Sun himself.

And *Nato'se* listened, for this man stood high in the regard of the spirits, and his medicine was good. He did not ask, and never had asked, for anything for himself, and to transform the Snake into a brave of the tribe was not a difficult task for the High Gods. The third day after the arrival of *Mo'ki-ya* at the Sun's abode, *Nato'se* said to him, "Return to your own lodge *Mo'ki-ya*, and build a fire of small sticks. Put many handfuls of sweet-grass on the fire, and when the smoke rises thickly, lay the body of the Snake in the middle of it."

And *Mo'ki-ya* came back to his own land.

The fire was built in the center of the Medicine lodge, as the Sun had directed, and when the sweetgrass smoldered among the embers, sending the smoke rolling in great billows through the tepee, *Mo'ki-ya* gently lifted the Snake, now very nearly dead, and placed him in the fire so that the smoke hid him.

The Medicine-drum whispered softly in the dusk of the lodge: the chant of the old men grew a little louder, and then the smoke obscuring the fire parted like a curtain, and a young man stepped out.

Great were the rejoicings in the camp that night. The Snake, now a hand-

some young brave, was welcomed into the tribe with the ceremonies befitting the reception of one shown to be high in the favors of the spirits. The chief gladly gave him his daughter, happy to have a son law-in-law of such distinction.

Many brave sons and beautiful daughters blessed the lodge of the Snake and at last, so the Old ones say, his family became a new tribe, the *Pe-sik-na-ta-pe*, or Snake Indians.

## The Mountain Giant

Source: *Lodge Stories,* by Edward W. Dolch and Marguerite P. Dolch, 1957. Illinois: Garrard Publishing Company, pp. 129-136.

One time there was an old woman who had a beautiful daughter. But the daughter had not married. For every time a young man came to see the daughter, the old woman would say,

"Daughter, Daughter. Marry no one but a great hunter."

But there was not a hunter in the village that pleased the old woman.

One night the daughter was sleeping in a little house outside the Lodge. She heard someone at the door.

"Who is there?" called the girl, for it was night and she could see no one.

"I have come to ask you to marry me," said a big man who was outside the door.

"You must be a great hunter or my mother will not let me marry you."

"In the morning," said the big man, "you will find a deer outside your door. Take the deer to your mother and tell her that I wish to marry you."

In the morning the girl found a deer outside the door. She took it to her mother and they had deer meat to eat.

The old woman was very pleased, but she said to her daughter,

"How do you know this man is a great hunter."

"I think he is very big," said the daughter, "and I like him very much."

That night the girl went to the little house outside the Lodge. But she did not go to sleep. Soon she heard someone at the door of the little house.

"Who is there?" called the girl.

"Did your mother say that I could marry you?" asked the big man at the door.

"How do I know that you are a great hunter?" asked the girl.

In the morning the girl found two deer outside the door. She took them to her mother and they had deer meat to eat. And the old woman said that the daughter could marry the big man that was such a great hunter.

Now the big man came only in the nighttime to see his wife.

One day the old woman said to her daughter, "Where is your husband? I want to see your husband."

That night the girl said to her husband, "My mother wishes to see you."

"Call your mother. I will stay until the sun comes up so that she can see me. But when she has seen me, if she says anything at all I will go away to the mountains and I will not come back."

The girl called her mother. The old woman came and looked into the little house outside the Lodge.

"OH! OH! OH!" cried the old woman. "I see the Mountain Giant. I see the Mountain Giant."

"Remember what I have told you," said the husband to the girl, "your mother could see me. But if she said anything after she had seen me, I would go away to the mountains and I would not come back."

And the Mountain Giant who was the greatest hunter of all times said goodbye to his wife and went back to the mountains. The wife of the Mountain Giant cried and cried for she wanted her husband to come back to her. Her mother cried too, for there was no more deer meat to eat.

## The Town Lodge in the Mountains

Source: *Lodge Stories,* by Edward W. Dolch and Marguerite P. Dolch, 1957. Illinois: Garrard Publishing Company, pp. 137-144.

The Mountain Giant had gone back to the mountains because his wife's mother had seen him and had told what she had seen. The wife and the mother were left alone.

The wife of the Mountain Giant had a little baby. The old woman was not good to the little baby. There was not much food to eat and the old woman wanted it all for herself. She did not want to give her daughter and the baby any of the food.

One night the young mother was sitting in the little house outside the Lodge. The baby was crying, for it was hungry. The young mother heard someone at the door.

"Who is there?" called the young mother.

"The old grandmother is not good to my wife and my child," said the Mountain Giant. "I have come to take them back to the mountains."

And now the old woman had no one to live with her, for her son was married and lived in another village.

One day the old woman's son said to his wife, "I must go and see my mother. I have heard that my sister is married to a great hunter and I want to meet him."

But when the son came to his mother's Lodge, he found the old woman crying, "I want my daughter to come back. I want my daughter to come back."

The old woman told her son that his sister was married to the Mountain Giant, who was the greatest hunter of all times, but the Mountain Giant had taken his wife and baby back to the mountains. Then the son said,

"Let us go to the mountains and ask the Mountain Giant to let my sister come back to your Lodge and live with you."

The old woman and her son went to the mountains. They went on and on for many moons. At last they came to a big Town Lodge in the mountains.

In the Square before the Town Lodge many people were dancing. The old woman and her son saw the wife of the Mountain Giant dancing in the Square with the people.

"My sister! My sister! Your Mother and your brother are here. Come and talk with us."

The wife of the Mountain Giant came and talked to her mother and to her brother. She was very glad to see them.

"We have come to talk to your husband," said the brother. "I want to ask your husband if he will let you come back and live in the Lodge of your mother."

Then a great wind blew in the mountains. The Mountain Giant called to his wife.

"Tell your mother and your brother that if they will eat no food for seven days, I will talk to them."

The wife of the Mountain Giant went into the Town Lodge to look after her baby. And then the old woman and her son sat on the side of the mountain and waited. They were very hungry. But they ate no food.

At last the old woman's son said, "Mother, I am cold and I am hungry. I think that I will die if I do not have something to eat. Look, the sun is almost coming up and this will be the seventh day. I am going to eat some food out of my food bag."

So the brother ate some food out of his food bag. Then he heard the thunder in the mountains. The Mountain Giant spoke in the thunder.

"Go back to your Lodge, for you shall never talk to the Mountain Giant again. My wife and my child shall stay with me in the mountains."

The Town Lodge in the mountains was gone. The Square and all the people were gone. And no one ever saw them again.

# The Chickasaw

Forcibly relocated to Oklahoma in the 1800s, the Chickasaw were once a large tribe spread throughout Mississippi. Their language is in the Muskogean family and is very closely related to the Choctaw. Their traditional word, *Lofa,* means "smelly, hairy being that could speak."

### Wiley and the Hairy Man

Source: Unknown.

Wiley's mama knew all about things that were magic, like the Hairy Man in the forest.

"The Hairy Man got your daddy, and if you're not careful, Wiley, he'll get you too!" Wiley's mama often warned.

"I'll be careful," Wiley promised every time.

Wiley had never once so much as caught a sniff of the Hairy Man. All the same, he felt better if he had his two dogs with him when he went into the forest.

One day, Wiley was chopping wood when a pig ran squealing by and his dogs raced after it. No sooner had they disappeared among the trees than something huge and hairy with sharp, pointy teeth came lumbering toward Wiley. It was the Hairy Man! Wiley saw that the Hairy Man had cow hoofs and couldn't climb, so he shot up a tree as fast as a squirrel.

The Hairy Man stood underneath the branches and grinned a razor-sharp grin at Wiley.

"Come down and I'll show you some magic," he said.

"My mama's warned me all about you," yelled Wiley, "and I'm not going to fall for that old trick! "

The Hairy Man stopped grinning. He picked up the ax that Wiley had dropped and began to hack away at the tree trunk. Soon the tree would come toppling down.

"Wait a minute, Mr. Hairy Man!" cried Wiley, thinking fast. "Let me say a short prayer before you eat me up."

"Very well," frowned the Hairy Man, leaning on the ax.

"*Hoooo-eeeeee*!" called Wiley at the top of his voice, and his two dogs came racing out from the trees, barking and snapping at the Hairy Man.

"Yikes!" gulped the Hairy Man, and he hurried away.

From that day on, the Hairy Man was determined to catch Wiley. He waited and waited until one day he saw Wiley in the forest without his two dogs. The Hairy Man sprang out of the bushes in front of Wiley. He waggled his hairy eyebrows at the boy and licked his hairy lips.

"Good afternoon, Mr. Hairy Man," said Wiley. "I'm glad I've bumped into you again. I've been thinking about what you said and I want to ask you something."

"Huh?" the Hairy Man shrugged, taken aback.

"You say you can do magic," continued Wiley. "So can you make things disappear–like all the rope in the area, for instance?"

"Of course," said the Hairy Man, scrunching up his eyes tightly, then opening them again. "There–it's done!"

"Oh good!" cried Wiley. "My dogs were tied up, but now they'll be free. *Hoooo-eeeeee!*"

"Yikes!" yelped the Hairy Man, fleeing into the forest.

Wiley's mama was very proud of her clever son and she was excited too. She knew that if you could trick a monster three times, he'd have to leave you alone forever.

The next day the Hairy Man came to Wiley's house.

"Where's Wiley?" he bellowed, bashing down the door.

"If I give you my baby, do you promise to leave us alone forever?" demanded Wiley's mama.

"Ummm... yes," nodded the Hairy Man.

"Then take him," she said, pointing to Wiley's bed.

The Hairy Man's eyes lit up. He pulled back the sheets and grabbed–not Wiley, but a squirming piglet!

"This isn't your baby!" the Hairy Man growled.

"Oh yes it is!" laughed Wiley's mama. "I owned the piglet's mother and I own him too–only now he's yours!"

As the Hairy Man howled with fury, Wiley crawled out from his hiding place under the sofa.

"That's the third time we've tricked you, Hairy Man!" he grinned. "So now you have to leave us alone forever. *Hoooo-eeeeee!*"

"Yikes!" cried the Hairy Man, and Wiley's two dogs chased him all the way back to the forest.

### The Wildcat Clan

Source: *The 44th Annual Report of the Bureau of American Ethnology*, by John R. Swanton, 1926.

This clan differs from other clans principally in what its members eat. They seldom go out in the daytime but roam about at night in search of food. They do not, however, try to steal.

They are swift of foot and when an accident happens to them they depend on their swiftness to escape. They care very little about women, but when they want anything they generally get it. They think more of their feet than of any other parts of their bodies and their eyes are so keen that they can see anyone before he detects them.

When one of them wants a wife he gets his parents to obtain one. They do not select any kind of woman but are careful in choosing. The younger always get a woman first. These generally sleep in the daytime. If they do not have good luck at night their rest is disturbed but if they have good luck they sleep through most of the day.

Once a number of men belonging to this clan went hunting and camped a

considerable distance from home. Afterward they scattered to see what they could find but remained within call of one another, having made an agreement that if anything happened to one of them he should shout for help. But one of them ventured farther than he was aware and got a long distance off. Presently he got tired and sat down to rest, but while he was there a *lofa* [means skinner] came along. The being was thought to have long hair like an animal. The *lofa* came up and said: "What are you doing here? You are intruding upon my land and had better get up and return to your own place."

But the Indian believed himself to be strong enough for any situation, so he sat still without speaking. Presently the *lofa* ordered him off again and added, "If you do not get up and go away I will tie you up and carry you to my place."

"You may do so if you can," the man replied, and upon this the *lofa* seized him.

At first it seemed as if the man were the stronger of the two and he was able to throw the *lofa* down, but the latter smelled so bad that it was too much for his antagonist, and the *lofa* overcame him, hung him up in a tree and went away.

The man hung there all night, and when he did not make his appearance at camp the other hunters began a search for him and, when they found him, cut the grapevine by which he was fastened so that he fell to the ground. They asked him what had treated him in this manner but he would not speak and they thought he might have seen a ghost or something of that sort. Some time later, however, he came to himself and related what had happened. Afterwards, though he was very fond of hunting and knew that he would be successful, he would not venture out unless someone was with him.

# The Choctaw

Originally from Mississippi, Alabama, and Louisiana, the Choctaw were forcibly removed to Mississippi and Oklahoma in the 1800s. Their language is part of the Muskogean stock and very closely related to Chickasaw. Their traditional names for a bigfoot are *Kashehotapalo* (cannibal man), *Nalusa Falaya* (big giant) and *Shampe* (giant monster).

## *Shampe*

Source: Unknown.

All of the evil spirits of the Choctaws have followed them on their long journey from the western part of North America. The witches, demons, and the monsters came with the Choctaw people.

But the most horrible frightening of all these beasts is the hideous monster the Choctaws call the *Shampe*.

A *Shampe* is a giant in the form of the ugliest Choctaw beast.

He lives in the deepest part of the woods. So far in the forest that no Choctaw has even been able to find the location of his huge, dark cave. The *Shampe* cannot stand the brightness of the sun or the open air.

The smell of blood will attract him and he will follow the person who has been hunting and carrying a wounded game. *Shampes* do not have very good vision but have a keen sense of smell. They can track any person or animal.

The *Shampe* makes a whistling noise as he stalks through the forest. His scent is so terrible, that many people have died from his odor. While he looks like a gigantic form of Choctaw, he smells like a skunk. Some of them are really hairy like an ape while others are hairless. The Choctaws won't live in an area where a *Shampe* will live or has been spotted. The Choctaws will often be caught or chased by a *Shampe*. If someone were to drop a small game such as a rabbit or a squirrel, the *Shampe* stops to eat it and may be drawn off your trail by the blood of the small animal.

*Shampes* have followed the Choctaw people along their journey from the western United States. They say that all *Shampe* have returned to the west now. But today, some Choctaws still hear whistling sounds in the woods and catch a strong odor. The Choctaws still drop small animals when they think a *Shampe* is near. You may never know that all *Shampes* have returned to the west.

# Little-Man-With-Hair-All-Over

Source: Unknown.

Little-Man was hairier than a skunk. Hair grew out of his nose and nostrils. He had thick, matted hair between his buttocks. He was not particularly good-looking and he smelled as if he didn't wash often, but he was a merry fellow who laughed a lot, and he never had any trouble finding pretty girls to share his blanket. He was always on the move, eager to discover new things.

Little-Man-with-Hair-All-Over was small, but he succeeded in everything he did. He was tough in a fight, so they called for him whenever there was something dangerous to do. When a bear monster went on a rampage, ripping up lodges with his huge claws and eating the people inside, Little-Man-with-Hair-All-Over had no trouble killing it. For this his grateful people gave him a magic knife.

One time when Little-Man was traveling, he met two brothers and asked what they were up to. "We're looking for adventure," they answered.

"That's exactly what I'm doing. Let's join up and travel together," said Little-Man. "What do they call you?"

"My name is Smoking Mountain," said one. "I'm the oldest. This one here is Broken War Club."

The three wandered on together and after a while came to a fine, large lodge with plenty of buffalo robes lying around. Outside there were racks with jerk meat, and someone had left a large cooking kettle. But the lodge was deserted; there was no trace of any human beings.

"I like this place," said Little-Man. "Let's stay a while."

"Somebody must own it," said Smoking Mountain.

"Well," said Little-Man, "if someone comes and claims it, I won't mind; and if nobody shows up I won't mind either." So they stayed.

Little-Man said to Smoking Mountain: "Let's go hunting. Broken War Club can stay and cook some of that jerk meat for supper." So the two of them took their bows and arrows and went.

But when the hunters came back to camp, there was no supper.

Broken War Club was lying under a buffalo robe moaning and groaning.

"What's the matter with you?" asked Little-Man. "You look as if you've been in a fight."

"I'm too embarrassed to tell," answered Broken War Club.

"Suit yourself," said Little-Man, and they ate some cold jerk meat. The next day Little-Man-with-Hair-All-Over said to Broken War Club: "Let's go out and hunt. Smoking Mountain can stay here and cook." But when the two came back, they found Smoking Mountain also laying under a buffalo robe moaning and groaning.

"What happened to you, friend?" asked Little-Man. "You look as if you've been in a fight."

"I'm too ashamed to tell," answered Smoking Mountain.

"You two are some fine cooks!" remarked Little-Man. Again they ate their jerk meat cold.

The next morning Little-Man told the brothers: "You go out and hunt; I'll stay and cook." And when the brothers came home with their meat, they found a fine supper waiting.

"Has anybody been here?" Smoking Mountain asked.

"Under that robe over there." said Little-Man, pointing to a buffalo robe

on the door, "there's a large hat stone, and under the stone there's a hole. Someone lifted the stone, came out of the hole, and crept out from under the robe."

"And what happened then?" asked the brothers.

"The same thing that happened to you. An ugly dwarf, only as big as my hand but monstrously strong, tried to beat me up with his whip. So that's why you were moaning and groaning. And you were ashamed to tell because he was so small."

"Ah," said the brothers, "he whipped you too."

"No," said Little-Man, "I didn't give him the chance. I killed him and threw him down that hole."

Smoking Mountain pushed aside the robe, lifted up the stone, and peeked down. "This is a very deep hole," he said. "It must lead to that dwarf's home. I wish I could go down and find out."

Little-Man-with-Hair-All-Over said: "That's easy." He took hold of the big cooking kettle and fastened a long rawhide rope to its handle. "Climb into this kettle," he told Smoking Mountain, "and we'll let you down. Then we'll draw you up and you can tell us about it."

They lowered Smoking Mountain down the hole and after a while pulled him up.

Smoking Mountain reported: "I landed right on top of that dwarf; you really fixed him good. It was dark and damp down there, and I could hear a strange noise like an animal snorting. I didn't feel comfortable in that place."

"Let me down," said Broken War Club. "I'm not afraid."

So they let him down and after a while pulled him up. He said: "I went a little farther. There's a door down there, a kind of hole in a cave wall, covered with a rock. I heard the noise too-it sounds like a deep growl rather than a snort. I didn't want to go in there."

"Let me down," said Little-Man-with-Hair-All-Over.

After they had lowered him, Little-Man found the entrance door and listened to the growling snort, or snorting growl. He rolled the rock out of the way and found himself in a cave-like room face to face with a two-headed monster. The monster growled: "Where is my son? Have you seen him? He is only so big."

"That must be the dwarf I killed," said Little-Man-with-Hair-All-Over. "I left his body outside."

At this the monster roared and attacked. Little-Man managed to cut-off one of its heads with his magic knife, but the monster continued fighting just as savagely. They struggled until Little-Man succeeded in cutting off the other head.

Looking past the monster's corpse, Little-Man saw another door opposite the first one. It too was stopped up with a big rock. From behind came a truly terrifying growling, snorting, and snuffling, as from a horde of strange beasts.

"I wonder who that can be," he thought, rolling the rock out of the way. In the next room he found a scaly man-monster with three heads, all three of which were snorting and growling and snuffling at the same time.

"Where is my son, the one with two heads?" the monster asked.

"Grandfather, or is it grandfathers? He is dead. I had to kill him because otherwise, I think he would have killed me. He was mad because I killed his son–your grandson, probably–the evil little dwarf with the whip."

At this the three-headed monster hurled himself at Little-Man. The three heads foamed at the lips, snarled and bit. "One at a time, one at a time," said Little-Man as he cut the three heads off one after the other.

"They really made me sweat," said Little-Man, looking around. He discovered yet another door, behind which he heard howling, shuffling, snarling, and growling. "This is getting boring," he said as he rolled the rock aside and met a horny-skinned, four-headed man-monster. This one asked no questions but immediately jumped at Little-Man with four sets of teeth biting, snapping, and tearing. The monster's skin was so tough, especially at the necks, that it resisted the magic knife. Even when Little-Man had finally cut off three of the four heads, the man-monster fought as fiercely as ever. The fourth head was the toughest; it bit a good-sized piece out of Little-Man's shoulder before he managed to cut it off. Panting, exhausted, Little-Man-with-Hair-All-Over kicked the giant body of the monster and said, "There, you wicked little thing!"

Again he looked around and saw a door. "Not again!" he said. But he listened and behind it he heard the sweet song of young girls. "This is much better," said Little-Man-with-Hair-All-Over as he rolled the last rock aside. He stepped into the last chamber and found three very pretty young women.

"Are the monsters out there relatives of yours?" asked Little-Man.

"No, no, in no way!" answered the maidens. "These horrible monsters have been keeping us prisoner for their own pleasure. We've been having a hard life."

"I believe it," he said.

"Handsome young warrior," said one of the girls, "surely you've come to free us."

"I don't know about handsome," said Little-Man, "but free you I will."

"And you are handsome," said the bold girl. "I like a little, hairy, lusty fellow."

"Then you've met the right man," he said. He looked around and saw wonderful things that the monsters had taken from their victims: buckskin robes decorated with multicolored porcupine quills, well-made weapons, war bonnets of eagle feathers, and much wore.

"Enough here for three friends to divide," said Little-Man, "and isn't it a lucky coincidence that there are three of you and three of us? For I have two friends waiting in the lodge above."

"Better and better," said the three good-looking girls.

Little-Man-with-Hair-All-Over gathered up the many fine things in a bundle and walked to the hole underneath the lodge. "Ho, friends," he hollered, "here are some good things for us to divide!" He placed the bundle in the kettle, and the two brothers in the lodge pulled it up.

They called down, "Are you coming up now?"

"Not yet," he answered. "First pull up three young pretty ones well worth meeting."

The brothers lowered the kettle and, one by one, drew up the women. Then Little-Man called out: "I'm coming up now." He climbed into the kettle. When they had pulled him halfway up, Broken War Club said to Smoking Mountain: "Let's drop him back down. Then we can keep these pretty girls and all the fine things for ourselves."

"No," said Smoking Mountain, "Little-Man has been a good friend to us." But Broken War Club had already cut the rawhide rope, and Little-Man fell all the way down with a big clatter.

He was stunned, but recovered quickly, saying: "Some fine friends I chose!"

Without the rope and the kettle, Little-Man-with-Hair-All-Over had a hard time climbing up into the lodge. He tried four times before he finally did it. "Now I'll find these no-good brothers," he said.

Traveling along what he believed to be the trail of Smoking Mountain and Broken War Club. Little-Man heard some people quarreling. He followed the sound and came upon the body of a big elk, over which a wasp, a worm, and a woodpecker were squabbling.

"My friends," Little-Man-with-Hair-All-Over told them, "there's enough here for all. Let me settle this for you and stop all the fuss." He gave the bones to the woodpecker, the fat to the wasp, and the meat to the worm, and everyone was satisfied.

"Thank you, uncle, for settling this matter and making peace between us," they said. "In return, if you ever find yourself in trouble, you can assume any of our shapes: you can turn yourself into a worm, a wasp, or a woodpecker."

"Thank you, I appreciate it," said Little-Man.

Always following the trail, he came at last to a lodge standing in a clearing of the forest. At once he turned himself into a woodpecker, flew up to a pole above the smoke hole, and looked down.

"Ah," he said to himself, "Here are the two no-good brothers talking to the three girls." Then he turned himself into a wasp and flew down into the lodge, where he settled on the shoulder of the bold girl. Nobody noticed him. The bold girl said: "I'm still angry with you men. It was mean to drop that nice little fellow. He was brave, and I was fond of him. I hope he's well, wherever he is."

Smoking Mountain added, "Yes, it wasn't right. I tried to stop it, but this one here had already cut the rope."

Broken War Club just laughed. "Brother, don't talk like a fool. It was so funny, dropping that hairy, useless man down there and listening to him squeal. Look at all the riches I got for us, and look at these pretty girls who, thanks to me, make our nights pleasant. Yes, I still have to laugh when I think of the hairy one clattering down, squealing."

"I don't remember having squealed," said Little-Man-with-Hair-All-Over, quickly turning himself back into a man. "Let's see who'll be squealing now."

Broken War Club tried to run away, but Little-Man seized him by the hair and cut his throat with the magic knife. Then he kicked Smoking Mountain in the backside.

"Coward! You could have defied your younger brother and gotten me out of that hole. If you ever cross my path again, I'll kill you the way I killed this one." Smoking Mountain slunk away.

Then Little-Man turned to the women. "Good-looking girls, will you take me for a husband? I'm man enough for three. I'm small, but not everywhere."

"Handsome one," said the bold girl, "since we three are sisters, it's only fitting for us to have one husband." So he married the girls, and they were all very happy together.

After Little-Man had lived with them for a while, he said: "Dears, I'm not made to stay always in one place. Now and then I just have to roam and discover things. I've left enough meat, pemmican, tongues, and back fat to last you a good many days. I won't be away for long, so don't be afraid."

Thus Little-Man-with-Hair-All-Over went traveling again. He came to a lodge, inside which a pretty young woman was crying. He went in and asked: "Good-looking one, what's the matter?"

"A slimy water monster is keeping me prisoner, and I hate his embraces.

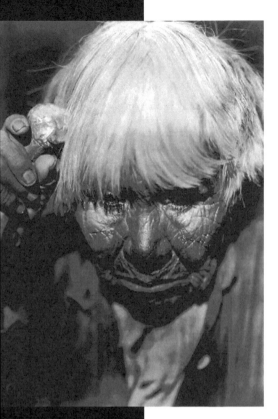

I've tried and tried to run away, but he always catches me and drags me back."

"Dry your tears," said Little-Man, "I'll kill this monster and marry you. I already have three wives, but I can easily take care of one more."

"I'd like that," said the woman, "but no one can kill him."

"I can kill any monster with my magic knife. I am forever rescuing pretty maidens imprisoned by evil monsters; I'm quite used to it."

"You can't kill this one, even with a magic knife, because he's many monsters in one. There's a secret way to kill him, and if you don't happen to know it, he'll kill you."

"And what is this secret way?"

"I don't know; I've never had a chance to ask. But tonight the monster comes back, and I'll try to get it out of him. Hide yourself in the meantime."

"That's easy," said Little-Man, turning into a woodpecker and flying to the top pole above the smoke hole.

At nightfall the water monster returned. Looking down from his perch, Little-Man thought: "This is indeed an ugly, slimy monster!"

The creature threw some meat to the girl, saying: "I just drowned and ate some humans, so I'm full, but here's some antelope meat for you."

"Just what I like," said the girl. "You know, that horn coming out of your forehead is dirty; let me clean it for you. It's really quite handsome."

"You're pleasant today for a change," said the monster, "instead of scowling and sour-faced. Perhaps you're beginning to appreciate me."

"How could anyone not appreciate you?" said the girl. "Tell me, so that in case of trouble I can help you: what's the only way to kill you?"

The monster grinned horribly and said: "Well, here I am, the great water monster. If you kill me, a huge grizzly bear will come out of me, and out of him a smaller brown bear, and out of him a panther, and out of the panther a wolf, and out of the wolf a wolverine, and out of that a fox, and out of that a rabbit. Out of the rabbit will come a quail, and out of the quail an egg. Only by dashing this egg against the horn in my forehead can I be killed."

Little-Man heard it all. At once he flew down into the lodge, resumed his own shape, and attacked the great water monster with his magic knife. One after the other, he killed all the animals coming out of the monster, and at last dashed the egg against the monster's horn.

"You're brave and powerful," said the girls. "I'm yours."

So Little-Man-with-Hair-All-Over took her as his fourth wife and carried her home to his lodge, together with all the treasures which the monster had amassed through robbing and murder. And Little-Man had been right: he was man enough for four wives, with a little left over.

# The Creek

The Creek, also known as the Muscogee, speak a language within the Muskogean stock. Prior to the 1700s, they occupied most of Georgia, but due to contact, their reservation lands now reside in Oklahoma, Georgia, and Alabama. Hairy man, in their traditional language, is called *Honka*.

### The *Honka*

Source: An interview with Ada M. Roach, 1937.

When the children were bad, they were warned that the "*Honka*" man would mark their arms. He was about the same as the "Bogey" man is to the white children. He walked on two legs and was hairy all over.

# The Natchez

The Natchez once occupied the area that is now Louisiana. However, their tribe was virtually destroyed after contact with the French and the survivors forcibly relocated to Oklahoma, where they were absorbed into the larger and more powerful Creek and Cherokee tribes. Their language was in the Gulf family.

## Panther Boy Takes a Wife

Source: *Lodge Stories,* by Edward W. Dolch and Marguerite P. Dolch, 1957. Illinois: Garrard Publishing Company, pp. 103-114.

One day Panther Boy went to the other side of the creek. He went a long way through the woods.

Panther Boy came to a river. Two girls were sitting beside the river. Panther Boy thought that one of the girls was the most beautiful girl that he had ever seen.

Panther Boy climbed a tall tree and when he was at the very top of the tree he called to the girls. "I am Panther Boy. And tell me, pretty girls, what will you be to me?"

The two girls looked up to the top of the tree and saw Panther Boy. "Come and play with us," they called.

But Panther Boy called again. "I am Panther Boy. Tell me, pretty girls, what will you be to me?" "I will be your sister," called one of the girls.

"No, No, No," cried Panther Boy. "I have no sister." "I will be your wife," called the other girl, and Panther Boy thought that she was the most beautiful girl he had ever seen.

"All right," cried Panther Boy. And he came down from the top of the tree.

The girls said, "Come with us, we will take you to our Father. Our father has great magic. He has never let us marry any young man that has asked us to be his wife."

"I am not afraid of your Father," said Panther Boy. And he went with the girls to their Lodge.

When the Father heard that Panther Boy wanted to marry one of his daughters, he said, "Three things you must do for me before you can marry my daughter."

And the Father of the girls had so much magic that he was sure that Panther Boy could not do any of the three things that he was going to ask him to do.

"First: You must get me the hair of the Giant that lives in the Big Lodge.

"Second: You must bring to me a ball of dirt from the bottom of the river."

"Third: You must run a race with me. If you cannot run faster than I can run, you cannot marry my daughter."

"I will go now," said Panther Boy. "But in three days I will be back with the hair of the Giant."

Panther boy went through the woods until he came to Father Panther's den. He told Father Panther about the beautiful girl that he wished to marry. He told Father Panther about the three things that he had to do before the girl's Father would give the beautiful girl to him for his wife.

Then Father Panther laughed and laughed.

"Do just as I tell you, my Boy, and you shall marry the beautiful girl."

All night long Father Panther talked to Panther Boy. And in the morning, Panther Boy went to the Big Lodge of the Giant. The Giant was not at home but his wife stood at the door of the Lodge. Panther Boy changed himself into a Granddaddy-Long-Legs. The Granddaddy-Long-Legs went into the Lodge and spoke to the Woman

The Woman heard someone talking to her and she did not see anyone in her Lodge. The Woman was very much afraid and cried out.

"Do not hurt me. Do not hurt me. I will do anything that you ask me to do. But do not hurt me."

The Granddaddy-Long-Legs that was in the Lodge said,

"Woman, do just what I tell you to do and nothing will hurt you. Tonight when the Giant is sleeping cut off his hair and put it outside the door of your Lodge."

Then the Granddaddy-Long-Legs went out of the Lodge. He turned himself back into Panther Boy and hid in the woods all night. In the morning Panther Boy went to the door of the Giant's Big Lodge. And there on the ground before the door, he found the hair of the Giant.

When Panther Boy gave the hair of the Giant to the girl's Father, he was very much surprised. But all he said was, "Bring me the ball of dirt from the bottom of the river."

Panther Boy went and sat beside the river for a long time. The turtles and the fish and the animals came and talked to him. He told all of them about the beautiful girl that he wanted to marry.

But no one with white around his neck came to talk to him. And Panther Boy remembered that Father Panther had said, "Wait until the one comes who has white around his neck, for he is the only one that can get the ball of dirt from the bottom of the river."

Panther Boy waited beside the river. And at last Kingfisher came to him. And Kingfisher had white around his neck.

"Kingfisher, Kingfisher," said Panther Boy. "Will you get me a ball of dirt from the bottom of the river?"

"That is a very hard thing to do," said Kingfisher. "But I will go down to the bottom of the river and see if I can get a ball of dirt for you."

At last Kingfisher came to the top of the water. He had a small ball of dirt and he gave it to Panther Boy.

Panther Boy took the small ball of dirt and hit it on a rock. The ball of dirt grew bigger and bigger. And then he took the big ball of dirt to the girl's Father.

When Panther Boy gave the big ball of dirt to the girl's Father, he did not know what to think. But all he said was, "Tomorrow we will have a race. If you can run faster than I run, you may marry my daughter."

The girl loved Panther Boy. And that night she came to talk to him.

The girl said, "In the race tomorrow, my Father will try to kill you. In the path where you will run is a very big hole. My Father has put many pointed sticks into the hole in the ground. He has covered the hole with leaves and dirt. My Father will run before you until he comes near to the hole in the path. Then he will drop back and let you run first. Then he will try to make you run into the hole. If you fall into the big hole you will be killed on the pointed sticks.

"I will look out," said panther Boy. "I do not want to be killed."

And in the race, it was just as the girl had told Panther Boy. But when the Father dropped back Panther Boy stepped to one side and the Father fell into the hole and was killed on the pointed sticks.

Panther Boy and the beautiful girl were married and went to live in the village by the creek. And the sister of the girl went with them. They were glad to get away from the Lodge in the woods where they had never been happy.

# The Seminoles

The Seminoles inhabited portions of Arkansas and Oklahoma in prehistoric times, moving into Florida when it was still ruled by the Spanish. The tribe maintains reservations throughout Florida. In their traditional Muskogean language, *Esti capcaki* means "tall man" and *Ssti capcaki* means "tall hairy man."

**Ssti capcaki**

Source: *Oklahoma Seminoles–Medicine, Magic, and Religion*, by James Howard and Willie Lena, 1984. Norman: University of Oklahoma Press, p. 211-212.

Tall Hairy Man or *Ssti capcaki* resembles a human being but of immense stature, ten feet or more in height, and covered with gray hair. He customarily carries a great wooden club made from a branch broken from a tree. Tall Man is reported to have a penetrating odor, like the smell of a stagnant muddy pond.

Willie Lena's father encountered Tall Man once when Willie was very young:

"When Daddy saw it he told Mamma and said that it looked like he had made his club from a limb of one of the trees on our place. Mamma said "If that is so, that tree he broke the limb from will soon be dead!" We all doubted this, but surely enough, the tree died. Where the branches had been there were big holes. It is in holes like this that Seminole women bury stillborn babies. I used to hear a baby crying at one of these trees near our house. There were little bones in there."

246

# The
# Southwest
# Culture

# Southwest Cultural Area

Hopi

Navajo

Taos

Pima

# The Hopi

The Hopi live on their traditional home-lands in Arizona. Their language is a part of the Uto-Aztecan family. The Hopi tradition-al words for bigfoot-like giants are *Chavcyu* and *Sio' Calako*. A female giant was called a *Suyuku*.

## The Poor Boys and the Sorcerers

Source: *The North American Indian,* Vol. 12, by Edward S. Curtis, 1930. Massachu-setts: The Plimpton Press, pp. 209-212.

*I-tdwu'ti!* People were living at *Kuchaptuvela* and at *Kisakobi*. The *Qita* [sorcerer] chief called in the members of his kiva, and when they had assem-bled, they said: "*Taai* [go on]! *Himuu* [what]?"

"*Owe!*" responded the chief. "There are too many children, and we must get rid of them. I have found the way. We will create a *chavcyu* [giant]."

"*Anchaaz!*" said the sorcerers.

So the chief appointed men to procure juniper-bark, and when it was brought they made it into a human effigy and put a crystal into it for the heart and shells for the liver and the lungs. Then they placed it between two cere-monial robes and sang over it. While they sang, it became alive, and they removed the covering. There lay a huge giant. He rose and spoke out in a loud voice, "What do you want of me?"

"*Owe!*" said the chief. "There are too many children and we want you to eat them."

"*Ali* [good eating]!" exclaimed the giant. "And what place will be my home?"

"You will go to *Siqi-teika* [a cliff a few miles north and west of Walpi on the opposite side of the valley]."

"*Anchaai!*" said the giant. He departed, and prepared his home in the cliff, and he excavated pits in the rock for roasting the children. That very night he went to *Kisakobi*, and passed from one house to another, demanding a child from each family, and he would not go until one was given to him. He put the children in a basket on his back, and thus carried away several children every night.

At *Kuchaptuvela* a poor old woman lived with her two little grandsons a short distance from the main part of the village. She became fearful that her two boys would be taken by the giant; for at the rate he was coming he would

soon reach her house. One day she sent them to the cliff at *Kanol-va* for wood of which to make bows and arrows. So they obtained the wood and prepared it for weapons. They secured wing-feathers of bluebirds and robins, and finished the arrows. This was done on the day before the giant in the course of his rounds in *Kuchaptuvela* would arrive at their house.

The next night they waited for him. They heard his heavy footsteps, and his rough voice demanding a child. But the old woman said, "No, I will not give my grandsons to you."

"You will!" he shouted. "I must have them!"

"If you want them so much, come yourself and get them," she said.

"I will," he rumbled. He came into the house. The two little boys were sitting beside the fire with their bows and arrows, and when he started toward them, they stood up and ran around him, one on each side, and shot him through the heart. He fell dead. Then the old woman was frightened, for she feared the sorcerers. So they dug a hole behind the ladder and buried the body, and she scraped up the blood and spread a new covering of earth.

Now the next night the sorcerers at *Kisakobi* wondered why their giant did not come as usual, and on the following day they sent two men to *Siqiteika*. They found his tracks going toward the village, and followed them to the house occupied by the two little boys and the poor old woman. Then they returned to their kiva and made their report. Some wondered if these children had been able to kill their giant, others doubted. It was decided to wait and see if he would not appear that night. But he did not come.

Nevertheless they waited until the next night, and then the *Qita* chief summoned his men. A young man said: "It might be that those little boys have killed our giant. Such things happen. A poor child sometimes has very good luck." So the mother of the sorcerers was sent for, a witch who was a member of their kiva. She bathed, and rubbed from her body some cuticle, which she made into the form of a wren, and by singing she gave it life.

"What do you want?" asked Wren.

"*Owe!*" said the chief. "Our giant has disappeared, and we want you to find him."

"*Anchaai!*" said Wren, and flitted away through the kiva hatchway.

The bird went hopping about the cliff at the giant's home, searching for him. Then it came to the house of the old woman and the two little boys, and hopped in. When the old woman saw it, she said: "That bird is a sorcerer! It is looking for the giant."

After flitting about the house, the Wren flew out and returned to the Qita-kiva, and reported that he had not been able to find the giant.

The witch-mother rolled another ball of cuticle, of which they made a *mastovi* [corpse fly]. The big, buzzing Fly asked, "What do you want of me?"

"We want you to find our giant," they said. And the Fly buzzed straight to the home of the poor old woman. It flew about the house, and then went in. The old woman said, "What is this fly doing here?" She suspected that it was an agent of the sorcerers. But the Fly found nothing until just as he was going out, when he detected the odor of a corpse. He went back and alighted on the floor, and when he was certain that he had found the body, he returned to the Qita-kiva.

"What have you found?" inquired the chief.

"Yes, I have found your giant. He is buried behind the ladder in the home of the two poor little boys and the poor old woman."

Then the young man said: "I have told you that poor people sometimes do such things. You see they have killed our giant."

It was agreed that the two boys and their grandmother should be killed, and a man was sent to them. The grandmother greeted him kindly. He filled his pipe and handed it to her, and she gave it to her boys, who passed it back and forth until it was smoked out. Then she asked, "What is it you want?"

"The sorcerers have decided to kill you and your boys in four days," said the man. And the old woman and the little boys were very downcast.

The next day she sent the boys to see if they could not find some green plants and thus prove themselves powerful. For it was midwinter. They went a short distance and on the side of the cliff they found a spring beside which green grass was growing. They pulled up the grass, put mud about its roots, and carried it a little way from the spring, where they placed it under a rock and sat down to rest. While they sat there a man appeared before them.

"What are you doing here?" asked he.

"We are just resting," they answered. "We have been wandering along, and now we are resting."

"I know what you are doing," he said, "and I have come for you."

"Where are you from?" they inquired.

"I am from *Kisiuf* [the home of the Kachinas]. You must go with me." He laid on the ground a *pa-tuwota* [water-shield]. The boys, at his direction, stepped on the shield with him, and it immediately began to revolve rapidly, rose in the air with them, and carried them quickly to *Kisiuf*. They were carried down into the spring, and the Kachinas treated them kindly. The chief said, "Have you come?"

"Yes," they said.

"I have sent this man for you, so that we may arrange about the way you shall escape from your trouble. The only thing you must do when they come to kill you is to call on the Kachinas. Tell your grandmother that she is the first one to call us, and you two will be the next. When we start, you will see clouds in this direction. Keep calling us, saying: 'They have started, they are on their way, they are coming.' Keep saying this until we reach the village. This is all you have to do. We will do the rest."

Then the Kachinas gave them melons and corn, and the man who had brought them took them home on the water-shield. When they arrived, their grandmother was surprised to see the fruits they had brought, and she was very happy. For she knew this to be a sign that they would in some way escape from their trouble.

The next evening the *Kisakobi* chief came to them. He said: "I will be on your side, and the Warrior Chief also will be on your side. We will see how it is to be done." One of the sorcerers, a young man, also was in favor of the poor family. Altogether there were eleven men against the sorcerers. When the chief had finished talking, he smelled the melons and said, "Where do you find melons?"

The boys said, "Give the poor man melons." So she gave the chief some of the fruit.

The chief went home, where the Warrior Chief and the friendly sorcerer were awaiting him. They asked what they were to do, and he told them to make *pahos* [offerings] the next day. The two boys also had been instructed to make *pahos* at their house. So the next day was the day for *paho*-making, and the sorcerers were in their kiva at this work.

On the morrow the boys and the old woman were to be killed. The sorcerers were the first to show their power, and they planted seeds and sang over them in the plaza. They were dressed like Kachinas. The corn sprouted and came up, but it did not grow high. They performed the ceremony now represented in the Kachina dance in which lightning is sent out from behind a curtain, and snow and rain are made to fall, and *Pa-lolokanu* [water bullsnake] knocks over the corn plants. When they had finished, they thought they had demonstrated greater power than the others could show, and bade the old woman and the little boys to show what they could do. All these three had was their pahos and a basket of meal. The old woman threw some meal toward *Kisiuui*, and called for the Kachinas, and clouds were seen in that direction. "There they are!" she cried. Then one of the boys threw meal toward *Kisiuu*, and said, "They have started." The other did the same thing, and said, "They are coming." The woman took the meal and cried, "They are coming in sight!"

While all this was being done, the sorcerers were angry and disgusted. "These people can do nothing," they said. "They are only taking up time." They wished to kill them at once. But the people said they would wait and see what happened.

The old woman again called for the Kachinas, and now they were seen coming up the trail. As they approached the village, the old woman said, "Let us go to meet them!" So the woman and the two boys met the Kachinas at the edge of the village and escorted them to the plaza, where the visitors at once prepared the ground, spreading sand in which they planted all kinds of seeds. Then they danced and sang, and real clouds appeared and real rain fell. It rained constantly while they danced, and the seeds at once sprouted and grew up, and quickly bore fruit, which in a little while was mature. Then they told the boys to distribute the fruits among all the people. The *Kisakobi* chief, the Warrior Chief, the old woman, and the two boys gave *pahos* to the Kachinas, who then departed.

Now the chief said that he did not wish any to be killed. "It is for the sorcerers to find a way to rid us of them. Since you boys have more power than anybody else, I do not want to be the chief hereafter. You must take my place." The sorcerer who had favored the poor family said: "I knew these boys would get out of trouble in some way. And now the sorcerers must find a way to die."

From that time the sorcerers began to die off. Some fell into the kiva and thus killed themselves, others died as they walked. All perished except the one who had favored the poor family, and from him are descended the sorcerers of the present day. *Paiyasava!*

### Destruction of the Giantess

Source: *The North American Indian, Vol. 12,* by Edward S. Curtis, 1930. Massachusetts: The Plimpton Press, pp. 212-213.

*I-tuwufsi*! People were living in *Kisakobi. Pokan-hoya* and his younger brother *Polonao-hoya* lived with their grandmother Spider Woman at *Si'kpi* on the trail that goes down the south point of the mesa. The two boys used to go down on the slope of the mesa to play with their shinny-balls. *Suyuku* [ogress] lived on the terrace. She used to steal little children, roast them in her firepit, and eat them. She had made away with most of the children of the village. Spider Woman often warned her grandsons not to go near that place to play. "Now, my grandchildren," she would say, "do not go over there to play ball any more, for fear *Suyuku* will catch and roast you, just as she does the little children from above." But they would answer: "She cannot do it! She will not be much of a person."

One morning they started out as usual to play ball on the slope, and as they moved back and forth along the terrace, they gradually came to where the giantess lived. She came out and spoke to them, "My little grandchildren, where are you going?" "We are just playing along here," they told her. "Do not go very far," she said: "a little way from here there is a giant woman. You had better come in and wait before you go on!"

Thus spoke *Suyuku*. The boys went into her house, and she gave them mumus-piki and meat; and they ate the mumis-piki, but the meat they only pretended to eat, throwing it on the ground, for it was the flesh of children. After they had finished, the old woman closed the door, seized the elder brother, and dragged him outside. Already she had the firepit heated. But the boys knew what danger threatened them, and *Pokan-hoya* had already said to his brother, "When she throws us into the pit, you must urinate into it and I will spit my medicine into it." So when *Pokan-hoya* was cast into the heated pit, he spat his medicine, and when *Palonao-hoya* was thrown in he urinated. Thus they checked the heat, and were not destroyed. After putting them into the pit, *Suyuku* closed it and sealed the opening with clay, and laid fire on the top; and when the sun went down, she began to grind corn. She had two young granddaughters, who were sleeping when she caught the brothers. After finishing her grinding, *Suyuku* went to bed, and when all was quiet, the boys opened the pit and crept out. They went into the house, and each chose one of the sleeping girls and cut off her head and dropped the body into the pit. The elder brother threw in some medicine that made it red-hot, and they sealed it up and placed the heads in the bed. In the morning when *Suyuku* awoke, she called to the two girls, but there was no answer. She scolded them, but still there was no reply, and the children did not move. She came to the bed to drag them out, but found only two heads. Then she knew that the two brothers had done this, and she wept aloud, and said that she would never take another child from *Kisakobi. Paiyasava*!

# The Navajo

The Navajo are a very large tribe residing in parts of Arizona, New Mexico, and Utah. Their language is in the Athabaskan family. The traditional Navajo word for a big giant is *Yé'iitsoh*.

## The Story of *Nagenatzani*

Source: Unknown.

The Ogre who kicked people off mountain paths was the next to be conquered by *Nagenatzani*. The ogre himself never fell because his coarse hair grew into the crevices of the rock to hold him. *Nagenatzani* walked along the path. He extended his wand and the kicker struck out. The young man dodged behind the Ogre's legs. The kicker was angered. Four times this was done. The kicker danced with rage, then with the big knife *Nagenatzani* slashed through his hair. As the Ogre crashed, a wailing sound was heard. The young man ran down to find that the kicker had fallen on his wife and family, who were now busy cutting up his body and eating it. *Nagenatzani* was angry that the Ogre's family would eat him. *Nagenatzani* threw the Ogre's wife and children into the sky and killed them.

## The Twin Brothers

Source: Unknown.

Now the only people who were still fulfilling the curse that First Woman and First Man had laid on their people were the descendants of *Yé'iitsoh*, the giant. So the twin brothers, *Nagenatzani* and *Thobaddestchin*, went together to a sacred spot that Sun had told them about. There they put down the black and red wind charm. They danced around it singing magical songs. The winds began to whirl, gathering power until they could uproot and toss great trees about. Then the winds were directed to the mountains where the giants lived. The wind took and tossed the giants to other areas so there were no more giants left in their lands.

# The Pima

The Pima, also known as the O'odham, currently live in their historic homelands of central and southern Arizona and Sonora, Mexico. Their language is part of the Uto-Aztecan family.

### Creation Myth

Source: *The North American Indian,* Vol. 2 by Edward S. Curtis, 1930. Massachusetts: The Plimpton Press, p. 19.

Not long afterward she bore a girl child, who had claws instead of fingernails and toe-nails. She was covered in hair. Before many years this malformed child, whom they called *Haak*, ran away into the hills and began killing game and even people, like a wild beast. A messenger was sent to beg help of *Suuhu*, who at the end of four days came to them and directed that they gather four kinds of poisonous plants, making them into four cigarettes.

Then all the people with *Suuhu* started toward the lair of *Haak*. While yet some distance away, they stopped to make a great feast and dance, and one was sent to bid *Haak* to the festivities. She at once began to dress for the occasion, putting on necklaces and bracelets of human bones, which rattled as she moved. Her dress, too, was fringed all about with these gruesome relics of her rapacity. When she reached the place of the feast, *Suuhu* was singing, and the people dancing about him in a great circle. The festivities continued through four days, and on each day one of the cigarettes was passed about; but the people merely put them to their lips without smoking.

*Haak*, however, smoked, and on the fourth day became crazed, as if drunken. *Suuhu* took her hand and danced with her, around and around, until she became very dizzy and fell down as if dead. Then he quickly bore her to a cave in the mountains, laid her upon a pile of wood at the farther end, and directed the people to fill the cave with logs and set fire to the whole. When the roaring flames reached *Haak*, she awoke, but was unable to escape through the fierce heat. She struck the roof of the cave with her head, trying to break through, and though the blow cracked the rock she could not completely disrupt it, so her body remained in the flames and the people were freed from this curse.

# The Taos

Located in north central New Mexico, the Taos live in their traditional Pueblo, which is also their native language group. The Taos word for giant is *Stsomu'lamux* and their words for big person are *T'oylona*, *Tsawane'itEmux*, and *TsekEtinu's*.

## Seed-Marked Boy Destroys the Giant

Source: *Taos Tales,* by Elsie Clews Parsons, 1996. New York: Dover Publications, pp. 9-11.

At Cottonwood were living *tqwaowia*, Seed-marked boy, and his grandmother. While living there the grandmother would go every day to bring in sticks of wood on her back. Every time she went she told her grandson not to go northward. The boy would play about the house. After a while the boy thought he would find out by going north why his grandmother told him not to go northward. So one day he went north-ward and found out that the giant [*toilana*, person big] was always around there. He learned that the people, men, women and children, never came back to their home because the giant was catching them and eating them up. So the people were diminishing all the time. They did not know what was becoming of them. Now Seed-marked boy was caught by the pants, and taken to [the giant's] home. His home was *antoilaenta* [his-giant-feet-at]. (It is a big, high, impassable rock.) When he was taken there he was bound hand and foot. The giant went out to gather stumps, he laid the boy underneath and piled the stumps on top of him and set fire to the stumps for Seed-marked boy to cook. Then the old giant lay down alongside his blazing fire, waiting for the boy to be roasted to eat him. He sang,

> *til'toao'wia til'toao'wia*
> *ilwi p'asiu pa'okilku'yuma*
> *wild celery trickle nicely flowing*
> *ilwi p'asiu pa'okilku'yuma*

The giant heard the song. Giant said to himself, "Oh, you little thing, why does it take so long for you to be roasted?" Then the giant took his wooden shovel and opened up the burning stump. Then he got the boy out. He was not burned. So the giant got hold of the boy and said to him, "You are such a small boy you must have some kind of power; but I will see who is *laietuwaiemu*, more powerful." So he took him up to the top of that precipitous rough wall of rock. Then he stood him up on the edge of the rock and said to him, "Here

is the place from which you will never come back." Then he pushed him down. Down he went. Then he went back, hollering, and alit as a soft eagle tail feather on top of the rock where the giant was. Then the second time the giant pushed him down. He said to him, "You are such a small boy, yet you know what to do!" Then he came back again, as a feather, hollering aloud. That was the second time. Then the giant pushed him down again. He came back again as the same feather, yelling and hollering. The fourth time he pushed him down. He came back hollering. (That was where the giant threw down all the people he killed.) Then the boy said to the giant, "Now, it is my turn. We will find out who is more powerful." The old giant liked the trick of the boy. He said to himself, "Now, I will try it, too." He got hold of the giant and took him down to the place where he had been put to be burned. He gathered old cedar stumps, put the giant under the stumps, and set them afire. It made a strong blaze, the fire sounded as if it was boiling *sss—s*! And the stumps all burned down to charcoal. Nothing was seen of the giant, nor could his voice be heard, only the blazing of the fire *sss—-s*! Until the charcoal burned away to ashes. So by his power [*tuwaiega*] he made a strong wind blow which blew the ashes away. The dead had been bound up by hands and feet, some sitting up, some lying down. Then by his power, he made all the dead come to life. They all exclaimed, "*Huwi, kitamena* [our father]! You are the man by whose power we shall see our world again." Then he looked for his grandmother and they went back to their home at Cottonwood. There they lived as before.

## Seed-Marked Boy Destroys the Giant, Variant 1

Source: *Taos Tales*, by Elsie Clews Parsons, 1996. New York: Dover Publications, pp. 11-13.

Seed-marked boy was living at Cottonwood with his grandmother. He used to go out hunting. He said to his grandmother, "Grandmother, do not go out when I have gone out hunting." Grandmother thought to herself, "I wonder why my grandchild does not want me to go out. I will go out today." So she left off grinding and went out. When she went out, a giant came to her. He had a basket water jar [*t'oamuluna*] and he told the old woman to get into it. He closed the mouth of the jar and carried the old woman on his back to his house. The giant lived far up in the mountain where nobody could go. When the boy came back from hunting, his grandmother did not come out to meet him. He thought to himself, "I wonder why my grandmother does not come running out to meet me." He threw down the deer and ran into the house and did not find his grandmother. The meal she was grinding was left there. Then he followed the tracks of the giant to *lakutuna* [wood spoon]. Wood Spoon called him and asked, "Where are you going?" He said, "I am going to look for my grandmother. " Wood Spoon gave him a spruce seed [*k'uowax-ona*]. "This will help you to get there," he said. "Cover this seed and it will grow." He took it and went on. He came to Spider old woman. She said, "Seed-marked boy, why are you around while you are living well at Cottonwood, with your grandmother? A good hunter, why are you around here now?" "Yes, I live there well and happily with my grandmother and bring deer to her all the time. But now the giant has taken her away, so I have to look for her." Spider old woman said, "Your grandmother is far up in the

mountain where nobody can go. I know that Wood Spoon gave you the spruce seed and now I will give something that will help you when you get up there." She gave him some medicine and told him to put it in his mouth and over his body so the giant would not kill him. Then Seed-marked boy went to the foot of the mountain and he dug a hole and, while he was putting in the seed, Squirrel came to him. Squirrel said, "I will help you to make this tree grow fast." While the tree was growing, he ran up and down the tree until the tree reached the top of the mountain. Then he ran down and told the boy the tree was close to his grandmother. So the boy climbed the tree and came to his grandmother. She said to him, "Grandchild, why do you come here? I am living with the giant. I know he will eat you up." As they talked together the earth was shaking because the giant was coming. Grandmother hid him underneath the thatch of the hatch. Then the giant came in and said, "I smell the blood of an Indian." Grandmother said, "Who would come here? Nobody can come here." "Yes, I smell, I smell!" And he began to search. She said, "Yes, my grandchild came." "He thinks he is one to tame me; but he is not." Then he pulled him out of the thatch. He did not cry, he hollered, "*Hip! Hip! Hip! Hip!*" Then the giant dug a fire and the giant put him there to roast. The giant lay beside the fire waiting for him to roast. "He is so small, I think it won't take long for him to roast," said the giant. The giant took down his wheel and rolled it so the ashes would disclose the boy. Then the boy jumped out hollering, "*Hip! Hip! Hip! Hip!*" The boy took the wheel and rolled it to the giant and killed him. He had the people and the *lachina* tied up (that is why it did not rain). So then the boy went and untied them. He went to another place where there were piles of human bones and he put medicine on them and they all turned to life. The women had the jars that they were carrying to get water when the giant caught them and the men had on their backs the ropes which they used when they were going to get wood. "Now you go back to your homes," he said. When the *lachina* were set free, it began to rain, too! He took his grandmother home and they lived happily.

## Seed-Marked Boy Destroys the Giant, Variant 2

Source: *Taos Tales,* by Elsie Clews Parsons, 1996. New York: Dover Publications, pp. 13-14.

Long ago, when the pueblos were first where they are now, everything was wild. They were always on the lookout, they never made fire at night, they did all their cooking in the daytime. They went out in the daytime for firewood. Someone noticed that some people were missing, one or two every day. They wondered why. They did not know what became of them. The old men kept watch to see if it was enemies hiding. No one could find out for years what became of the missing persons. There was an old man then that went out after firewood. He made a bundle of wood to carry on his back. He started home. He came to a place where he rested. While he was resting he saw some kind of a human walking, but he looked different–kind o' naked, long hair on his body like an animal, big feet, hands, big muscle arms, big head, mouth. The man got scared. This creature came up and grabbed the man. It was a giant. The giant killed him and took him to his cave. It was late. The family missed the old man. The War captain and the officers went out to look for him. They came to where he had rested. They examined the place. They saw the footprints of the giant. They wondered what it could be. They tracked him to the foot of a hill–clear to the entrance of his cave. They saw blood on the edge of the cave. They finally decided it was a giant that had killed the man. They looked around. They found where the giant had thrown the bones and head. They saw lots of bones there. They did not know how to get the giant, but they were going to try to get him some way. Everyone who could carry weapons finally started out to fight the giant. They decided to cut brush and make a big fire at the mouth of the cave and smoke him out. The giant gnashed his teeth. He stuck his head out. The people stood back. Then the giant came out–furious. The people attacked him with bows and clubs. They could not kill him. Finally he ran away, angry.

The people kept shooting. There were arrows sticking in his body, but he did not mind. They chased him, followed his trail of blood on the ground. They chased him to the north. He crossed Lucero River. The blood is still there, you can see it in the rocks and on the earth. He went on to Qgesta. Finally they surrounded him near Qgesta. He went into a cave and died. You can see that red line there now today. The medicine men had helped on the last day of the fight. That is how they were able to kill him. It clouded up like a storm. There was a noise above (thunder). Lightning killed him.

## Seed-Marked Boy Destroys the Giant, Variant 3

Source: *Taos Tales,* by Elsie Clews Parsons, 1996. New York: Dover Publications, pp. 14-15.

When at the Canyon of the Red Willows people (*ialapai'mu pahoatel t' ainemu*) they first came to live, the giant came there. The people did not know he was there. All the men would go out for firewood, to carry in on their backs. Sometimes some were caught by the giant and carried up to his cave. He killed them. As the people, men, boys, women, would go out, he would catch them and carry them to his cave. For a long time they could not find out why these people were disappearing. They were not able to find out. So they went out to see what they could learn about these missing people. They kept searching in the hills and mountains. Finally they found the track of the giant, larger than men's tracks. They tracked him wherever he went. Sometimes they would lose the track on hard ground, and then they would find it in soft dirt. They kept tracking that way many days. Finally they found a fresh footprint and they followed and found where he had been sitting on top of the hill. His tracks led them to his cave. They saw him lying down asleep near his cave. The giant was a very big bodied man. So they went back to the village. They told the people to get ready to go and try to kill him. They went up there and began to shoot with their bows and arrows. He got angry and they could not kill him. Their arrows could not penetrate his hard body, they only scratched him where they hit. The blood was dripping from his body. He ran in to his cave. They poked at him with long sticks, and he caught their sticks and took them away. So they could not do anything and at night they went home. The next day they went back again. He had gone out from the cave, and they tracked him, across the hill, toward the north. They followed him, but could not overtake him. Then went back home. They went back the next day, to where they left the track. They could see his blood stains on the ground, the dirt on the hillside was covered with blood. So they followed him, to the side of the mountain, still to the north. They overtook him at *tohse'uba*. There they killed him. That's why at *tohse'uba* the mountain side is red all over, with the giant's blood. Then they came home, and ever since then the people increased.

### Seed-Marked Boy Destroys the Giant, Variant 4

Source: *Taos Tales,* by Elsie Clews Parsons, 1996. New York: Dover Publications, pp. 15-16.

Once were living Turkey and his wife. They had one daughter. They used to tell their daughter not to go out in an easterly direction lest an accident or some misfortune happen to her. One day the girl came to a decision and said, "I will go toward the east and see why my father and mother do not want me to go that way." So she went in the direction she was forbidden. As she descended she came to a pumpkin field. She picked the pumpkin flowers. As she was picking, the big giant came to where she was. The giant said to her, "What are you doing?" The girl replied, "I am picking pumpkin flowers." Then Giant said to her, "Come on here! I have some nice ones here in my big jar. Look in!" Then Giant said to the girl, "Go in!" That girl went in. Then Giant took the girl away off to his home in a cave. There the Turkey girl saw dead people, their hands and feet bound with yucca string. The girl was not killed like the others in the cave but merely became the wife of the giant. The girl was treated nicely by her husband. Giant would go out during the day and at nightfall bring in a whole dead deer for the girl to eat. The next day he would go out and bring in dead people for himself to devour. The girl did not like this, Giant eating dead humans, nor did she like being at the center of bloody butchering. She kept asking her husband where he had his life. He said he had no life anywhere, but that he feared God only in making solemn promises, in making crosses with his fingers (in making the sign of the cross). The next day he went out. In the evening he brought in a big dead deer. The girl

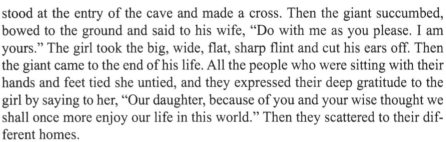

stood at the entry of the cave and made a cross. Then the giant succumbed, bowed to the ground and said to his wife, "Do with me as you please. I am yours." The girl took the big, wide, flat, sharp flint and cut his ears off. Then the giant came to the end of his life. All the people who were sitting with their hands and feet tied she untied, and they expressed their deep gratitude to the girl by saying to her, "Our daughter, because of you and your wise thought we shall once more enjoy our life in this world." Then they scattered to their different homes.

## The Striped Ones Save Him from the Giant

Source: *Taos Tales,* by Elsie Clews Parsons, 1996. New York: Dover Publications, pp. 16-17.

They were living at *palilapahana* [hot springs], *Tsiuha'a* and his grandmother. He was always going out rabbit hunting. His grandmother said, "My grandson, you may not go to the north." He was out hunting rabbits and he said, "I wonder why it is my grandmother said I was not to go hunting north, past the pine tree. I think I will go." When he went to the pine he found lots of rabbits. He camped there and put around a string of rabbits. He took two rabbits to cook. "*Maku*, grandchild!" he heard, "where?" "Somebody hunting," he said. "Grandchild, where?" "*Yaipi*, here, grandfather!" "Grandchild, where?" "Here, grandfather!" Came a giant. "Grandchild, you have had good hunting?" "Yes, grandfather. You may sit down." "Grandchild, *Tsiuha'a*, your rabbit is cooking?" "Yes, grandfather, you may have it." He thought, "This is Giant. If I don't give him everything he asks for, he will swallow me." He gave him the second rabbit. "Grandchild, *Tsiuha'a*, you may give me the string of rabbits you have here." "Yes, grandfather, I will give it to you if you dance for it. Giant danced with his arms out and sang:

*Y aaipus! pus!*
*Yaaipus! pus!*

Giant made a grab at *Tsiuha'a*, but he sneaked away. "Well you are mine. I am going to get you." *Tsiuha'a* got to the *kawiuna*. "*Kawiuna*, can you help me? Giant is after me." "Yes, brother, come in!" They painted him like themselves. "We must hurry, before Giant comes." They started dancing and singing:

*Hili kitaiwan taiwan*
What our people came people came
*Milmawa talapapu talapapu*
Don't make yourselves heard heard
*Haiya haiya*

"Grandchildren, didn't *Tsiuha'a* come here?" They did not answer. They kept on dancing and singing:

*Hili kitaiwan Taiwan*
*Milmawatalapapu talapapu*
*Haiya haiya*

"Listen! I am asking you if *Tsiuha'a* got here." They stopped. "Well, grandfather, is it this one you are looking for?" "No." "Is it this one?" "No." "Is it this one?" "No. I want you to bring him out. I will eat you all up." "I don't know which you want. Come in and get him!" "How can I come in this small place?" "We can make it larger." Just as he came in they took hold of him and threw him down and trampled him and danced on top of him. They sang:

*Kawiunmama*
*Powahaha powahaha*

They trampled him to pieces. "He is not holy or fortunate like us and he is always trying to be." They put him into the fire and burned him into ashes. They called to Wind old woman, "You may come and blow away the ashes!" They said, "Now, *Tsiuha'a*, your grandmother is swelling from sadness. You go home! Now you can go hunting wherever you want without fear of the giant." When he got home he found his grandmother sitting by the fireplace, swelling with sadness. Then she got well and they lived happily. People say *Tsiuha'a* lived at hot springs and he was a good hunter, and *Tsiuha'a* said, "Those who want to be good hunters, they can come and ask (pray to) me."

## The Striped Ones Save Him from the Giant, Variant

Source: *Taos Tales,* by Elsie Clews Parsons, 1996. New York: Dover Publications, pp. 17-18.

At *wepuavada* [pine-near-water] lived *Saiofaa* who was a rabbit hunter. He always had a string of rabbits hanging in a bunch. Then the giant came after him, calling him by his name, "*Saiofaa*, grandchild, grandchild!" "Who is that? Somebody who must know me is about here." He was sitting on his little shack of pine brush. Then the giant got to his shack. He saw a kind of human that he had not seen before or known. Then he asked him to give him his rabbits. He was afraid. He told the giant he would give him the rabbits. The giant took the rabbits, one by one, and swallowed them. When the giant ate all the rabbits, he said, "*Saiofaa*, my grandchild, you look fat, too." Then *Saiofaa* ran out underneath his little shack. The giant chased *Saiofaa*. At *hiohkualdah* [stone fence] lived *Kawiyonah*. *Saiofaa* ran into the house. The giant arrived there. *Saiofaa* said to the *Kawiyonah*, "My grandchildren, hide me! A giant is after me." *Saiofaa* was spotted as *Kawiyonah* were spotted. They were all spotted just the same. The giant said, "My grandchildren, is *Saiofaa* here?" They told the giant he was there. Then they all began to dance. The giant did not listen, he went into the house. All the *Kawiyonah* said, "Is it I? Is it I?" and so on. They were all spotted just the same, all of them. *Saiofaa* was there, but the giant did not know him. Then they killed the giant. They danced, kicking him, trampling on him all they could, as in the war dance, singing:

*Kawiyoyo Kawiyoyo*

*Saiofaa* was safe. The *Kawiyonah* took the skin of the giant and measured themselves dresses and leggings, moccasins, gloves and all. Then they hid the giant under water.

## The Whistling Cannibals

Source: *Legends Beyond Psychology,* by Henry James Franzoni III and Kyle Mizokami.

Once upon a time there was a mountain-goat hunter. While he was hunting he met a white bear, which he pursued. Finally he came near enough to shoot it, and he hit it. The bear, however, ran on, and finally disappeared in a steep rock. After a short time a man came out of the mountain, approached the hunter, and called him in. He followed, and found that there was a large house in the mountain. The person who called him asked him to sit down on the right-hand side of the house. Then the hunter saw four companies of people in the house, and saw what they were doing. In one corner were the *Mela*; in the second corner, the *Nolem*, who ate dogs; in a third corner, the *Wihalaid*, the Cannibals; and in the fourth one, the *Semhalaid*. The first group and the last group were very much afraid of the other two. The hunter stayed in the house for three days, as he thought, but in reality he had only been away for three years. Then the supernatural being sent him back, and ordered him to imitate all that he had seen in the mountain.

The White Bear took the hunter back to his home, and put him down on the top of a tree. There the people saw him. He slid down the tree on his back, attacked a man, and devoured him. Then he attacked another one, tore him to pieces, and ate him; and thus he killed many people. Finally the tribe succeeded in overpowering him, and they cured him by means of medicine. When he had quite recovered his senses, he taught them the dances of the four companies that he had seen in the mountain, and since that time the people have had the Cannibal dance and the Dog Eaters' dance.

# The Cannibal Dance

Source: *Legends Beyond Psychology,* by Henry James Franzoni III and Kyle Mizokami.

There was a young prince in a village of the *Gitqada* whose name was "Gather on the Water." One winter, when the time had come for his dance, his father called the companies of the Cannibals to let his son join them. Therefore one day these people took the young man, took him around the village, knocked at every house, and, after had been to every house, all the men shouted, and said that this young man had gone up into the air or that the supernatural power had taken him away to his home in the mountains. They deceived many common people. These dancers were chiefs and princesses, and all the head men, old and young.

They took this young man and placed him in the trunk of a large tree secretly. They put a long ladder against the tree and sent the young man up. He went up the tree and entered a small hut. Then they took the ladder away from the tree, intending to come back at the end of ten days.

The young man staid on the tree; and the first night when he was there, some one came up to his hut and asked him, "What are you doing in there, young man?"

He replied, "I am a dancer."

Then the visitor laughed at him, and said, "That is not the way of your dance for the dancer to stay on a tree. Wait until I come again! I will show you the ways of a true dancer."

So he went away. After he had been away a short time, he came back with a dead child; and he said to the young man who lived in the hut on the tree, "Now open your mouth and eat this dead child!"

The young man was afraid. The person who held the dead child in his arms said again, "If you don't do it, I will eat you right here!"

Therefore the young man opened his mouth and swallowed the dead child's body whole.

The supernatural being asked him, "Do you feel satisfied now?" The young man replied, "No, I do not feel that I ate anything."

"Now come with me," said the supernatural being. They flew down to the village, and the supernatural being said to him, "Now shout and catch one of the people!" Then he shouted, "Hop, hop!" caught one of the young men, and ate him as a cat eats a mouse. Thus he did to the young men; and he acted like the supernatural being, which was glad to see that he had eaten a whole man. Then they went back to the tree; and the supernatural being said to him, "Whenever you feel hungry, take a person and eat him in front of the village." Then the being went away.

The people in the village always heard a terrible whistle on the tree behind the village, and everybody noticed that before he came down he shouted twice, and then he would fly down and kill some one in front of the village, and everybody was afraid of him. His fame spread all over the different villages, and all the Cannibals gathered and tried to kill him.

All these companies of dancers gathered in one house; and they prepared a mixture of poisonous herbs, urine, and other bad things, and they began to sing. While they were singing, they hear a cry from the tree. Then they heard a noise on the roof of the house in which they were assembled, and caught a person in the house. Then they threw the mixture over him and caught him. They were pouring the mixture into his mouth, and they made a heavy ring of red-cedar bark mixed with white for him, and they gave him a large griz-

zly-bear skin to be his garment, and they put a red band of red-cedar bark on each leg, and rings of cedar bark on each hand; and everybody was glad because they had tied him hand and foot.

While he was sleeping a terrible whistling was heard in his hair, although there was nobody with him. They watched over him for four nights. Then they did not give him any more medicine, and they all went to sleep. Now the great Cannibal threw off all his cedar-bark ties around his neck, and the large grizzly-bear skin, and he shouted and caught one of the men who was holding his foot bands of red-cedar bark, and he ate him right there. Then he flew up to his house on the tree, and the noise of the whistles struck terror to those in the houses.

He came down twice a day to catch people, and he ate them, and we went everywhere to devour people.

Then the chief said, "Let all the people of the village move tomorrow!" On the following morning they moved, leaving the young man behind; and he flew to every place, caught people, and devoured them. Once he flew away, and alighted on a very high mountain on the Nass River. Then he ran down, and saw a fish lying on a sandbar at low water. He started a little fire at the foot of a large tree, gathered some fuel, and roasted the fish by the fire. Then a supernatural being came to him and asked him, "What are you doing here?"

He replied, "I am roasting fish."

The supernatural being said, "This fish is not fit for you to eat. Are you not ashamed of yourself? Is that the way of dancers? Fly away to yonder place on the large tree!" Then he flew back to his own place.

He continued to eat live people as well as the bodies of the dead, and all the villages were in great distress on account of him.

They held a council in order to determine how to catch him. They made a large trap of wood; and in the night, after they had finished the trap, the companies of dancers assembled. They sang and beat time on their wooden drums, and beat with sticks on planks. He came down from the roof right into the house, and the trap shut and he was caught there. Then they all went to him, caught him, and threw the medicine over him, and they invited all the companies of their village and all the various companies assembled at the appointed time. They brought slaves to feed the dancers; and as they all came there, the dancers came forth and they gave slaves to him. He ate them all. Now his stomach was full of the flesh of many slaves, and he was satisfied. Then they put a large grizzly-bear skin on him, and a large ring of red-cedar bark on his neck and one on his head, and red-cedar bark rings on his hands and on his feet; and at the end of four days, in the morning, they beat a wooden drum and beat their sticks on the planks with thundering noise to drive away his supernatural power; and he went out alone, walking down to the beach; and at low water he sat down on a large rock, his face toward the village, and everybody came out to see him. Then the tide rose, and the rock on which he was seated was floating on the water; and when the tide was out, the rock grounded at the same place where it had been before. When the sun set, he walked up to the house where all the people were assembled. As soon as he came in, they all ran up to him. They took a heavy pole, threw him on the ground, and put his neck under the pole, trying to kill him; but the supernatural power came and helped him and delivered him from their hands. He escaped, and he would always come down to the village; but he did not take so many people as he had done before. He just killed some one, but did not eat him. Many years passed, and he still lived on the tree. After two generations passed, his voice ceased. That is the end.

## The Lytton Girls Who Were Stolen By Giants

Source: *Legends Beyond Psychology,* by Henry James Franzoni III and Kyle Mizokami.

Once some people were camped on the hills near Lytton, and among them were two girls who were fond of playing far away from the camp. Their father warned them against the giants, who infested the country. One day they rambled off, playing as usual, and two giants saw them. They put them under their arms, and ran off with them to their house on an island in a large river, a long distance way. They treated them kindly, and gave them plenty of game to eat. First they brought them grouse, rabbits, and other small game; but when they learned that the girls also ate deer, they brought to them plenty of deer, and the girls made much buckskin. The giants were much amused when they saw how the girls cut up the deer, how they cooked the meat and dressed the skins. For four days the girls were almost overcome by the smell of the giants, but gradually they became used to it.

For four years they lived with the giants, who would carry them across the river to dig roots and gather berries which did not grow on the island. One summer the giants took them a long distance away, to a place where huckleberries were very plentiful. They knew the girls liked huckleberries very much. They left them to gather berries, and said they would go hunting and come back in a few days to take them home. The elder sister recognized the place as not many days travel from their people's home, and they ran away.

When the giants returned for them, they found them gone, and followed their tracks. When the girls saw that they were about to be overtaken, they climbed into the top of a large spruce-tree, where they could not be seen. They tied themselves with their tump-lines. The giants, who had lost their tracks, thought they must be in the tree, and tried to discover them. They walked all around and looked up, but could not see them. They thought, "If they are there, we shall shake them out." They shook the tree many times, and pushed and pulled against it; but the tree did not break, and the girls did not fall down. Therefore the giants left.

After they had gone, the girls came down and ran on. The giants were looking all around for their tracks, when at last they came to a place where the girls had passed. They pursued them; and when the girls saw that they would be overtaken, they crawled, one from each end, into a large hollow log on a side-hill. They closed the openings with branches which they tied together with their tump-lines. The giants lost their tracks again, and thought they might be in the log. They pulled at the branches, but they did not move. They peered in through some small cracks, but could not see anything. They tried to roll the log down the hill, to shake out whatever might be inside, but it was too heavy. After a while they left. When they were gone, the girls ran on as before, and after a time reached a hunting camp of their own people in the mountains. During their flight they had lived on berries and fool-hens. Their moccasins were worn out, and their clothes torn. They told the people how the giants lived and acted. They were asked if the giants had any names besides *Tsawane'itEmux*, and they said they were called *Stsomu'lamux* and *TsekEtinu's*.

# THE
# SUBARCTIC
# CULTURE

# Subarctic Cultural Area

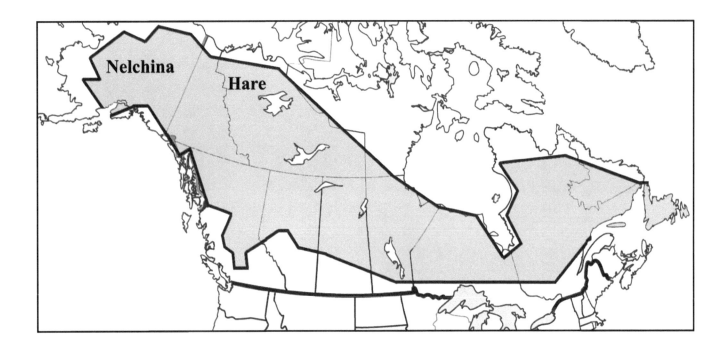

Nelchina

Hare

# The Hare

The Hare have been known by several different names, including Slavey and Slave. Today, as in prehistoric times, the Hare occupy the Northwest Territories of Canada, the Yukon, northern British Columbia and Alberta. In their traditional language of the Athabaskan family, a bigfoot-like animal is called a "bushman" or *Lariyi n* and *Naka*.

### *Lariyi n*

Source: *The Hare Indians and their World,* by Sue Hiroko Hara, 1980. Diamond Jenness Memorial Volume, National Museum of Canada, Canadian Ethnology Service Paper No. 63.

A *lariyi n* is a human-like being who roams around in the bush during the summer and steals women and children. They are considered to be foreign people who lost their way and became transformed into evil dwellers of the wilds.

Bushmen make house under the ground. They stay there all winter. In springtime they come out. They never make fire. They kill moose, and any animal. They might have guns, but usually they have knives, snares. I do not know if they have matches or not. They might smoke tobacco, maybe. They wear any kind of hide in winter. They are just men. There are not women in bushmen. They steal women but not children. They are in all sorts of ages–old ones and young ones. When there is no grub, they die and lie on the ground. *Ewe' n* [ghosts] might come out from the bushmen, too.

During the winter, they eat fresh meat. Even in winter, there is no fire. One or two people live together. But never three or more. They whistle. [It is taboo for the Hare to whistle in the dark.] They do not have dogs. I do not think they start forest fires. I don't know how they would do with mosquitoes. They speak white man's language. All the white people who got lost in the [Indian] wars became bushmen. I have never seen a bushman.

But my dad saw a bushman's track.

# The Nelchina

There is not a lot of detail about the Nelchina available. Likely the term referred to a variety of tribes in Alaska who spoke languages within the Eskimaun family. Although the *Gilyuk* were known as fearsome black giants who ate people, their apparent cannibal nature did not translate well into their traditional name, which means "The-Big-Man-With-The-Little-Hat." Nevertheless, according to Murphy, Green and Steenburg (*Meet the Sasquatch*, 2004) this name came about because from a distance, the creature's pointed head (sagittal crest) made it appear as though it is wearing a little hat.

***Gilyuk***

Source: *Sasquatch–The Apes Among Us*, by John Green, 1978. Blaine, Washington, Hancock House, p. 336.

*Gilyuk* is the shaggy cannibal giant sometimes called "The-Big-Man-With-The-Little-Hat." The Indians knew that *Gilyuk* was around because they had seen his sign, a birch sapling about four inches through that had been twisted into shreds as a man might twist a match stick.

# Appendix A

## Traditional Native American/First Nations' Names for Bigfoot

### Table 1. Organized by Name

| Traditional Name | Translation | Tribe |
|---|---|---|
| *Ahoo la huk* | Unknown | Yupik |
| *Ah-wah-Nee* | Giant | Me-Wuk |
| *Albatwitch* | "Man of the Woods" | Susquehannocks |
| *Atahsaia* | Cannibal demon | Zuni |
| *At'at'ahila* | Female monster | Chinook |
| *Atshen* | Unknown | Tete de Boule |
| *Ba'oosh* | Ape or monkey | Tsimshian |
| *Be'a'-nu'mbe* | "Brother of the Woods" | Kwakiutl |
| *Boqs* | "Bush Man" | Bella Coola |
| *Bukwas* | "Wildman of the Woods" | Kwakiutl |
| *C'amek'wes* | Hairy man | Lummi |
| *Chavcyu* | Giant | Hopi |
| *Che-ha-lum'che* | "Rock Giant of Calaveras County" | Me-Wuk |
| *Chenoo* | Devil cannibal | Micmac |
| *Chiha tanka* | "Big Elder Brother" | Dakota East/Sioux |
| *Chiye-tanka* | "Big Elder Brother" | Lakota West/Sioux |
| *Chiye-tanka* | Big man | Sioux |
| *Choanito* | Night people | Wenatchee |
| *Ciatqo* | Stick Indian | Twana |
| *Cyatkwu* | Tall hairy animal | Pugent Sound |
| *Djeneta`* | Giant | Chippewa |
| *Dzo'avits* | Cannibal giant | Shoshone |
| *Dzunukwa (Dsonoqua)* | "Wild Woman of the Woods" | Kwakiutl |
| *Eeyachuba* | Wild man | Alabama-Coushatta |
| *El-Ish-kas* | Unknown | Makah |
| *Esti capcaki* | Tall man | Seminole |
| *Gagiit* | "Wildman that lives in the woods" | Haida |
| *Ge no sqwa* | Stone giants | Iroquois/Seneca |
| *Ge no'sgwa* | Stone giants | Seneca |
| *Get'qun* | Unknown | Lake Lliamna |
| *Gilyuk* | "Big-Man-With-Little-Hat" | Nelchina |
| *Goo tee khl* | Unknown | Chilkat |
| *Gougou* | Unknown | Micmac |
| *Gyaedem gilhaoli* | "Men of the woods" | Tsimshian |
| *Ha'yacatsi* | Lost giants | Caddo |
| *Hecaitomixw* | Dangerous being | Quinault |
| *Honka* | Hairy man | Creeks |
| *Iekshthehlo* | Female cannibal | Chinook |
| *Iktomi* | "The Trickster" or "Double Face" | Sioux |
| *Itohiul* | Big feet | Chinook |
| *Itssuruqai* | Cannibal monster | Shasta |
| *K!a;waq!a* | Female cannibal | Bella Bella |

| Traditional Name | Translation | Tribe |
|---|---|---|
| *Kala'litabiqw* | Unknown | Skagit |
| *Kashehotapalo* | Cannibal man | Choctaw |
| *Kecleh-Kudleh* | Hairy savage | Cherokee |
| *Kokotshe* | Unknown | Tete de Boule |
| *Kwai-a-tlatl* | Tree striker | Nanaimo |
| *La'-lum-me* | "Rock Giant of Wennok Valley" | Me-Wuk |
| *Lariyi n* | Bushman | Hare |
| *Lofa* | Smelly, hairy being that could speak | Chickasaw |
| *Loo-poo-oi'yes* | "Rock Giant of Tamalpais" | Me-Wuk |
| *Madukarahat* | Giant | Karok |
| *Mai-a-tlatl* | Hairy giant | Comox |
| *Manabai'wok* | The Giants | Menomini |
| *Matah Kagmi* | Bigfoot | Modoc |
| *Matlox* | Hairy giant | Nootka |
| *Mayak datat* | Hairy Man | Yokuts |
| *Mesingw* | "The Mask Being" | Lenni Lenape |
| *Miitiipi* | Bad luck or disaster | Kawaiisu |
| *Misinghalikun* | "Living Solid Face" | Lenni Lenape |
| *Mu pitz* | Cannibal monster | Comanche |
| *Na'in* | Brushman | Gwich'in |
| *Naka* | Bushman | Hare |
| *Nalusa Falaya* | Big giant | Choctaw |
| *Nantiinaq* | Unknown | Kenai Peninsula |
| *Nant'ina* | Unknown | Dena'ina |
| *Nashlah* | Cannibal monster | Klickitat |
| *Neginla'eh* | Wood man | Alutiiq/Yukon |
| *Nun' Yunu' Wi* | Stone man | Cherokee |
| *Nu'numic* | Giant | Southern Paiute |
| *Nuwa'deca* | Man eater | Bannock Shoshone |
| *Oh Mah* | "Boss of the Woods" | Hoopa |
| *Okohl* | Female monster | Chinook |
| *Olala* | Hairy giant | Haida |
| *Olayome* | Hairy giant | Patwin |
| *Omah* | Unknown | Yurok |
| *Oo'-le* | "Rock Giant of the Chowchilla Foothills" | Me-Wuk |
| *Oo-wel'-lin* | Rock giant | Me-Wuk |
| *Ot-ne-yar-hed* | Stonish giant | Iroquois |
| *Papay'oos* | Hairy creature | Nanaimo |
| *Piamupits* | Cannibal monster | Comanche |
| *Puck Wudj Ininees* | Wild man | Ojibwa |
| *Qagwaai* | Giant | Northwest Coast |
| *Qah lin me* | Unknown | Yakama/Klickitat |
| *Qe'ku* | Wild woman | Nehalem/Tillamook |
| *Qelqelitl* | Female *Sesquac* | Coast Salish |
| *Qui yihahs* | The Brothers (hairy) | Yakama/Klickitat |
| *Rugaru* | Unknown | Turtle Mt Ojibwa |
| *Sachacha* | Ogre | Me-Wuk |
| *Sasahevas* | "Wild Man of the Woods" | Coast Salish |
| *Saskehavis* | Wild man | Chehalis |
| *Saskets* | Giant | Salishan/Sahaptin |
| *Sc'wen'ey'ti* | "Tall Burnt Hair" | Spokane |

| Traditional Name | Translation | Tribe |
|---|---|---|
| *Seat ka* | Unknown | Yakama |
| *Seatco* | Stick Indian | Yakama/Klickitat/Puyallup |
| *Seeahtkch* | Unknown | Clallam |
| *See'atco* | "One who runs and hides" | Coast Salish |
| *Sesquac* | "Wild Man of the Woods" | Coast Salish |
| *Shampe* | Giant monster | Choctaw |
| *Shoonshoonootr!* | Bigfoot | Yokuts |
| *Sio' Calako* | Giant | Hopi |
| *Si-Te-Cah* | People eaters | Northern Paiute |
| *Skanicum* | Stick Indian | Colville |
| *Skookum* | "Evil God of the Woods" or Mountain devil | Chinook |
| *Skukum* | "Devil of the Forest" | Quinault |
| *Slalakums* | The Unknown | Upper Stalo |
| *Snanaik* | Female cannibal | Bella Coola |
| *Sne nah* | "Owl Woman" | Okanogan |
| *Squee'noos* | Hairy creature | Nanaimo |
| *Ssti capcaki* | Tall hairy man | Seminole |
| *Ste ye mah* | "Spirit Hidden by Woods" | Yakama |
| *Steta'l* | "Spirit Spear" | Puyallup/Nisqually |
| *Stsomu'lamux* | Giant | Taos |
| *Supchet* | Giant man | Wintu |
| *Suskia* | Giantess | Washoe |
| *Suyuku* | Giantess | Hopi |
| *T'oylona* | Big Person | Taos |
| *Tah tah kle' ah* | "Owl Woman Monster" | Yakama/Shasta |
| *Tarhuhyiawahku* | Giant monster | Iroquois |
| *Tsadjatko* | Giant | Quinault |
| *Tsawane'itEmux* | Big person | Taos |
| *TsekEtinu's* | Big person | Taos |
| *Tse'nahaha* | Giant | Southern Paiute |
| *Tsiatko* | Wild Indians | Puyallup/Nisqually |
| *Tso'apittse* | Cannibal giant | Shoshone |
| *Tsonaqua* | "Wild Woman of the Woods" | Kwakiutl |
| *Tsunukwa* | Female giant covered with hair with bigfeet | Kwakiutl |
| *Urayuli* | Unknown | SW Alaskan Eskimo |
| *Wappeckquemow* | Giant | Hoopa |
| *Wetiko* | Unknown | Cree |
| *Windago* | "Wicked Cannibal" | Eastern Athabascan |
| *Witiko* | Unknown | Tete de Boule |
| *Wsinkhoalican* | "The Game Keeper" | Lenni Lenape |
| *Yah'yahaas* | Bigfoot | Modoc/Klamath |
| *Yalali* | Hairy giant | Me-Wuk |
| *Yayali* | Hairy giant | Me-Wuk |
| *Yayaya-ash* | "The Frightener" | Klamath |
| *Yeahoh* | Wild man | Algonkian |
| *Yeahoh* | Monster | Mosopelea |
| *Yé'iitsoh* | Big giant | Navajo |
| *Yi' dyi'tai* | Wild man | Nehalem/Tillamook |
| *Zoe'ah'vich* | Hairy man | Bannock Shoshone |

## Table 2. Organized by Tribe

| Tribe | Traditional Name | Translation |
| --- | --- | --- |
| Alabama-Coushatta | *Eeyachuba* | Wild man |
| Algonkian | *Yeahoh* | Wild man |
| Alutiiq/Yukon | *Neginla'eh* | Wood man |
| Bannock Shoshone | *Nuwa'deca* | Man eater |
| Bannock Shoshone | *Zoe'ah'vich* | Hairy man |
| Bella Bella | *K!a;waq!a* | Female cannibal |
| Bella Coola | *Snanaik* | Female cannibal |
| Bella Coola | *Boqs* | "Bush Man" |
| Caddo | *Ha'yacatsi* | Lost giants |
| Chehalis | *Saskehavis* | Wild man |
| Cherokee | *Kecleh-Kudleh* | Hairy savage |
| Cherokee | *Nun' Yunu' Wi* | Stone man |
| Chickasaw | *Lofa* | Smelly, hairy being that could speak |
| Chilkat | *Goo tee khl* | Unknown |
| Chinook | *Okohl* | Female monster |
| Chinook | *At'at'ahila* | Female monster |
| Chinook | *Iekshthehlo* | Female cannibal |
| Chinook | *Itohiul* | Big feet |
| Chinook | *Skookum* | "Evil God of the Woods" or Mountain dev |
| Chippewa | *Djeneta`* | Giant |
| Choctaw | *Kashehotapalo* | Cannibal man |
| Choctaw | *Nalusa Falaya* | Big giant |
| Choctaw | *Shampe* | Giant monste |
| Clallam | *Seeahtkch* | Unknown |
| Coast Salish | *Sasahevas* | "Wild Man of the Woods" |
| Coast Salish | *Sesquac* | "Wild Man of the Woods" |
| Coast Salish | *See'atco* | "One who runs and hides" |
| Coast Salish | *Qelqelitl* | Female *Sesquac* |
| Colville | *Skanicum* | Stick Indian |
| Comanche | *Mu pitz* | Cannibal monster |
| Comanche | *Piamupits* | Cannibal monster |
| Comox | *Mai-a-tlatl* | Hairy giant |
| Cree | *Wetiko* | Unknown |
| Creeks | *Honka* | Hairy man |
| Dakota East/Sioux | *Chiha tanka* | "Big Elder Brother" |
| Dena'ina | *Nant'ina* | Unknown |
| Eastern Athabascan | *Windago* | "Wicked Cannibal" |
| Gwich'in | *Na'in* | Brushman |
| Haida | *Gagiit* | "Wildman that lives in the woods" |
| Haida | *Olala* | Hairy giant |
| Hare | *Lariyi n* | Bushman |
| Hare | *Naka* | Bushman |
| Hoopa | *Oh Mah* | "Boss of the Woods" |
| Hoopa | *Wappeckquemow* | Giant |
| Hopi | *Chavcyu* | Giant |
| Hopi | *Sio' Calako* | Giant |
| Hopi | *Suyuku* | Giantess |
| Iroquois | *Ot-ne-yar-hed* | Stonish giant |
| Iroquois | *Tarhuhyiawahku* | Giant monster |

| Tribe | Traditional Name | Translation |
|---|---|---|
| Iroquois/Seneca | *Ge no sqwa* | Stone giants |
| Karok | *Madukarahat* | Giant |
| Kawaiisu | *Miitiipi* | Bad luck or disaster |
| Kenai Peninsula | *Nantiinaq* | Unknown |
| Klamath | *Yayaya-ash* | "The Frightener" |
| Klickitat | *Nashlah* | Cannibal monster |
| Kwakiutl | *Be'a'-nu'mbe* | "Brother of the Woods" |
| Kwakiutl | *Bukwas* | "Wildman of the Woods" |
| Kwakiutl | *Dzunukwa (Dsonoqua)* | "Wild Woman of the Woods" |
| Kwakiutl | *Tsonaqua* | "Wild Woman of the Woods" |
| Kwakiutl | *Tsunukwa* | Female giant covered with hair with bigfeet |
| Lake Lliamna | *Get'qun* | Unknown |
| Lakota West/Sioux | *Chiye-tanka* | "Big Elder Brother" |
| Lenni Lenape | *Mesingw* | "The Mask Being" |
| Lenni Lenape | *Misinghalikun* | "Living Solid Face" |
| Lenni Lenape | *Wsinkhoalican* | "The Game Keeper" |
| Lummi | *C'amek'wes* | Hairy man |
| Makah | *El-Ish-kas* | Unknown |
| Menomini | *Manabai'wok* | The Giants |
| Me-Wuk | *Ah-wah-Nee* | Giant |
| Me-Wuk | *Che-ha-lum'che* | "Rock Giant of Calaveras County" |
| Me-Wuk | *La'-lum-me* | "Rock Giant of Wennok Valley" |
| Me-Wuk | *Loo-poo-oi'yes* | "Rock Giant of Tamalpais" |
| Me-Wuk | *Oo'-le* | "Rock Giant of the Chowchilla Foothills" |
| Me-Wuk | *Oo-wel'-lin* | Rock giant |
| Me-Wuk | *Sachacha* | Ogre |
| Me-Wuk | *Yalali* | Hairy giant |
| Me-Wuk | *Yayali* | Hairy giant |
| Micmac | *Chenoo* | Devil cannibal |
| Micmac | *Gougou* | Unknown |
| Modoc | *Matah Kagmi* | Bigfoot |
| Modoc/Klamath | *Yah'yahaas* | Bigfoot |
| Mosopelea | *Yeahoh* | Monster |
| Nanaimo | *Squee'noos* | Hairy creature |
| Nanaimo | *Kwai-a-tlatl* | Tree striker |
| Nanaimo | *Papay'oos* | Hairy creature |
| Navajo | *Yé'iitsoh* | Big giant |
| Nehalem/Tillamook | *Qe'ku* | Wild woman |
| Nehalem/Tillamook | *Yi' dyi'tai* | Wild man |
| Nelchina | *Gilyuk* | "Big-Man-With-Little-Hat" |
| Nootka | *Matlox* | Hairy giant |
| Northern Paiute | *Si-Te-Cah* | People eaters |
| Northwest Coast | *Qagwaai* | Giant |
| Ojibwa | *Puck Wudj Ininees* | Wild man |
| Okanogan | *Sne nah* | "Owl Woman" |
| Patwin | *Olayome* | Hairy giant |
| Pugent sound | *Cyatkwu* | Tall hairy animal |
| Puyallup/Nisqually | *Steta'l* | "Spirit Spear" |
| Puyallup/Nisqually | *Tsiatko* | Wild Indians |
| Quinault | *Hecaitomixw* | Dangerous being |

| Tribe | Traditional Name | Translation |
|---|---|---|
| Quinault | *Skukum* | "Devil of the Forest" |
| Quinault | *Tsadjatko* | Giant |
| Salishan/Sahaptin | *Saskets* | Giant |
| Seminole | *Esti capcaki* | Tall man |
| Seminole | *Ssti capcaki* | Tall hairy man |
| Seneca | *Ge no'sgwa* | Stone giants |
| Shasta | *Itssuruqai* | Cannibal monster |
| Shoshone | *Dzo'avits* | Cannibal giant |
| Shoshone | *Tso'apittse* | Cannibal giant |
| Sioux | *Chiye-tanka* | Big man |
| Sioux | *Iktomi* | "The Trickster" or "Double Face" |
| Skagit | *Kala'litabiqw* | Unknown |
| Southern Paiute | *Nu'numic* | Giant |
| Southern Paiute | *Tse'nahaha* | Giant |
| Spokane | *Sc'wen'ey'ti* | "Tall Burnt Hair" |
| Susquehannocks | *Albatwitch* | "Man of the Woods" |
| SW Alaskan Eskimo | *Urayuli* | Unknown |
| Taos | *Stsomu'lamux* | Giant |
| Taos | *T'oylona* | Big Person |
| Taos | *Tsawane'itEmux* | Big person |
| Taos | *TsekEtinu's* | Big person |
| Tete de Boule | *Atshen* | Unknown |
| Tete de Boule | *Kokotshe* | Unknown |
| Tete de Boule | *Witiko* | Unknown |
| Tsimshian | *Ba'oosh* | Ape or monkey |
| Tsimshian | *Gyaedem gilhaoli* | "Men of the woods" |
| Turtle Mt Ojibwa | *Rugaru* | Unknown |
| Twana | *Ciatqo* | Stick Indians |
| Upper Stalo | *Slalakums* | The Unknown |
| Washoe | *Suskia* | Giantess |
| Wenatchee | *Choanito* | Night people |
| Wintu | *Supchet* | Giant man |
| Yakama | *Seat ka* | Unknown |
| Yakama | *Ste ye mah* | "Spirit Hidden by Woods" |
| Yakama/Klickitat | *Qah lin me* | Unknown |
| Yakama/Klickitat | *Qui yihahs* | The Brothers (hairy) |
| Yakama/Klickitat/Puyallup | *Seatco* | Stick Indian |
| Yakama/Shasta | *Tah tah kle' ah* | "Owl Woman Monster" |
| Yokuts | *Mayak datat* | Hairy Man |
| Yokuts | *Shoonshoonootr!* | Bigfoot |
| Yupik | *Ahoo la huk* | Unknown |
| Yurok | *Omah* | Unknown |
| Zuni | *Atahsaia* | Cannibal demon |

# Appendix B

## Language Families of the Native American/First Nations' Tribes

| Language Stock | Tribe | Language Stock | Tribe |
|---|---|---|---|
| Algic | Yurok | Penutian | Chinook |
| Algonquian | Cheyenne | | Clackamas |
| | Micmac | | Kalapuya |
| | Ojibwa | | Klickitat |
| | Shawnee | | Me-Wuk |
| Athabaskan | Hare | | Modoc |
| | Hoopa | | Nehalem |
| | Navajo | | Nez Perce |
| | Tlingit | | Wintu |
| Caddoan | Caddo | | Yakama |
| | Pawnee | | Yokuts |
| | Wichita | Salishan | Bella Coola |
| Eskimaun | Nelchina | | Chehalis |
| | Nunivak | | Coeur d'Alene |
| | Yupik | | Colville |
| Gulf | Natchez | | Flathead |
| Hokan | Shasta | | Puyallup |
| | Washoe | | Spokane |
| Iroquoian | Cherokee | | Upper Skagit |
| | Iroquois | | Wenatchee |
| Kitunahan | Kootenai | Siouan | Mosopelea |
| Kiowa-Tanoan | Taos | | Sioux |
| Muskogean | Alabama-Coushatta | Uto-Aztecan | Commache |
| | Chickasaw | | Hopi |
| | Choctaw | | Northern Paiute |
| | Creek | | Pima |
| | Seminoles | | Shoshone |
| | | | Southern Paiute |
| | | Wakashan | Bella Bella |
| | | | Kwakiutl |

# Photograph Credits, Copyrights and Additional Information

## General Photograph Credits

The National Archives
Library of Congress
U.S. Fish and Wildlife Service library system
Northwestern University Library, Edward S. Curtis, *The North American Indian,* Photo Images, 2001
Western History/Genealogy Department, Denver Public Library
The University of Washington Libraries
U.S. Department of the Interior Photo Library

## Specific Photograph Credits/Copyrights

Page 78:  Painting of Yosemite Paiutes by Frederick Dielman, 1891.

Page 79:  Photo of Lovelock Cave by Robert Strain.

Page 140: Logo, Chehalis First Nation.

Page 141: Photo of mask by Chris Murphy–Murphy/Hancock Photo Library.

Page 148: Painting by E. Demenech, 1860.

Page 152: Painting by Paul Kane, Royal Ontario Museum.

Page 154: Photo of totem by John Green–Murphy/Hancock Photo Library.

Page 157: Photo of mask–Murphy/Hancock Photo Library.

Page 162: Photo of dancer by David Hancock–Murphy/Hancock Photo Library. Dancer is in a traditional
          Dsonoqua mask performing for Chief Don Assu Potlach in Campbell River, B.C. in 2002.

Page 163: Photo of mask by Chris Murphy–Murphy/Hancock Photo Library.

Page 167: Photo of mask by David Hancock–Murphy/Hancock Photo Library. This Kwakiutl transformer mask
          is related to the dancer on Page 162. The mask is used in ceremonies by manipulating pulleys to
          "transform" or reveal different characters.

Page 189: Painting by George Catlin.

Page 194: Drawing by witness.

Page 225: Painting of Sequoyah, inventor of Cherokee alphabet, by Charles Bird King, 1828.

Page 234: Painting of Choctaw ballplayer by George Catlin.

Page 235: Painting of Choctaw by George Catlin, 1846.

Page 246: Painting of Osceola by George Catlin, 1838.

## Additional Information on Selected Photographs

Page 67:  The Hairy Man Pictographs from Painted Cave, Tule River Indian Reservation, California.

Page 69:  Yokuts basket with the Hairy Man motif in the lower row. For comparison, human figures adorn the
          upper row.

Page 75:  Photo of Sarah Winnemucca, well known Northern Paiute.

Page 146: Petroglyph of "She Who Watches."

Page 153: Totem of Dsonoqua.

Page 154: Totem of Dsonoqua and her son, Bukwas.

Page 155: Mask of Dsonoqua.

Page 161: Mask, appears very "ape-like."

Page 165: Totem of Dsonoqua.

Page 197: Photo of Chief Joseph, Nez Perce.

# General Index

# Story Index

# Other **Hancock House** *cryptozoology titles*

**Bigfoot Encounters in
New York & New England**
*Robert Bartholomew
Paul Bartholomew*
978-0-88839-652-5
5½ x 8½, sc, 176 pages

**Raincoast Sasquatch**
*J. Robert Alley*
978-0-88839-508-5
5½ x 8½, sc, 360 pages

**Sasquatch:
The Apes Among Us**
*John Green*
0-88839-123-4
5½ x 8½, sc, 492 pages

**Meet the Sasquatch**
*Christopher Murphy, John Green,
Thomas Steenburg*
0-88839-580-9
8½ x 11, hc, 240 pages

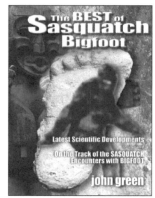

**The Best of
Sasquatch Bigfoot**
*John Green*
0-88839-546-9
8½ x 11, sc, 144 pages

**Bigfoot Encounters
in Ohio**
*C. Murphy, J. Cook,
G. Clappison*
0-88839-607-4
5½ x 8½, sc, 152 pages

**The Bigfoot Film
Controversy**
*Roger Patterson,
Christopher Murphy*
0-88839-581-7
5½ x 8½, sc, 240 pages

**Sasquatch Bigfoot**
*Thomas Steenburg*
0-88839-312-1
5½ x 8½, sc, 128 pages

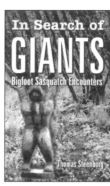

**In Search of Giants**
*Thomas Steenburg*
0-88839-446-2
5½ x 8½, sc, 256 pages

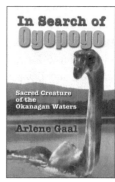

**In Search of Ogopogo**
*Arlene Gaal*
0-88839-482-9
5½ x 8½, sc, 208 pages

**The Locals**
*Thom Powell*
0-88839-552-3
5½ x 8½, sc, 272 pages

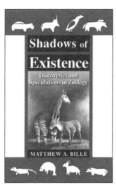

**Shadows of Existence**
*Matthew A. Bille*
0-88839-612-0
5½ x 8½, sc, 320 pages

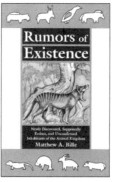

**Rumours of Existence**
*Matthew A. Bille*
0-88839-335-0
5½ x 8½, sc, 192 pages

**Strange Northwest**
*Chris Bader*
0-88839-359-8
5½ x 8½, sc, 144 pages

**UFO Defense Tactics**
*A.K. Johnstone*
0-88839-501-9
5½ x 8½, sc, 152 pages

*View all* **Hancock House** *titles at* **www.hancockhouse.com**

Made in United States
Troutdale, OR
04/04/2024

18944289R00164